Investing in Africa

Wiley Frontiers in Finance

SERIES EDITOR: EDWARD I. ALTMAN
NEW YORK UNIVERSITY

Investing in Africa

An Insider's Guide to the Ultimate Emerging Market

Justin F. Beckett
and
Michael E. M. Sudarkasa

John Wiley & Sons, Inc.

New York • Chichester • Weinheim • Brisbane • Singapore • Toronto

JUSTIN BECKETT:
To Mom, Dad, Dorika, and Maceo.
Thank you for your love, guidance and support.

MICHAEL SUDARKASA:
To my family—Joyce, Jasmine, Jonathan, Maya, Mari-elle, and Nigel.
Thank you for believing in me and in Africa.

This book is printed on acid-free paper. ∞

Copyright © 2000 by Justin F. Beckett & Michael E. M. Sudarkasa. All rights reserved.

Published by John Wiley & Sons, Inc.

Published simultaneously in Canada.

This publication is designed to provide accurate and authoritative information in regard to the subject matter covered. It is sold with the understanding that the publisher is not engaged in rendering professional services. If professional advice or other expert assistance is required, the services of a competent professional person should be sought.

ISBN: 0-471-37951-4

Printed in the United States of America

10 9 8 7 6 5 4 3 2 1

Contents

Preface

"I WAS COUNTRY WHEN COUNTRY WASN'T COOL!"

We are not sure whether famed American country singer Barbara Mandrell said it first, but in the 1980s she popularized country music for the crossover audience with her song titled "I Was Country When Country Wasn't Cool." In this poignant piece Mandrell quite simply professed her adoration for country music and the style of life that influenced it. For her, the music and the lifestyle had never been a fad, but rather always a passion. Hence, her refrain . . . "Oh, I was into country [music], when country wasn't cool!"

In many ways, that sentiment is a fitting overture for the reason why we are writing this book. Long before Africa was fashionable; before U.S. Vice President Al Gore teamed up with current South African President Thabo Mbeki to create the U.S.–South Africa Binational Commission; before Reverend Leon Sullivan, of apartheid-era "Sullivan Principles" fame, began his first African/African-American Summit; before the U.S.-based Corporate Council on Africa was founded; before the U.S. Congress and President Bill Clinton began advocating an American foreign policy of "Trade, not just Aid" and promoting the U.S. Growth and Opportunity Act (aka the African Trade Bill); and lastly, before there was an identifiable "African Renaissance," as the aforementioned South African leader Thabo Mbeki has eloquently described this current era, both of this book's authors were attracted by the vast untapped potential of the continent. At early ages we committed ourselves to learning about Africa's promise—and to sharing that knowledge with others (particularly others in the United States) whom we felt could benefit financially from the business and investment opportunities that we identified there.

Under our premise, most foreign investors did not know Africa. But if we could show them the dynamic, investor-friendly Africa that we knew, they would be more able and inclined to objectively explore it.

At the beginning of the 1990s, we began our respective efforts to promote business between the United States and Africa—Justin in the investment arena, and I (Michael) principally in the trade arena. Over the course of the decade our paths crisscrossed quite frequently, and we compared notes and pursued collaborative initiatives. In 1997, our discussions about ways in which we could work synergistically culminated in my being invited to join the Board of the Calvert New Africa Fund, of which Justin was also a member. While working with the Fund, we had even more frequent occasions to discuss means by which we could inform the investment community about the significant opportunities we were aware of on the African continent. As I was then an adjunct professor at Georgetown University's Graduate School of Management, teaching a course on U.S./Africa business development, I was painfully aware of the dearth of substantive African investment-related publications. *The African Business Handbook,* which I first published in 1991, was still the only relatively comprehensive text available. It was then that I broached the idea that we collaborate on a practical, straightforward book about investing in Africa.

At that time Justin was based in Johannesburg, South Africa, irrefutably Africa's commercial center and economic crossroads, and I was based in Washington, D.C., arguably the world's Africa economic information capital and home of the World Bank and the International Monetary Fund. From our respective vantage points in those two nations, we thought we would be particularly well-suited to bring greater focus on the mechanics, available resources, opportunities, and risks related to pursuing foreign direct investment and portfolio investment in Africa. Furthermore, having both spent most of the decade promoting investment and business opportunities in one of the world's fastest growing continents, we relished the thought that we would once again—but in a more lasting fashion—be undertaking a meaningful project to illuminate Africa. In our opinion, the continent was, and is, the ultimate emerging market. To all of those readers who have yet to enjoy the rich opportunities that the continent provides, we hope that this book provides the spark and guide to help explore them. For those of you who are already acquainted with the continent, we hope that you will find this a useful reference in your continued business and investment pursuits in Africa.

Acknowledgments

With our sincerest appreciation, we would like to thank the following individuals for their assistance on this project: Jeff Bacote, Lucrecia Bartman, Francis Daniels, Kirk Jackson, Rosalind Johnson, Anne Luusah, Aletha McManama, Noelle Elaine Media, Kofi Mensah, Elam Muchira, Roy Mutooni, Nomsa Ngakane, Kote Nikoi, Leslie Noukelak, Sydney Njai, Byron Otieno, Michael Raeford, Zarina Tilley, and Melina Van Renen.

We would also like to extend a special thank-you to the following institutions for allowing us to reprint selected graphic material from their publications:

The African Development Bank
The World Bank Group
UNCTAD
The World Economic Forum

Introduction

TARZAN DOES NOT LIVE HERE ANYMORE

It may be awkward for some readers to have us begin our book with that somewhat loaded heading. But it is necessary to deal with the still-present and often vivid images that Hollywood continues to produce about a mythical, romanticized, and primitive era when Africa was supposedly a place for great adventures where you had to worry about the natives "getting restless" and where you could count on an all-knowing European (who spoke the natives' language(s) and could even talk to the animals) to guide you, the "civilized" visitor to this "godforsaken wilderness," back to safety.

A distinguishing reality of today's postcolonial, post–Cold War, and postapartheid Africa is the increasing level of independence and functional autonomy experienced by African businesses and governments. In fact, as anyone who has been able to travel to the continent recently will tell you, there is an overall undeniable buzz of evolving self-determination.

This said, the goal is not to distort or misstate the still-present legacy of Africa's colonial past. Multinational corporations, mostly from Europe, still play very significant roles in most African economies, and the professionals they second to their African subsidiaries often have a better lay of the land than many other foreign entrants into the African market. The governments of Western Europe (or better put, the government of the European Union) have far more involvement with and impact upon the continent's geopolitical structure, future, and plans, than do their counterparts in any other region of the world. From providing balance of payments assistance to offering debt relief, preferential trade access to markets, disaster relief, and peacekeeping support, the European Union of today, and the countries that constitute this market, still have vast influence in Africa. Yet, in twenty-first-century Africa, capital, contacts, and content will be king!

CAPITAL

There is no economy in the world today growing as fast as the U.S. economy. And although there may be periodic market corrections, there are no signs that the fundamental aspects of America's push for and role in globalization will end in the near term. This fact has not been lost on African business and political leaders. So in unprecedented numbers they are reaching out to American political and business leaders, in order to develop and strengthen their ties with America. U.S. President Bill Clinton's visit to Africa in 1997 may remain the most visible example of how far the effort to establish an economically focused relationship between Africa and the United States has come, but in the past 15 years there have been numerous lesser publicized efforts to close the expanse of the Atlantic Ocean. U.S. corporations, in particular, have been successfully investing in Africa for decades, albeit disproportionately in the mineral extraction arena. Blue chip U.S. multinational corporations like cereal maker Kellogg's, computer giant IBM, world beverage market leader Coca-Cola, and global financial giant Citigroup, have long had a significant presence on the African continent. More recently these corporations have been joined by other major companies such as Microsoft, Cisco Systems, Dell Computers, General Motors, Oracle, Southwest Bell Corporation, Exxon, Chrysler, Ford, McDonald's, Kentucky Fried Chicken, and Domino's Pizza, as well as professional service providers such as McKinsey and Company and Bain and Company, law firms such as White & Case, and financial institutions such as Chase Manhattan Bank, J.P. Morgan, Merrill Lynch, and First Boston. The establishment of the Corporate Council on Africa in 1995, with a corporate membership of over 150 major U.S. corporations and firms significantly involved with Africa, is indicative of the growing U.S. involvement in Africa. And lastly, the emerging market focus and entry of U.S. financial giants like Alliance Capital, Morgan Stanley, and the Calvert Group into the African capital markets arena through the establishment of mutual funds has also had a globally illuminating influence on the opportunities and investment potential of Africa.

CONTACTS

One of the key people-driven contributors to the efforts to increase U.S. political and economic collaboration has been the rapid increase in the depth and variety of ways in which African and American people are interacting. In the past 10 years an unprecedented number of Africans seeking higher education have come to the United States for their formal educational training. At the same time, the number of American universities offering Africa-related courses (particularly on African business and economics) and including Africa in their study abroad curricula has expanded exponentially. Sister city relationships between U.S. and African communities have grown significantly, and more U.S. states than ever before are establishing offices or at least representation on the continent and sending annual trade delegations to explore business and investment opportunities there. Tourism involving Americans traveling to Africa is also on the rise, and the development of the Internet and the penetration of CNN have made it a bit easier for Americans to get information about Africa—and for Africans to learn about America.

CONTENT

Content—or technology—is another key catalyst for the development of closer ties between the United States and Africa. To the extent that American products and services, particularly in the information technology area, have become world industry leaders (e.g., Microsoft, Cisco Systems, Oracle, Lucent Technologies), there has been a sea change in Africans' attitudes about who their global suppliers should be. And while both Europe and Asia still have strong market share in Africa, U.S. product and service exports—directly from the U.S., and often through European subsidiaries as well—continue to grow.

America's dominance of the Internet, and the content provided therein, also have helped foster greater African interest in establishing ties with the United States. And lastly, the rapid (or some might say continued) expansion of America's media presence globally through music, television, and films has captivated the younger generations in Africa. On a continent where approximately 70% of the more than 750-million-person population is below the age of 30, this has had a big impact.

Today, unlike in Tarzan's era, there are vast, rapidly growing African metropolises. There is a corporate Africa and many African Wall Streets. Although there is continued lament about the brain-drain effect of Africans studying in the West and not returning to work at home, and of skilled Africans emigrating north to find better lives for their families, an unprecedented number of Harvard, Yale, Stanford, and even Oxford and Sorbonne-trained young Africans are returning home and playing catalytic roles in their nations' economies. This is the Africa that the authors know: the backward-looking but forward-moving Africa symbolized in the Ghanaian mythical image of Sankofa—the bird that is cognizant of the past but boldly stepping into the future. In this Africa, if you want to see the animals, you must go on safari to a game park or reserve! And if you mention bears and bulls, some-one will ask you if you're referring to events on the Johannesburg Stock Exchange or on the Cairo Stock Exchange.

It is this Africa—modern Africa, the new Africa—that we want to illuminate for our readers. Furthermore, it is our hope that through this work we will also be able to provide a readable, compelling, and clear analysis of the investment opportunities that await smart investors in twenty-first-century Africa.

PART 1

The African Financial Renaissance Considered

For many potential investors, the idea that *Africa* and *investment opportunity* are presented in the same sentence may seem an odd combination. Yet, the fact is that an increasing number of institutional investors and multinational corporations have found markets in Africa to be some of their best-yielding investment destinations. Paradoxically, African markets are often these same investors' best-kept secrets. Most such investors do not mind the fact that they have limited competition in the African markets. If the rest of the world wants to believe that Africa is a monolithic, backward region beset by war, disease, poverty, and ethnic conflict, so be it, they surmise—all the more opportunity for them.

Thus, we recognize that before we get into any great detail about how to find and pursue the many investment opportunities that Africa offers, we must first provide a more contemporary picture of the continent and an overview of the regions, countries, and sectors where opportunities lie. Thus, in the next four chapters, we provide an overview of the investment environment in Africa and discuss why it is more favorable today than at any time in the past. We also provide our thoughts about why the successes of Africa, from an investment standpoint, have not received the same extensive global coverage that some of the continent's failings have. We also discuss who is currently investing in Africa, and we analyze African portfolios and direct investments from a performance standpoint, as compared with other regions of the world.

1
Africa, Inc.!

Mobius Rules: "The Final Frontier (Africa)"

Rule #1: Your best protection is diversification.

Rule #81: By the time everyone and his brother believes that it's the right time to invest, the right time will have long since come and gone.

Rule #83: Political uncertainty—like any other form of uncertainty—can be your green light to move into a market. Uncertainty depresses stock prices. If you have faith in your own crystal ball—or, better yet, your own independent analysis—an uncertain atmosphere can be just the break you've been looking for to pick up large-cap, blue-chip stocks that would otherwise be too expensive to consider.

Rule #84: Once uncertainty becomes certainty, and anyone with two nickels to rub together can with some degree of accuracy predict the likely outcome of events, that beautiful risk premium will have evaporated in a puff of smoke.

Africa, Incorporated! Corporate Africa! In the past, with the African continent's history of political difficulty, ethnic conflict, and poor infrastructure and social services, it would have been very difficult to envision images that represent either of these phrases. And if the words did conjure up such visions, they would most likely be images placed in a far-off future. An

"Africa, Incorporated" that draws to mind an image of one economically focused region aggressively engaged in production and marketing, and offering client-driven services in a competitive global environment, would most likely be criticized as unrealistically idealistic. Similarly, to promote a vision of a "Corporate Africa" made up of African professionals in dark blue Brooks Brothers suits, establishing and serving on boards of directors, focusing on issues such as corporate governance and ethics, and working to define profit-making, mutually beneficial public-private partnerships, would probably lead to claims that one was describing the small exception, not the rule.

Yet, the reality is that this future is now! As Mark Mobius (arguably the world's most widely respected expert on emerging market investments) acknowledges in his recent book *Passport to Profits,* Africa, as the investment world's last frontier, offers unique unexplored opportunities for development, growth, and economic success. And the continent, its businesses, and its governments offer these opportunities today!

Never before have so many Africans educated and trained in Europe, the United States, and Asia, decided to return to the countries of their birth to become actively involved in commerce, industry, and investment. Never before have so many African nations focused consistently and concertedly on promoting their investment opportunities, improving their business environments, and developing accords with their neighbors to enhance their collective market size. And, frankly, never before have so many of the world's economic leaders—most notably in the United States—worked so hard to redefine their engagement with Africans away from that of donor-donee toward that of mutually respected trade and investment partners.

Without a doubt the Information Age has played a tremendous role in Africa's realization that there are almost irreversible penalties for being excluded from the world economy. Thus, the development of telecommunications infrastructure has become a priority. The liberalization of the financial sector to allow freer and safer transfers of capital, intraregion and globally, has also assumed precedence. Furthermore, a renewed focus on marshaling global assistance from Africans living outside of the continent (via Internet, wire transfer, and old-fashioned savings clubs) has strengthened Africa's resolve to pursue economic independence over the next 30 years—as vigorously as the region has pursued political independence during the last 30 to 40 years.

The terms regionalization, global competitiveness, connectivity, privatization, democracy, and free enterprise—since the late 1980s, in the multilateral and emerging market investment community—have become the collective benchmark for assessing the progress of all of the regions of the developing world, including Africa, Asia, Latin America and the Caribbean, Eastern Europe, and the Newly Independent States region. In the 1990s, in a quiet, determined, and often unheralded manner, the 53 nations occupying the African continent have made great strides toward successfully achieving these tenets of the development holy grail (see Figure 1.1).

Often African countries have forged ahead on a one-by-one basis, while in other cases, as in the French-speaking countries of West and Central Africa, they have made collective strides. Devisive regional economic competition between neighbors such as Ghana and Côte d'Ivoire in West Africa, Kenya and Uganda in East Africa, and Zimbabwe and South Africa, while still existent, are giving way to far more constructive dialogue about collaboration, joint venturing, and economic partnership.

Admittedly, some of the countries of Africa have been more successful than others in their economic endeavors. Ghana, Uganda, and Botswana are three examples of countries that at various times during the 1990s have been heralded for their efforts in the previously mentioned areas. On the other hand, Angola, the Democratic Republic of Congo, Sierra Leone, Somalia, Algeria, and Sudan are all countries that continue to struggle to make the grade as successful emerging markets.

As Africa enters the next millennium, one set of factors in particular makes the continent a unique and attractive region—and that is that, economically speaking, as a market for products, as an overseas destination for outsourced manufacturing operations, and as an investment destination for institutional portfolio capital, Africa is the world's least-explored region. Fierce competition among companies, skyrocketing prices for public equities valuations for publicly traded securities, mature markets with low growth prospects—all of these negative elements have yet to arrive on the continent. The emerging market investment phenomenon of the mid-1990s to a large extent bypassed Africa. Strides were made in the establishment of various open-ended, closed-ended, private equity, venture capital, and multilateral funds, but for the most part, the geographical focus and size of the funds were limited (see Figure 1.2).

However, one such fund, the Simba Fund, effectively summarized in its offering memorandum the trends in Africa which today warrant further exploration of the continent's investment opportunities. The Simba Fund was established in November 1995 to target African stocks in industries with products (primarily extractive minerals) that are likely to be sought by the rapidly industrializing Asian nations. The Simba Fund identified 11 trends that in the minds of its managers underpin Africa's attractiveness as an investment destination today:

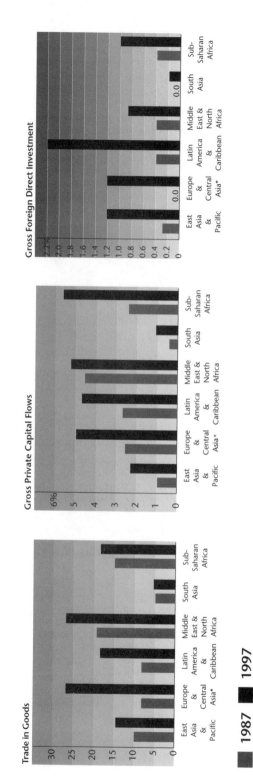

FIGURE 1.1 "Joining the World"
Source: Wall Street Journal, September 27, 1999, World Bank

* Excludes nations of the European monetary union. *Note:* Figures are calculated as percentages of GDP converted to international dollars using purchasing power parities.

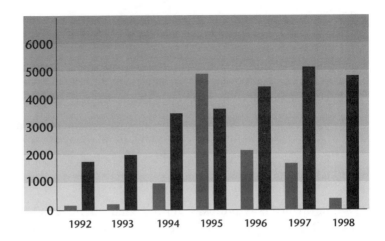

Foreign Direct Investment

Portfolio Investment

FIGURE 1.2 Foreign Investment Flows to Africa, 1992–1998
Source: World Bank, Global Development Finance, 1999

1. Africa's resources are increasingly in demand, especially from emerging Asian economies.

2. Africa's governments are now promoting private-sector-led, export-oriented economies.

3. Africa's resource-based companies have become more productive and globally competitive.

4. Domestic political considerations are becoming less intrusive on the business environment.

5. Privatization is reviving key sectors of the economy.

6. The opening of new stock markets and the rejuvenation of existing ones are enhancing the role of capital and so broadening opportunities for portfolio investors.

7. Foreign investment is returning, especially in the natural resource sector.

8. Regional economic cooperation is occurring in such key areas as infrastructure, development, and transportation.

9. The end of the era of fixed exchange rates is allowing more realistic, market-determined economic conditions.

10. Liberalization of agricultural marketing boards is reviving export-oriented crop production (which is important since nearly 70% of the continent's labor is involved in the agriculture sector).

11. The advent of accountability in government is seeing the political appointee replaced by the technocrat; and South African corporations are now spreading their skills, technologies, products, and capital across the African continent.

Harvard University professor Jeffrey Sachs, in the 1999 Global Competitiveness Report, further corroborates the fact that a number of African nations are on the move upward in their ranking globally. Of the 59 countries included in the annual survey, Mauritius, which was unranked globally in 1998, is ranked 29 in 1999. Other African nations showing up on the radar screen include South Africa, no. 47, Egypt, no. 49, and Zimbabwe, no. 57. In a related comparison of the projected annual per capita gross domestic product (GDP) growth of these same 59 countries, Egypt was the highest African nation surveyed, with a 3.06% growth projected, followed by Mauritius (2.82%), South Africa (2.26%), and Zimbabwe (2.05%). See Figures 1.3 and 1.4.

Measuring African nations in a class by themselves, the World Economic Forum has further explored the relative competitiveness of 23 African countries based on estimates of their medium-term economic growth. Each country's overall competitiveness is measured based on an average of six indices that are also useful in assessing the progress that has been made by Africa's nations in general: openness, government, finance, labor, infrastructure, and institutions (see Figure 1.5).

Four aggregate indices which illustrate the relative development, growth, and opportunity within the surveyed countries are: (1) the overall 1998 African Competitiveness Index, (2) the 1992–1997 Improvement Index, (3) the 1997–1999 Optimism Index, and (4) the Global Economy Trade Index (see Figures 1.6 through 1.9).

Today, African nations are striving to forge closer ties with one another and with the global business community generally. As they respectfully acknowledge that their 750-million-plus population represents a virtually untapped consumer market, they are equally focused on the development of two-way business opportunities with the rest of the world.

With some of the world's most concentrated mineral, oil, and gas reserves, Africa's nations recognize that there is yet-untapped value to be developed

Rank	(1998)		Rank	(1998)		Rank	(1998)	
1	(1)	Singapore	21	(18)	Chile	41	(44)	Greece
2	(3)	United States	22	(19)	Korea	42	(36)	Argentina
3	(2)	Hong Kong SAR	23	(22)	France	43	(49)	Poland
4	(6)	Taiwan	24	(27)	Belgium	44	(40)	Turkey
5	(5)	Canada	25	(24)	Germany	45	(48)	Slovakia
6	(8)	Switzerland	26	(25)	Spain	46	(n/a)	El Salvador
7	(10)	Luxembourg	27	(26)	Portugal	47	(42)	South Africa
8	(4)	United Kingdom	28	(29)	Israel	48	(39)	Vietnam
9	(7)	Netherlands	29	(n/a)	Mauritius	49	(38)	Egypt
10	(11)	Ireland	30	(21)	Thailand	50	(45)	Venezuela
11	(15)	Finland	31	(32)	Mexico	51	(46)	Brazil
12	(14)	Australia	32	(28)	China	52	(50)	India
13	(13)	New Zealand	33	(33)	Philippines	53	(n/a)	Ecuador
14	(12)	Japan	34	(n/a)	Costa Rica	54	(47)	Colombia
15	(9)	Norway	35	(41)	Italy	55	(n/a)	Bolivia
16	(17)	Malaysia	36	(37)	Peru	56	(n/a)	Bulgaria
17	(16)	Denmark	37	(31)	Indonesia	57	(51)	Zimbabwe
18	(30)	Iceland	38	(43)	Hungary	58	(53)	Ukraine
19	(23)	Sweden	39	(35)	Czech Republic	59	(52)	Russia
20	(20)	Austria	40	(34)	Jordan			

FIGURE 1.3 1999 Competitiveness Rankings
Source: World Economic Forum

Rank	Annual GDP growth per capita($)	Rank	(1998)	Rank	(1998)
1	Singapore 5.02	21	Korea 3.35	41	Belgium 2.57
2	Taiwan 4.29	22	Peru 3.34	42	Israel 2.49
3	Malaysia 4.19	23	Thailand 3.33	43	Poland 2.36
4	Hong Kong SAR 4.13	24	El Salvador 3.31	44	Turkey 2.36
5	United States 4.07	25	Norway 3.31	45	South Africa 2.26
6	Canada 4.03	26	Luxembourg 3.25	46	Czech Republic 2.20
7	Ireland 3.91	27	Denmark 3.25	47	Bolivia 2.11
8	United Kingdom 3.88	28	Egypt 3.06	48	Slovakia 2.08
9	New Zealand 3.86	29	Sweden 3.04	49	Zimbabwe 2.05
10	Finland 3.81	30	India 2.96	50	Argentina 1.92
11	Indonesia 3.78	31	Spain 2.91	51	Ecuador 1.76
12	Switzerland 3.74	32	Costa Rica 2.88	52	Ukraine 1.75
13	Netherlands 3.73	33	Austria 2.87	53	Greece 1.69
14	Philippines 3.65	34	Mexico 2.84	54	Brazil 1.69
15	Australia 3.64	35	Iceland 2.83	55	Bulgaria 1.68
16	Vietnam 3.62	36	Mauritius 2.82	56	Italy 1.57
17	China 3.59	37	Portugal 2.75	57	Venezuela 1.47
18	Chile 3.54	38	Hungary 2.69	58	Colombia 1.17
19	Japan 3.50	39	France 2.67	59	Russia 0.91
20	Jordan 3.36	40	Germany 2.62		

FIGURE 1.4 1999 Growth Projections, 2000–2008
Source: World Economic Forum

FIGURE 1.5 High, Middle, and Low Performing Economies
Source: World Economic Forum

through the enhancement of their natural resources (see Figure 1.10). But no longer is it deemed necessary for the state to try to manage or even to control all of the entities that operate in these sectors.

For many African countries, commodities export earnings (including agricultural cash crops such as cocoa, sugar, rubber, coffee, and cut flowers) still comprise the major component of foreign exchange export earnings (see Figure 1.11). However, textile, manufactured goods, and services exports (particularly in South Africa) have grown significantly in the past decade.

Notwithstanding the predominance of extractive and natural resources as contributors to the foreign exchange income of African nations, it is critical to point out the strides being taken to improve the region's manufacturing capacity. The United Nations Industrial Development Organization (UNIDO),

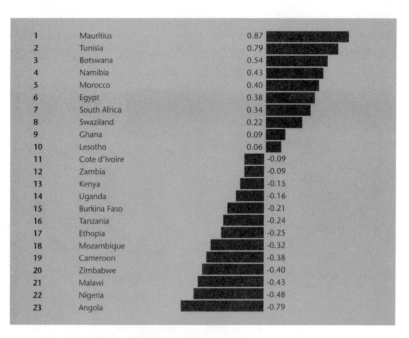

FIGURE 1.6   1998 African Competitiveness Index
Source: World Economic Forum

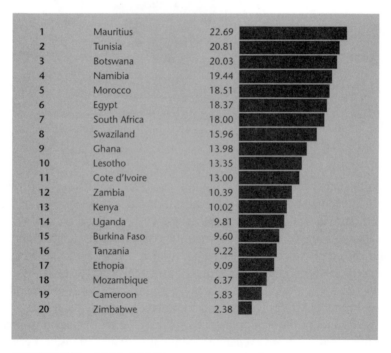

FIGURE 1.7   1992–1997 Improvement Index
Source: World Economic Forum

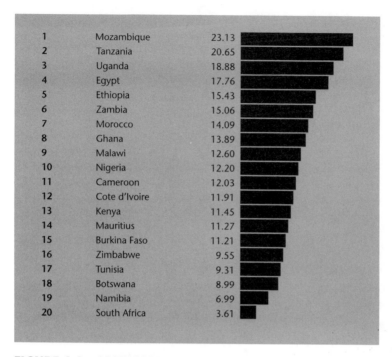

1	Mozambique	23.13
2	Tanzania	20.65
3	Uganda	18.88
4	Egypt	17.76
5	Ethiopia	15.43
6	Zambia	15.06
7	Morocco	14.09
8	Ghana	13.89
9	Malawi	12.60
10	Nigeria	12.20
11	Cameroon	12.03
12	Cote d'Ivoire	11.91
13	Kenya	11.45
14	Mauritius	11.27
15	Burkina Faso	11.21
16	Zimbabwe	9.55
17	Tunisia	9.31
18	Botswana	8.99
19	Namibia	6.99
20	South Africa	3.61

FIGURE 1.8 1997–1999 Optimism Index
Source: World Economic Forum

which supports the industrial development of emerging market countries, measures industrial output capacity in terms of a standard it has coined as MVA, or *manufacturing value added.*

Africa's top 10 industrial companies in 1997 as measured by MVA included South Africa, Egypt, Morocco, Algeria, Libya, Tunisia, Sudan, Cameroon, Côte d'Ivoire, and Zimbabwe.

The critical factor noted by studies of Africa's industrialization is the rapidity with which it is taking place. Overall, UNIDO notes that Africa is industrializing at a nearly 5% per annum rate of improvement, which is deemed to be a very positive factor. Certain countries, such as Uganda (13+%), Lesotho and Libya (10%), and Ethiopia and Mauritius (6%) are even exceeding the 5% average.

What South Africa's relative industrial superiority has translated into within the concept of Africa, Inc. is the emergence of this country as the African continent's supplier of choice. Since 1992, when trade sanctions ended for the country, South Africa's exports to the other countries of the continent have grown by 335%, totaling over $3 billion in 1998. For foreign

Country	Mean Response	
Mozambique	3.85	
Uganda	4.00	
Zambia	4.13	
Ghana	4.18	
Malawi	4.33	
Nigeria	4.43	
Botswana	4.57	
Tanzania	4.80	
Zimbabwe	4.80	
Kenya	4.86	
Cote d'Ivoire	4.90	
Cameroon	4.94	
Namibia	5.19	
Egypt	5.21	
Morocco	5.25	
Ethiopia	5.25	
South Africa	5.38	
Tunisia	5.44	
Mauritius	6.02	

1-restricts economic opportunity for your firm
7-opens economic opportunity for your firm

FIGURE 1.9 Global Economy Trade Index
Source: World Economic Forum

manufacturers looking to establish facilities on the African continent, South Africa has emerged as a favorite destination. And growth within that country's indigenous manufacturing sector has also been fueled by the flow of capital into the continent's largest stock market.

Private-sector-led growth and the inclusion of the vast informal market into the recorded GDP market is another of the key tenets of African nations today. African leaders recognize that the public sector, although shrinking, still remains active in a number of commercial areas in Africa's economies that would be better suited to private management (see Figure 1.12). Thus, privatization and commercialization programs continue to gain momentum, and stock markets and private equity and venture capital funds continue to facilitate the growing flow of private capital into African businesses.

Commodities	Africa's Production of the World Total
Cobalt	76%
Cocoa Beans	54
Vanadium	50
Diamonds (Industrial)	49
Platinum	48
Diamonds	44
Chromium Ore	40
Uranium	38
Cassava	37
Gold	31
Manganese Ore	28
Phosphate Rock	21
Bauxite	16
Olive Oil	16
Copper	12
Green Coffee Scans	12
Crude Petroleum	11
Tea	9
Peanuts	8

FIGURE 1.10   Africa's Share of World Supply of Selected
Commodities
Source: African Business Handbook

As Africa enters the twenty-first century, a new theme guides the continent's leaders. And that theme is that economic integration into the global
community is of critical import to the region's long-term success. After a
decade of implementing change, it is time to unveil the new-model Africa,
the more confident and qualified partner-Africa.

	%		%
Algeria	97	Libya	100
Angola	87	Madagascar	69
Benin	80	Malawi	94
Botswana	95	Mali	98
Burkina Faso	75	Mauritania	98
Burundi	92	Mauritius	69
Cameroon	81	Morocco	42
Central Africa Republic	87	Mozambique	98
Chad	94	Niger	98
Comoros	87	Nigeria	99
Congo	98	Rwanda	93
Dem. Rep. of Congo	95	Sao Tome/Principe	89
Cote d'Ivoire	69	Senegal	62
Djibouti	38	Seychelles	86
Egypt	94	Sierra Leone	62
Equatorial Guinea	100	Somalia	98
Eritrea	88	South Africa	38
Ethiopea	88	Sudan	68
Gabon	94	Swaziland	54
The Gambia	48	Tanzania	61
Ghana	91	Togo	72
Guinea	93	Tunisia	47
Guinea-Bissau	66	Uganda	99
Kenya	75	Zaire	95
Lesotho	72	Zambia	98
Liberia	89	Zimbabwe	55

FIGURE 1.11 Commodities as a Share of Total Export Earnings in African Countries
Source: African Business Handbook

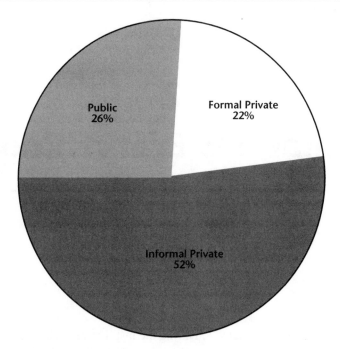

FIGURE 1.12   Structure of African Economies
Source: IFC

For those seeking above-average returns and to benefit from being a first mover in the world's last great market, the time to explore Africa is *now*. For some, the investment opportunities in Africa will stimulate a long-term presence and economic involvement with the continent. For others, African investment will provide short-term diversification and a chance to take part in some of the world's highest-yielding investment opportunities.

2

Image Is Everything

Riddle: Which continent (1) During the last five years, has been home to the world's top performing stock markets? (2) Has the least expensive stock prices in the world? (3) Has given birth to the most new stock markets in the last decade? (4) Has over 2,000 publicly traded securities? (5) Is the world's second largest continuous land mass?

If your answer to any of these five questions was Africa, then not only are you correct but you are also part of an increasing pool of individuals and institutions who have begun to acknowledge Africa's dynamic investment potential. Sparked during the 1980s by an international economic climate that was increasingly shaped more by globalization and less by the waning Cold War, certain African nations began to experience fundamental improvements in their economies. Subsequently, since the early 1990s the number of African investor success stories has increased dramatically. Additionally, investors have discovered the unique performance characteristics of Africa's capital markets that make African securities an ideal diversification option.

Although the African continent has long been dismissed as economically insignificant, recent success stories have prompted investors to take a closer look. Today, sophisticated investors no longer view the entirety of Africa with the Joseph Conrad–inspired perception as the "dark continent." Instead, investors are examining this vast region of over 11 million square miles and over 750 million people and judging the economies of Africa's 53 independent countries on their own merits.

Unfortunately, if you answered any of the questions to the riddle correctly, you are part of what is still a minority. Although far more investors have Africa on their investment radar screens today than did at the beginning of the 1990s, the majority of corporate executives and institutional investors worldwide still have difficulty grasping the fact that the continent offers viable and profitable opportunities.

Why is this? Because the information that is globally disseminated about Africa (e.g., through the media, by filmmakers and television executives, and by donor organizations) consistently presents Africa from a glass-is-half-empty perspective. That is to say that instead of giving due attention to the positive political and economic transformations that are taking place on the continent, the majority of the stories and pictures highlight Africa's shortcomings. These shortcomings may be real, but when the various media focus almost exclusively upon such issues it becomes very difficult to then cast the continent as an attractive place to put one's hard-earned investment capital to work.

Like numerous innovations of the Information Age, the creation and subsequent mass proliferation of CNN can be viewed as both a blessing and a curse. A blessing, because of the network's pioneering commitment to a global versus a national news format; and a curse, because of the inevitable news repetition that results from a profit-driven, 24-hour news network committed to a global format. While CNN deserves credit for sparking a global news awareness for western (and in particular U.S.) viewers, the network all too often provides our sole source of visual imagery of developing nations. The fact that news broadcasts in general disproportionately focus on tragedy and human drama has meant that what media focus emerging markets do get is usually presented within the context of natural disaster, war, poverty, health crisis, or some other tragedy. This is a fact which has unfortunately led to some deeply ingrained misperceptions of Africa.

To be fair, one cannot blame CNN exclusively for reinforcing the image of Africa as a region drastically inferior to the West. Unfortunately, we rarely see positive images of Africa on any other television networks or in films. Moreover, the diversity of Africa is almost always understated to the point that when "Africa" is discussed, it is as if it is one homogenous country. The fact that the continent is over three times the size of the United States, with its populations speaking thousands of different languages, living in countries with drastically different climates and cultures, and comprised of peoples with quite varied histories, is rarely presented.

Perhaps the most inhibiting factor regarding our perception of Africa is that we rarely are shown any normal contemporary pictures of Africa's modern cities, with their Wall Streets, their universities, their industries, and their suburbs. But we do get a fairly constant flow of images depicting poverty, war, and disease, with an emphasis on jungle and tribal scenes. Even when President Bill Clinton made a historic visit to five countries in Africa in 1997, becoming the first sitting U.S. president to do so, the images that made it back to America were of Clinton and his party on safari in Botswana, and the key story covered by the press told of his remorse that more had not been done to stop the ethnic cleansing which had taken place in Rwanda.

Not that these were not worthwhile images and stories, but by focusing on them an opportunity was missed, for example, to draw attention to the growing dynamism of Ghana's economy by capturing pictures of the modern industrial plants there. Highlighting the relatively impressive infrastructure of Nairobi or Johannesburg would also have gone a long way toward impressing upon western viewers that by and large Africans in the continent's major cities have the same concerns as their peers in the Americas, Europe, and Asia—enjoying equal opportunities, holding good jobs, obtaining adequate education for their children, and securing quality health care and other social services.

Part of the problem is that the countries of Africa historically have not had the financial wherewithal nor the technological sophistication to present their own images to the world. Their overall ability to engage in public relations efforts to get across the positive developments occurring in their countries has thus been quite limited. Also, notwithstanding the nearly 40 years of independence that most African countries have had, global media have tended to view Africa through the interpretations of the former colonialists, France, Belgium, England, Portugal, and to a lesser extent, Germany. This Europerspective romanticizes a bygone era in which "civilization" was "brought" to Africa, and in doing so helps to maintain economic hegemony and political influence by these European countries within the continent. A strong, democratic, economically vibrant and self-sustaining Africa is not the image that those who benefit most from the continent's perceived weaknesses want the world to see. As long as African nations are debtors, their creditors have the upper hand, and as long as these nations are donor aid recipients, the donors can dictate the type, pace, and extent of development assistance that will be provided. It is safe to say that this development assistance is unlikely to help African countries directly compete with the donors in the global economy.

An important aim of African countries over the next decade will be to not only continue improving their investment climates, but also to play a greater role in disseminating the news of investment successes on the continent. Further, efforts to ensure a more balanced coverage from a news and media standpoint are also being planned in the continent's major markets, particularly in South Africa and Nigeria. Today, those working to promote investment in Africa are recognizing that improving the realities of investing there is only half of the solution to effectively attracting capital to the continent. Changing investors' existing perceptions about the risks, real and imagined, the types of opportunities available, and the potential for significant returns related to investment in Africa will be the next big hurdle to overcome.

3
Finding Needles in a Haystack

There is somewhat of a herd mentality in the investment world. If the "big boys"—meaning the large institutional investors in the asset management/ portfolio investment arena and the large blue chip multinationals in the foreign direct investment arena—with all of their tools and resources for research and due diligence are putting their money in a particular market or sector, then I, the new investor/company, will piggyback off of their analysis and park my money there as well.

However, in the case of Africa, the investment success of the big boys has not being heralded in a manner that can serve to illuminate similar opportunities that others can take advantage of. Most often the performance numbers attributable to Africa are hidden in a broad Africa/Europe or Africa/Middle East analyst report. Furthermore, few African companies are profiled in global trade and finance publications, or are featured on the growing number of international business television programs. So, unfortunately, most African businesses still remain faceless and nameless. Thus, we recognize that it is still quite difficult to determine which countries provide the best potential investment opportunities, which sectors offer the greatest amount of growth, and which companies have the strongest and most experienced management teams. In the vastness of the continent, looking for the right investment opportunity can indeed be like searching for the proverbial needle in the haystack.

THE REGIONAL MARKETS

Although the African investment landscape is comprised of 53 potential markets, if one segments the markets into regional groupings, there are 6 major markets for consideration: North Africa, Southern Africa, Central Africa, East Africa, West Africa–CFA Zone, and West Africa–Non-CFA Zone.

North Africa

The economies of North Africa (see Figures 3.1 and 3.2) are principally involved in the export of oil and in the production of agricultural products. However, tourism is a fast-growing contributor to the gross domestic product (GDP) for a number of this region's members. The North Africa region is economically the strongest on the continent, and its members account for 47% of Africa's GDP and 22% of its population. As members of the Arab Maghreb Union, the countries of North Africa are working to remove tariff and nontariff

FIGURE 3.1   North Africa Region

Percentage

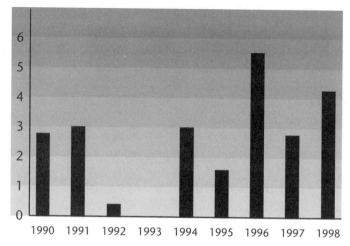

FIGURE 3.2   GDP Growth in North Africa
Source: African Development Report 1999

barriers between themselves to promote intraregional business development. Two members, Morocco and Tunisia, have gone even further and have signed association agreements with the European Union (EU). These agreements provide for extensive trade liberalization between the two countries and the EU and are aimed at promoting cooperation in a number of other areas.

Southern Africa

Southern Africa (see Figures 3.3 and 3.4) is one of the continent's most richly endowed regions, and most of the economic activity revolves around the extraction, and to a lesser degree the processing, of selected metals, oil, diamonds, gold, and copper. Agriculture and tourism are other important contributors to Southern Africa's GDP, with crops, cattle, and fisheries being the key sectors of agriculture-related activity. The service sector is also quite dynamic in this region, providing nearly 46% of the regional GDP. Industry provides 41% and agriculture approximately 14% of regional GDP. South Africa is by far the leading engine of the region, accounting for approximately 80% of the region's GDP. Other rapidly growing countries in the region include Mozambique and Botswana. Lastly, it is noteworthy that after South Africa, Zimbabwe is the region's second-largest industrial power.

The most prominent economic community in this region is the Southern African Development Community (SADC), headquartered in Botswana. With its focus on fostering intraregional trade and investment, SADC is arguably the continent's best-functioning regional community.

FIGURE 3.3   Southern Africa Region

Central Africa

The Central Africa region (see Figures 3.5 and 3.6) is a diverse one. As one of the (if not *the*) foremost producers of African crude oil, the region has both relatively extreme wealth—in terms of per capita income—and extreme poverty. A number of the countries in the region have tremendous untapped or underutilized economic potential in the area of natural resource development. The oil-producing countries in the region are Cameroon, Chad, Gabon, and Equatorial Guinea, and those richly endowed with mineral wealth include the Democratic Republic of Congo, which has an abundance of diamonds and gold reserves.

Cameroon has the largest economy in this region, followed by Gabon. Both are Central African members of the Banque des Etats de L'Afrique Centrale (BEAC), which is a central bank for the French-speaking countries of the region. Other BEAC members include the Central African Republic, Chad, Congo, Equatorial Guinea, and São Tome & Principe. These countries

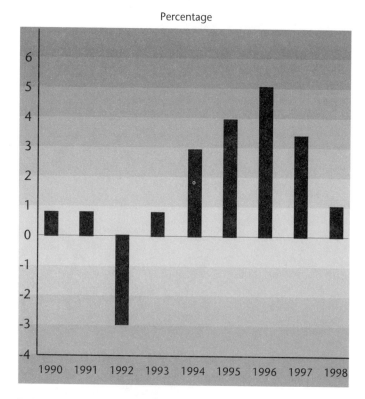

Percentage

FIGURE 3.4   Gross Domestic Product Growth in
Southern Africa
Source: African Development Report 1999

are also members of the CFA Zone, and as such have benefited from the currency stability provided by the fact that the BEAC historically maintained its operations account with the French treasury, and currently does so with the European Union Treasury.

East Africa

The East Africa region (see Figures 3.7 and 3.8) is one in which agriculture and services play a large roll in the economy. It is a diverse region, where some countries, such as Uganda, Mauritius, Madagascar, and Kenya, have lush, arable land, while others, such as Somalia and Djibouti, are natural-resource poor and located primarily on desert terrain. Uganda and Mauritius are two of the more consistently dynamic economic performers in the region. Mauritius' steady 5+% GDP growth rate is attributable to rapid expansion in the sugar industry; the strong performance of companies in its export processing zones; progress in

FIGURE 3.5 Central Africa Region

its efforts to become a regional financial center; and positive performance in the tourism sector. Economic growth in Uganda has been attributable to strong services and industrial sectors. In East Africa's agricultural sector, coffee and tea exports account for a large share of foreign revenue generation. These two products account for 82% of Ethiopia's export earnings (EE), 64% of Uganda's EE, 36% of Kenya's EE, 18% of Tanzania's EE, and 14% of Madagascar's EE. Kenya, Mauritius, and Seychelles also have the region's strongest tourism sectors and rank among the top tourist destinations on the African continent.

West Africa Region—CFA Zone

The countries of West Africa (see Figures 3.9 and 3.10) can best be classified by denoting those which are within the CFA franc monetary zone and those that fall outside of it. These countries, like the members of the BEAC central bank in the Central Africa region, share a currency that until 1994 was pegged to the French franc at a value of 2CFA: 1 Franc. In 1994, the CFA was devalued by 50 percent,

Percentage

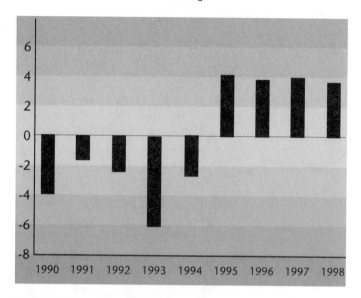

FIGURE 3.6 Gross Domestic Product Growth in Central Africa

Source: African Development Report 1999

and on January 1, 1999 it became pegged to the euro at a rate of 655.957 CFA francs per euro. The industrial sector in this region is relatively small, accounting for only 17.9% of GDP. Agriculture accounts for 29.4% of GDP, and the service sector accounts for the balance of 50.9% of GDP. In West Africa overall, tourism has become a fast-growing contributor to GDP, accounting for 11% of all tourism revenues in Africa. Two of the three leading regional tourist destinations, namely Côte d'Ivoire and Senegal, are within the CFA Zone. Ghana is the other leading tourist destination. Monetary policy within this region is set by the West African Economic and Monetary Union (UEMOA), which supports the intraregional harmonization of macroeconomic and legal policies.

West Africa Region—Non-CFA Zone

Ghana and Nigeria possess the dominant economies outside of the CFA Zone in West Africa (see Figures 3.11 and 3.12), with Nigeria being the predominant economy in the region when considering both CFA and non-CFA countries. Oil in Nigeria and gold, cocoa, and tourism in Ghana are the key contributors to these countries' GDP. In the smaller economies of the region, agriculture is the primary contributor to GDP. Along with the CFA Zone countries, the non–CFA-Zone countries are part of the 16-member Economic

FIGURE 3.7 Map of East Africa Region

Community of West African States (ECOWAS). Although to date ECOWAS has not been very successful in stimulating intraregional trade, significant strides have been made in the area of macroeconomic harmonization. Also, visa and entry permit requirements have been abolished in the region, allowing the free movement of labor.

PROMISING COUNTRY MARKETS

The process of segmenting Africa's markets cannot stop with a brief analysis of the key regions of the continent. There are a number of other factors that one needs to consider when deciding where to invest. Some of these discriminators include the population size of the market, the size of the economy, the presence or lack thereof of peace and political stability, the absence or degree of corruption, the existence of capital markets, the standard of education and degree of

Percentage

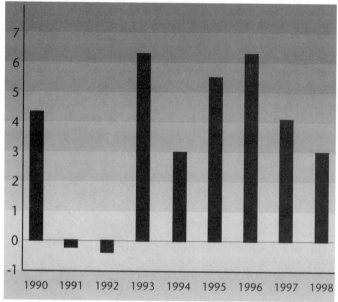

FIGURE 3.8   Gross Domestic Product Growth
in East Africa
Source: Africa Development Report 1999

adult literacy, the competitiveness of the labor force, the proximity to ocean/river trade routes, the endowment of natural resources, and the state of development of the energy/electricity telecommunications, transportation, and water/sewage infrastructure. When you compensate for these factors, the number of promising target investment markets in Africa shakes out to a much more manageable size.

We believe that there are two tiers of countries worth targeting: (1) those with immediate investment opportunities and potential, and (2) those that are promising markets with midterm investment opportunities but which still have to overcome certain political, economic, and/or social hurdles before they can reach their maximum investment attraction potential. The tier-one countries include Botswana, Côte d'Ivoire, Egypt, Ghana, Mauritius, Morocco, Namibia, Nigeria, South Africa, Tunisia, and Uganda (see Figure 3.13). The tier-two countries include Cameroon, Ethiopia, Gabon, Kenya, Mozambique, Senegal, Tanzania, and Zimbabwe (see Figure 3.14).

Also worth mentioning because of their longer-term economic possibilities are Angola and the Democratic Republic of Congo, two of Africa's potentially richest countries. Both are richly endowed with natural resources but

FIGURE 3.9 West Africa Region—CFA Zone

have been embroiled in political conflict, and at times war, during the past 15 years. Except for offshore oil exploration potential in Angola, they do not offer many short-term attractive investment opportunities—but they are countries to monitor during the next decade.

All of the tier-two countries offer unique and attractive investment opportunities for the sophisticated investor. However, because of political instability/ undemocratic governance (Cameroon, Kenya, Zimbabwe), engagement in regional conflicts (Ethiopia), or the emergent size of their economies (Gabon, Mozambique, Senegal, Tanzania), these countries require more prudence from an investment standpoint and therefore present opportunities that are riskier than those offered within the tier-one countries.

A key additional point that a shrewd investor in Africa must keep in mind when evaluating countries and specific deal opportunities within the context of the aforementioned two-tier system is that it is important to use it only as a rough guideline for opportunity selection. Change can happen fast on the con-

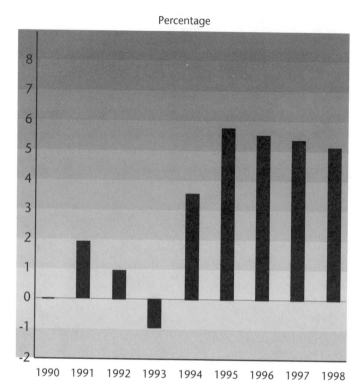

Percentage

FIGURE 3.10   GDP Growth in West Africa
Source: Africa Development Report 1999

tinent, and a second-tier country today, with a change in leadership; a cessation of conflict, internally or in a neighboring country; and/or renewed support from the multilateral community, can quickly emerge as a tier-one investment target. Similarly, a tier-one country today, with a change in leadership, the withdrawal of multilateral support, or the emergence of internal civil unrest, can quickly become an unattractive investment destination.

Flexibility, patience, research, and deal-by-deal analysis are ultimately the best determinates of probable investment success in each of Africa's 53 markets.

INFRASTRUCTURE AND COMPETITIVE ADVANTAGE

For the investor appraising opportunities in Africa, an additional way to rank countries from a risk and attractiveness standpoint is to assess the competitive advantages that access to adequate infrastructure in one region/country/company lends to a particular target company/industry/region, versus a region/industry/company with comparably less infrastructure.

FIGURE 3.11 West Africa Region—Non-CFA Zone

The premise here is that given better and more cost-effective access to infrastructure, a company in one region/country is likely to perform better than a competitor situated in a region or country that is less endowed infrastructurally. Hence, a manufacturer in South Africa's eastern region of Kwa Zulu Natal is likely to have a competitive advantage over a manufacturer in the same field based just a few hundred miles away in Mozambique, because of the better overall infrastructure (among other things) in South Africa versus Mozambique (see Figure 3.15).

A comparative look at Africa's infrastructure sectors can be instructive in helping to isolate prospective target investment markets and companies.

Telecommunications

In today's Information Age, telephone connectivity has become a vital source of not just voice communication but also video, data, and Internet communication as well. Thus, access to cheap and reliable telecommunications infra-

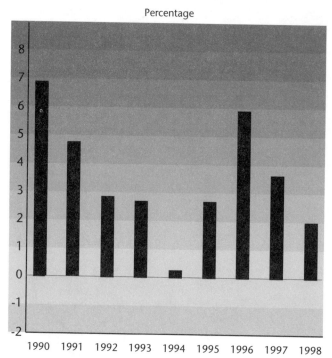

Percentage

FIGURE 3.12   GDP Growth in West Africa
                 Non-CFA Zone
                 Source: Africa Development Report 1999

structure is an important component of a country's investment attractiveness and competitiveness.

From an overall standpoint, Africa is still a way from being fully integrated into the global communications network. Using the standard measurement of telephone access—*teledensity*—which provides an analysis of the ratio of telephone land lines to inhabitants in a country, Africa's telephone coverage ranks among the lowest in the world. Africa accounts for only 2% of the world's telephone lines, versus 32% for America, 28% for Asia, and 36% for Europe (see Figure 3.16).

Today, there are only about 14 million telephones in Africa, 2 million of which are in the 7 countries of North Africa, 5 million of which are in South Africa, and the remaining 2 million of which are disbursed among the remaining 45 countries of the continent. Outside of South Africa, in Sub-Saharan Africa, the additional 7 million telephone lines are so widely dispersed that the average person lives more than two hours away from the nearest telephone. Various references have noted that there are more phones in a num-

FIGURE 3.13 Tier-One Target Investment Countries
Source: African Development Report 1999

Country	Area ('000 Sq. Km)	Population 1998	GNP Per Capita (US$) 1997	Gross National Savings (Percentage of GDP) 1998	Gross Domestic Investment (Percentage of GDP) 1998
Botswana	600	1.55	3260	31.7	27.9
Cote d'Ivoire	323	14.57	690	14.2	18.2
Egypt	1001	65.67	1180	19.5	18.5
Ghana	239	18.86	370	13.6	18.2
Mauritius	2	1.15	3800	26.4	28.0
Morocco	447	28.01	1250	23.5	22.5
Namibia	823	1.65	2220	25.5	21.1
Nigeria	924	121.77	260	8.1	14.8
South Africa	1220	44.30	3400	14.2	15.9
Tunisia	164	9.50	2090	24.5	27.7
Uganda	236	21.32	330	17.7	24.7
Africa	30,060	777.53	677	15.7	20.0

Country	Gross Domestic Product, Real (Millions of US Dollars) 1998	International Reserves (Millions of US Dollars) 1998	Total External Debt (Millions of US Dollars) 1997	Adult Literacy (%) 1995	Life Expectancy at Birth (Years) 1997
Botswana	5016	6026.3	759.8	70	51
Cote d'Ivoire	14081	701.5	17680.0	30	52
Egypt	53827	19103.0	28774.0	51	67
Ghana	8268	102.5	6317.1	64	49
Mauritius	3922	613.7	1235.6	83	72
Morocco	31948	4569.0	19999.9	44	67
Namibia	3295	234.0	343.4	44	56
Nigeria	35898	----	28660.0	57	53
South Africa	116863	4326.0	25200.0	82	66
Tunisia	17646	2129.9	10858.6	67	70
Uganda	7333	751.0	3972.3	62	43
Africa	376,856	53,806.4	314,688.7	56	54

FIGURE 3.13 Tier-One Target Investment Countries (*continued*)

Country	Area ('000 Sq. Km)	Population 1998	GNP Per Capita (US$) 1997	Gross National Savings (Percentage of GDP) 1998	Gross Domestic Investment (Percentage of GDP) 1998
Cameroon	475	14.32	650	14.7	18.4
Ethiopia	1104	62.11	110	3.5	20.3
Gabon	268	1.17	4230	24.7	28.0
Kenya	583	29.02	330	20.1	18.7
Mozambique	802	18.69	90	16.0	35.2
Senegal	196	9.00	550	13.1	17.5
Tanzania	945	32.19	210	15.8	19.4
Zimbabwe	391	11.92	750	22.1	22.2
Africa	30,060	777.53	677	15.7	20.0

FIGURE 3.14 Tier-Two Target Investment Countries
Souce: African Development Report 1999

Country	Gross Domestic Product, Real (Millions of US Dollars) 1998	International Reserves (Millions of US Dollars) 1998	Total External Debt (Millions of US Dollars) 1997	Adult Literacy (%) 1995	Life Expectancy at Birth (Years) 1997
Cameroon	11743	1.2	9990.2	63	57
Ethiopia	8760	330.1	4166.8	35	51
Gabon	7606	107.7	4147.6	63	56
Kenya	9944	685.2	6400.0	78	56
Mozambique	3139	523.7	7431.6	40	48
Senegal	7122	403.5	3256.8	33	52
Tanzania	5211	557.2	7799.9	68	52
Zimbabwe	10126	173.8	4708.7	85	49
Africa	376,856	53,806.4	314,688.7	56	54

FIGURE 3.14 Tier-Two Target Investment Countries (*continued*)

Percentage Respondents All Firms

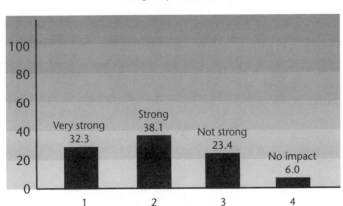

FIGURE 3.15 Impact of Infrastructure on Foreign Direct
Investment
Source: Africa Development Report 1999

ber of other emerging world markets, and indeed in some cities in the more
developed countries of the world, than in the entire continent of Africa.
Brazil, for example, has more phones than Africa, and Tokyo, Japan, and the
borough of Manhattan in New York each have more phones than all of Africa.
For world distribution of telephone lines, see Figure 3.17.

In 1996, Africa's teledensity averaged 2 (2 persons out of 100 had access
to a telephone), compared to 6.02 in Asia, 30.38 in North and South America
combined, 30.60 in Europe, and 40.39 in Oceania. Thirty-four countries in
Africa still have a teledensity of less than 1, and only five countries have a
teledensity of 10 or more: South Africa, Mauritius, Namibia, Gabon, and
Gambia. Today, the continent's teledensity is a disappointing 1.2.

Inequities in the per capita GDP levels of Africa's various countries underlie,
in large part, the distinctions between which countries have the greatest and least
levels of teledensity. Countries such as Botswana, Libya, Mauritius, Morocco,
South Africa, and Tunisia that have relatively higher GDP per capita rates also
have higher telephone penetration rates. Landlocked countries with lower GDP
per capita rates, such as Chad, Mali, and Niger, have lower penetration rates.
From a regional perspective, North African countries have roughly three times
the teledensity rates of African countries south of the Sahara Desert.

From the standpoint of the ratio of teledensity splits between rural and
urban areas, the greater teledensity can be found in the major urban areas,
where over 80% of the average telephone coverage in African countries is
concentrated. Thus the rural areas of Africa possess less than 20% of the con-

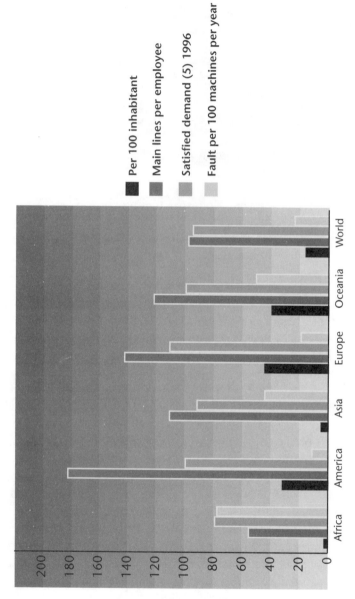

FIGURE 3.16 Comparative Telecommunications Statistics for Africa and the Rest of the World
Source: African Development Report 1999

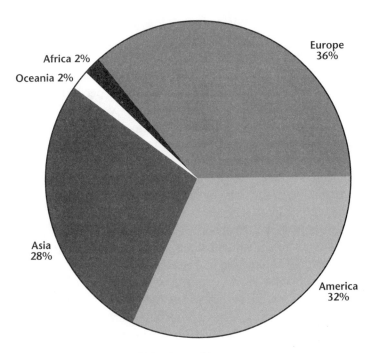

FIGURE 3.17　Main Telephone Lines
Source: African Development Report 1999

tinent's telephones; yet, paradoxically, these are where the access needs are greatest, since in many cases up to 80 percent of the African populations reside in the outlying regions.

An interesting outgrowth of Africa's teledensity challenges has been the phenomenal interest in cellular telephony in many of the continent's countries. Powered by satellite technology, cellular communications have been able in a number of cases to effectively supplement the aging analog landline telephone systems. From an investment perspective, as discussed elsewhere in this book, cellular telephone deals have also been some of the best performing and highest yielding deals in the past decade.

The success of cellular companies in Africa has also been partially due to the pent-up demand for phone service existent on the continent. Although in South Africa and Morocco the average waiting period for telephone installation among new clients is only 3 and 6 months, respectively, the overall average waiting time for telephone services in Africa is the highest in the world. In 1996, this average connection period was 3.5 years, compared to an average of 7 months in Asia and 3 months in the United States, inclusive of under-privileged rural and urban areas.

Waiting lists for telephone service are common in a number of African countries, including Cameroon, Ghana, Kenya, Nigeria, South Africa (particularly in the rural areas, where teledensity averages about 1 phone per 100 people), Tanzania, and Zimbabwe. In 1996, Egypt, in the relatively affluent North Africa region, had a waiting list of nearly 1.3 million people. Algeria, Eritrea, Ethiopia, Gambia, Malawi, Mozambique, São Tome & Principe, Sierra Leone, and Tanzania all have recorded waiting periods for connection that exceed 10 years.

Positive changes are, however, on the way. At Africa Telecom 98, the International Telecommunications Union (ITU)-supported annual meeting of African telecommunications ministers and experts, more than 6,000 people met in South Africa to strategize about ways to improve the continent's telephone infrastructure. Telecommunications ministers attending the forum signed policy agreements pledging to privatize and liberalize the sector by June 2000, and to work toward the implementation in Africa of the Global Information Infrastructure (GII) protocol put forth by the United States at the First World Telecommunications Development Conference in 1994. Furthermore, the ITU revealed that plans were underway to increase Africa's telephone user base to 20 million subscribers by the year 2000, and that in support of this mission it was expected that more than $20 billion of new infrastructure development projects would be undertaken by 2003.

Electricity

Just as connection to the global information highway has been recognized as a key catalyst for the improvement of the African investment climate, improving available sources of power generation has also been targeted as a critical investment promotion-related agenda item for the next decade.

Power availability in Africa, like the availability of telephone access, is disproportionately concentrated in the urban areas. In terms of regional distribution (see Figure 3.18), North Africa accounts for one-third of the continent's energy production. West Africa accounts for 9% of the continent's capacity, Central Africa, 4%, and East Africa, 3%. Southern Africa has the most developed electric infrastructure on the continent, producing 55% of the entire continent's energy.

Overall, Africa's power generation mix is dominated by fossil fuel generating plants, which account for 81% of total electricity generation. Oil-related power generation is fairly evenly distributed throughout Africa, while coal-based generation is principally concentrated in Southern Africa, specifically in Botswana, Mozambique, South Africa, and Zimbabwe. Morocco and Niger are North and West Africa countries, respectively, that also have significant

REGION / PERCENT		ENERGY SOURCE
East Africa	3%	Oil and hydroelectricity
West Africa	9%	Hydroelectricity, oil and gas
Central Africa	4%	Hydroelectricity
North Africa	33%	Coal and natural gas
Southern Africa	55%	Hydroelectricity and coal burning

FIGURE 3.18 Africa's Energy Production by Region and Type
Source: African Development Report 1999

coal-fueled electricity generation. In Algeria, Nigeria, and Tunisia, gas-fueled energy systems are becoming increasingly important.

Notwithstanding Africa's abundant waterways, only a small fraction (15%) of Africa's power generation comes from hydroelectric sources, with 64% of this amount originating in East and Southern Africa, 34.2% in West Africa, and only 1.2% in North Africa. This is primarily because there are often short-falls in water flow associated with climate changes in a number of countries, low demand in some countries endowed with immense hydroelectric re-sources, and often significant power losses during long-distance transmission because of deteriorating infrastructure.

Beginning in the latter 1990s, a number of alternative and renewable energy projects have been launched that focus on harnessing the continent's abundant solar and wind resources. Providing rural electrification has been a major theme of such initiatives. Although some strides have been made in West Africa in this area, the greatest developments of renewable energy sources have been achieved in Southern Africa, particularly in Botswana and South Africa.

A review of selected electrical power performance indicators in Africa (see Figure 3.19) and other emerging markets provides illustration of the progress that is needed in this area. Fortunately, major global power-generation–related corporations such as Enron and ABB are becoming active in Africa. South Africa's Eskom is also becoming active in other African nations. And new private equity funds such as the $500 million Africa Infrastructure Fund and the $350 million New Africa Infrastructure Fund are being organized with an end toward providing and helping to mobilize additional capital for power generation projects in Africa.

Country	Transmission and distribution losses (per cent)	Rate of return on net asset (per cent)
Ghana	17.8	6.0(1993)
Cote d'Ivoire	16.3	NA
Mali	21.2	1.2(1994)
Guinea	27.0	-6.2(1993)
Sierra Leone	38.5	-16.0(1993)
Nigeria	30.0	-8.2
Senegal	14.3	3.7(1993)
Cameroon	13.0	NA
Zambia	8.0	-8.0(1994)
Zimbabwe	11.0	5.8(1993/4)
Kenya	12.5	15.0(1994)
Uganda	38.0	0.0(1994)
South Africa	7.0	11.5(1994)
Chile	10.6	8.1(1994)
Malaysia	15.8	8.2(1994)
Argentina	25.4	7.0(1994)

FIGURE 3.19   Power Sector Performance Indicators of Selected African
Countries
Source: Turkson and Rowlands 1998

Roads

Road transportation remains the most important mode of transportation in
Africa. Africa's inland waterways have never been fully developed for larger
vessels, and the rail networks have historically only been constructed for slow
freight moving over limited distances, generally from inland areas toward the
coastal ports. Thus, even where rail and water transport routes have been
available, roadway travel has remained an integral component of the transport
route for significant lengths of the cargo or passenger's route.

In 1996, the latest year for which statistics were available, Africa had
approximately 311,000 kilometers of roads. However, with the exception of
Mauritius and the North African countries (Algeria, Egypt, Morocco, and
Tunisia), paved roads account for less than half of the road network in Africa.

Indicative of the growth necessary in this infrastructure development area is the fact that in the region south of the Sahara, paved roads account for only 17% of all roads—and many countries have fallen below even that average. Overall, in Africa road density per square kilometer is among the lowest in the world; significantly less than in Asia and Latin America. (See Figures 3.20 and 3.21.)

As vital to economic growth as Africa's roadways are, many countries simply are unable to bear the often significant costs necessary to develop, maintain, and rehabilitate their existing road infrastructure, let alone build and/or expand new roads. A critical focus of Africa's nations in the next decade will be to develop a more comprehensive and trade-route-reflective interregional and intraregional road grid.

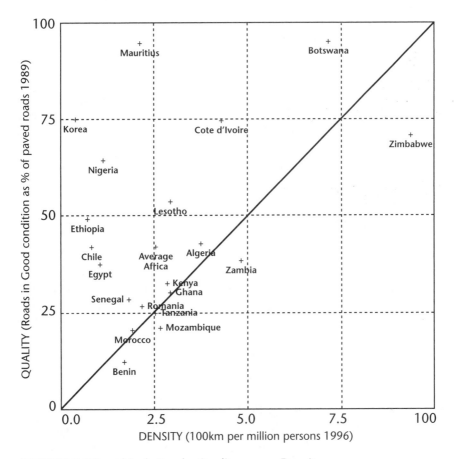

FIGURE 3.20 Africa's Roads: Quality versus Density
Source: African Development Report 1999

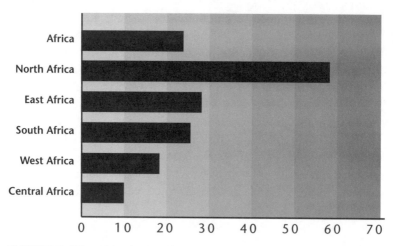

FIGURE 3.21   Africa's Paved Roads as a Percentage of the Total Road Network by Region
Source: African Development Report 1999

Apart from North Africa, Southern Africa, given the past regional hegemony of South Africa, arguably has the continent's best intraregional road network. This network links Botswana, Lesotho, Malawi, Mozambique, Namibia, South Africa, Swaziland, Zambia, and Zimbabwe with easily accessible, relatively uniformly maintained multilane highways. Large trucks move goods across the region—principally from the main regional ports in South Africa and Namibia.

From the perspective of individual countries with fairly sound roadway systems in North Africa, Algeria, Egypt, Morocco, and Tunisia all have significant kilometers of paved roads; in East Africa, Kenya has the best roads, although for the past 15 to 20 years maintenance has been a problem; in Central Africa, none of the countries have significant paved road coverage; in West Africa, Côte d'Ivoire has the best-maintained road system, while Ghana is aggressively working to catch up. Nigeria has the overall largest network of paved roads, but as in Kenya, maintenance has been a perennial problem. In Southern Africa, Botswana, Lesotho, Namibia, South Africa, Swaziland, and Zimbabwe share a relatively seamless network of paved road connectivity.

Water Supply and Waste Management

In addition to assessing the telecommunications, road, and electricity/energy sectors of any particular African country, the investor seeking to make the soundest investment decisions possible should not fail to also analyze the water and waste management capacities of that nation.

In Africa, water management is a critically important issue. The World Health Organization has identified waterborne organisms as one of the leading contributors to diarrheal and other disabling illnesses in the developing regions of Africa. Guinea worm disease (dracunculiases), trachoma infection (which can cause blindness), and louse- and fly-borne diseases are but some of the many maladies that can be transmitted and contracted in environments where potable water is available but where significant water purification/treatment facilities do not yet exist.

In terms of impact on industry, wastewater management is critical to companies that need adequate water for the cleaning and disposal process within their manufacturing/processing operations. Water management is also important in countries where significant flows of electrical energy are achieved from hydroelectric power sources. Given the vagaries of rainfall in Africa, efficiently managing water resources has been a constant challenge and national priority for most of the nations on the continent. As agricultural production is an important contributor to national GDP in almost all of the countries of the continent, water irrigation, conservation, and transportation are also key focal points.

Many African countries have battled with the challenge of providing safe water to citizens. In 1995, only 60% of the residents of urban centers on the continent had access to safe water, and a mere 40% had such access in rural areas. African nations with comparatively better overall water systems include Côte d'Ivoire in West Africa; Mauritius, South Africa, and Zimbabwe in Southern Africa; Kenya in East Africa; and Egypt in North Africa. In all of these countries, however, there is greater access to safe water in the urban areas than in the rural areas (see Figure 3.22).

In the next decade, water management, sanitation, and purification will be among the greater infrastructural development priorities for the continent. Those countries which are most successful in addressing the challenges related to this sector will be able to achieve an important relative comparative advantage for investment attraction into the twenty-first century.

THE INVESTOR'S WHO'S WHO—THE BEST COUNTRIES FOR INVESTMENT AS CHOSEN BY THE AFRICAN INVESTMENT PROMOTION AGENCIES

During the 1990s, globalization has progressed, and transnational corporations have expanded into Africa. The African countries that have become the principal recipients of foreign direct investment on the continent share a few common attributes: market size, natural resource wealth, and adequate publicly (or privately) supplied infrastructure.

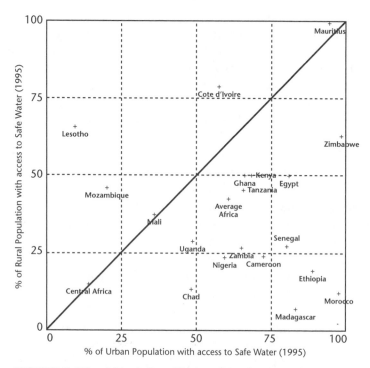

FIGURE 3.22   Africa's Rural/Urban Distribution of Water
Source: Africa Development Report 1999

In 1998, $8.3 billion of foreign direct investment (FDI) was made in Africa. Africa's share of FDI in developing countries was 5% (but only 1.2% of global FDI). However, in comparison to the early 1990s, this marked significant improvement, although it was slightly less than the $9.4 billion record high recorded in 1997. What is of particular note is that for the sixth consecutive year, the 33 least-developed countries in Africa experienced an increase in FDI flows, thus raising their share in total FDI received in the region from one-fifth in 1997 to one-quarter or $2.2 billion in 1998 (see Figure 3.23).

In 1998, the top recipients of African FDI were Nigeria and Egypt. In 1997, these two countries and South Africa had shared top billing, but investment in South Africa fell off significantly in 1998 (principally due to lower privatization-related FDI inflows). From 1996 to 1998, key target areas of investment included the following sectors: telecommunications, food and beverages, tourism, mining and quarrying, and textiles and leather (see Figure 3.24).

(Billions of dollars)

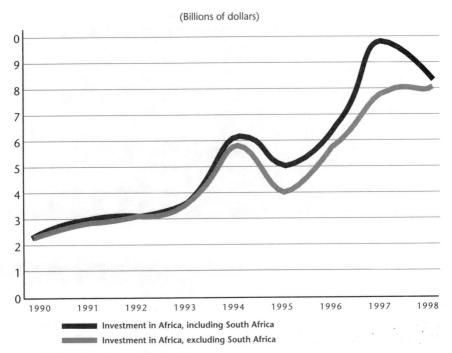

Investment in Africa, including South Africa
Investment in Africa, excluding South Africa

FIGURE 3.23 FDI Inflows to Africa, 1990–1998
Source: UNCTAD

Many of the foreign investors active in these sectors were significantly involved in privatization programs. Among the lesser developed countries receiving FDI, Equatorial Guinea, Ethiopia, Mozambique, Uganda, and Tanzania received the majority of the investments made, and they were principally targeted toward the natural resource and manufacturing sectors (see Figure 3.25).

The main sources of FDI into Africa have historically been France, the United Kingdom, the United States, and, to a lesser extent, Germany and Japan. However, while these countries have remained important investors in Africa, in recent years other countries such as Canada, Italy, and The Netherlands have become more active. In 1997, the latest year for which figures are available, U.S. companies were the largest foreign direct investors in Africa ($3.7 billion), followed by Belgium ($1.2 billion), the United Kingdom ($1.1 billion), and France ($600 million).

Although South African FDI fell off in 1998 due to less privatization-related investment activity, the fact that most of the FDI in this country is driven by mergers and acquisitions (M&A) is a relevant phenomenon to

(Percentage)

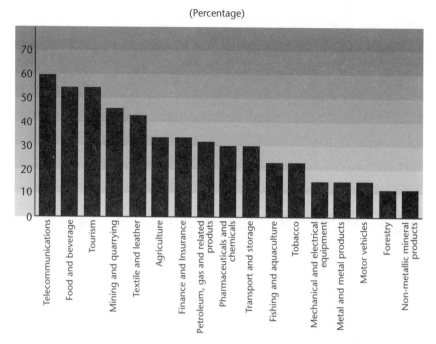

FIGURE 3.24   Industries in Africa that Received Considerable FDI Flows in 1996–1998
Source: UNCTAD

acknowledge. In 1998, over $50 billion in M&A transactions took place. South African companies continue to be perceived as attractive partners by foreign corporations—principally from Germany, Italy, Malaysia, Switzerland, the United Kingdom, and the United States. The leading target sectors for investment in South Africa have included energy and oil sectors, mining and quarrying, construction and materials, motor vehicles and components, and food and beverages.

From the standpoint of acknowledging the African countries that have been most successful at attracting foreign direct investment throughout the 1990s, the United Nations selected six African nations in 1998 as *FDI Front-runners* for their dynamism in attracting FDI. These countries included Botswana, Ghana, Mozambique, Namibia, Tunisia, and Uganda. In a broader effort, the United Nations surveyed African investment promotion agencies to request their rankings of the most attractive African FDI destinations. Their responses were quite illuminating. The top 10 countries projected to receive

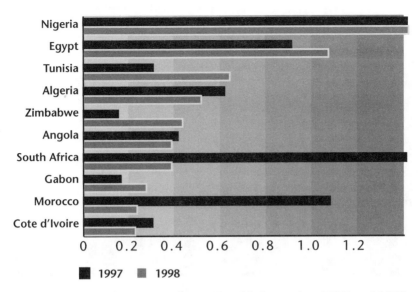

FIGURE 3.25   Africa: FDI Inflows, Top 10 Countries, 1997 and 1998
Source: UNCTAD

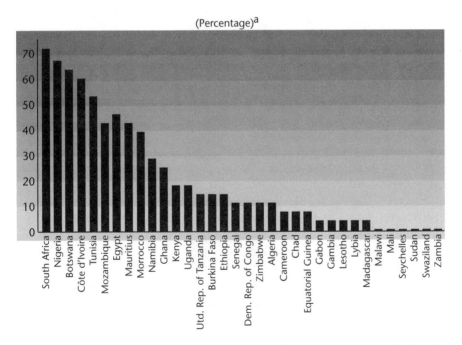

FIGURE 3.26   African Countries Ranked According to their Attractiveness
for FDI in 2000–2003
Source: UNCTAD

(Percentage)

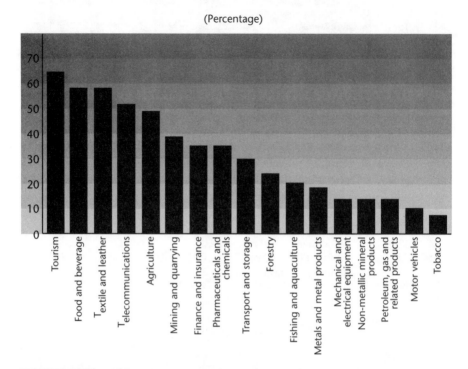

FIGURE 3.27   Africa: Most Attractive Industries for FDI in 2000–2003
Source: UNCTAD

FDI, in order of ranking, were South Africa, Nigeria, Botswana, Côte d'Ivoire, Tunisia, Mozambique, Egypt, Mauritius, Morocco, and Namibia (see Figure 3.26).

The top 10 projected most attractive industries for investment included: tourism, food and beverages, textiles and leather, telecommunications, agriculture, mining and quarrying, finance and insurance, pharmaceuticals and chemicals, transport and storage, and forestry (see Figure 3.27).

With a sound understanding of the overall African macroeconomic environment, and regional information that permits an investor to further segment the continent, it becomes much easier for the interested investor to explore specific opportunities as they are presented. And against this background it also becomes much easier to assess the opportunities that are emerging within Africa's maturing universe of stock markets.

4

A Walk down Africa's Wall Streets

Once investors have developed a sense of which countries they want to target, an analysis of those nations' capital market structures can assist the research process. We believe that the ideal way to explore the African investment landscape is by beginning to follow the activity on and performance of the continent's stock markets.

Today, more than 2,100 public companies in Africa are listed on the region's 16 stock exchanges (see Figure 4.1*). With a combined market capitalization of more than $270 billion, Africa's markets have an average annual trading volume of nearly $100 billion.

A casual glance at Figure 4.1 reveals that without question South Africa's Johannesburg Stock Exchange (JSE) is by far the largest of Africa's stock markets, representing more than 80% of the continent's market capitalization. Other import exchanges on the continent include those of Egypt, Morocco, and Tunisia. Rapidly growing but much smaller African exchanges include those in Zimbabwe, Ghana, Mauritius, Côte d'Ivoire (BRVM), Kenya, and Nigeria.

The 1999 Global Development Finance report published by the World Bank noted that as recently as 1995 nearly $5 billion of portfolio capital was

---

* Because the stock exchanges of Tanzania, Uganda, and Mozambique are very thinly capitalized they have been omitted from Figure 4.1. Tanzania has only three listed companies and does not permit foreign investors to invest in its stock exchange. Uganda has only one listed company, and Mozambique does not have any listed companies to date, although one government treasury bill was floated in 1999.

Country	Founded	Listed Companies	Market Cap. ($millions)	Annual Trading Value ($millions)
Botswana	1989	14	724	70.0
BRVM(Abidjan)	1998	35	1818	39.0
Egypt	1881	861	24381	5028.0
Ghana	1990	21	1384	60.0
Kenya	1954	58	2024	79.0
Malawi	1995	3	100	0.6
Mauritius	1989	40	1849	102.0
Morocco	1929	53	14676	1385.0
Namibia	1992	15	429	13.0
Nigeria	1960	186	2887	161.0
South Africa	1887	668	248600	58444.0
Sudan	1995	34	500	3.5
Swaziland	1990	5	85	0.0
Tunisia	1989	38	2268	188.0
Zambia	1995	8	293	0.0
Zimbabwe	1896	67	1310	166.0
TOTAL		2106	287797	65739.1

FIGURE 4.1   Africa's Stock Exchanges
Source: IFC, Emerging Stocks Markets Factbook 1999

invested in Africa's stock exchanges. It was further noted that between 1992 and 1997 the majority of the investment inflow (86%) went to one market, South Africa. Other markets that were significant recipients of investment capital included Ghana (7%) and Morocco (5%). The top 10 African stock markets from the standpoint of net equity inflows are listed in Figure 4.2.

Notwithstanding the fact that the lion's share of investment has gone to the JSE, more and more African countries during the 1990s have launched efforts to establish a local capital market. In fact, Africa has given birth to more new stock exchanges during the last decade than has any other continent. Principal among the reasons cited for establishing local stock markets has been the realization that such markets offer an additional vehicle for attracting foreign investment. In 1997, portfolio equity flows accounted for just under 10% of the total investment received by Sub-Saharan and North Africa. Stock markets are also becoming catalysts and conduits for the mobilization of domestic savings in Africa. Active stock/bond and money markets are starting to help both companies and governments to finance expansion and investment.

The establishment of stock markets in Africa also has had the effect of raising the national and corporate profiles of listed companies and the countries where the listings take place. The hugely successful listing of Ashanti Gold-

Country	$ (millions)
South Africa	24860
Egypt	24381
Morocco	14676
Nigeria	2887
Tunisia	2268
Kenya	2024
Mauritius	1849
Côte d'Ivoire (BRVM)	1818
Ghana	1384
Zimbabwe	1310

FIGURE 4.2 Top 10 African Capital Markets, 1999
Source: IFC, Emerging Stock Markets Factbook, 1999

fields on the Ghana Stock Exchange and internationally (including, among other foreign exchanges, the New York Stock Exchange) greatly contributed to the enhanced recognition that company has enjoyed over the last few years, notwithstanding its more recent financial troubles. Furthermore, that one listing helped put Ghana on the emerging market investor map. Carrying this theme further, the establishment of a stock exchange has increasingly become a sign that a country is moving positively along the development continuum. In addition to contributing to domestic savings, stock markets also are a welcome sign to foreign direct and private equity investors.

Privatization has become an increasingly important component in the economic development strategy of African countries. Stock markets have been identified as important tools through which to mobilize local and foreign capital for the purchase of public assets. African governments in Ghana, Malawi, South Africa, Botswana, Egypt, Morocco, Tanzania, and Zimbabwe have successfully used their stock markets to support their privatization programs. African stock markets have also helped African governments to spread the ownership of privatized companies to local investors, entrepreneurs, and financial institutions such as pension funds. And they have also served as a vehicle to attract capital from Africans living and working abroad. Lastly, the establishment of a stock exchange has come to be viewed as a clear way to promote a country's efforts toward the development of a transparent, disciplined, and free-market-oriented economy—factors that have been proven to be necessary for any meaningful attraction of foreign capital.

Developing secondary markets and liquidity is one of the key areas of focus of today's African exchanges. In 1997, total market activity on the continent was $47.7 billion, 94% of which took place in South Africa. Morocco, with a turnover of approximately $1 billion, had the continent's second-busiest exchange, and Zimbabwe, with a turnover of $532 million, had the third-most-active exchange.

The low liquidity within African stock exchanges is caused by the dearth of shares available for trading, execution hurdles, and limited investor awareness. However, in some markets, including South Africa, Zimbabwe, Nigeria, and Tunisia, increasing investor awareness and improved operating efficiency has lead to a greater liquidity and performance.

AFRICA'S BLUE CHIP COMPANIES

As investor interest in African securities has grown, so too have the companies and the markets that host them. Interestingly, the portfolio capital of today has also helped change the composition of Africa's top blue-chip companies. Given the abundant natural resources of the continent, the perception is that Africa's largest companies would, almost by default, be found among those involved in the extraction and processing of metals and minerals or in agriculture and agribusiness. Although these types of corporations remain significant contributors to Africa's overall GDP, the listed companies of Africa today are far more likely to be in the services sector. Financial services, tourism, and bottling are just a few of the areas in which Africa's blue chip companies are involved.

A Standard Bank African Equities Research unit survey in 1998 found that in 10 of Sub-Saharan Africa's largest markets—Botswana, Ghana, Kenya, Malawi, Mauritius, Namibia, Nigeria, Tanzania, Zambia, and Zimbabwe—the finance sector was the largest sector among the exchanges, accounting for

27.8% ($3.1 billion) of the exchanges' collective $11.2 billion capitalization (see Figure 4.3). Services made up 16% ($1.8 billion) of the total, followed by beverages and tobacco, which together accounted for 14% ($1.6 billion).

The research further showed that 33 listed companies, outside of the larger exchanges of South Africa and North Africa, had a market capitalization of over $100 million. Among the largest of these companies were Ashanti Goldfields, a Ghanaian multinational involved in gold mining, worth $714 million; Delta Corporation, a Zimbabwean industrial conglomerate worth $457 million; and State Bank, a Mauritian financial institution worth $340 million.

Eight of the top 20 companies that made the over $100 million club were financial institutions. British multinational Barclays Bank, whose three primary African subsidiaries (in Kenya, Zimbabwe, and Botswana) were together valued at $611 million, represented 5.4% of the capitalization of the 10 exchanges. Standard Chartered Bank, also a British multinational, through operations in Botswana, Ghana, and Kenya, accounted for an additional $389 million in capitalization.

From an investor security standpoint, it is also worth noting that subsidiaries of foreign multinationals comprised a significant portion of the markets of the 10 exchanges surveyed. Along with the British banks, the top-40 list included a handful of other European multinationals such as Nestle,

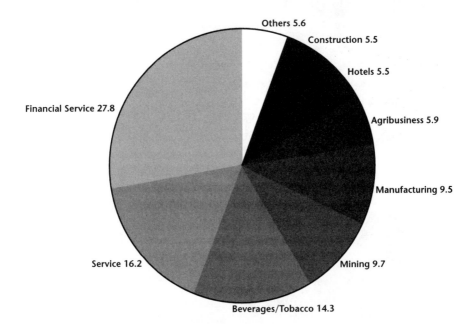

FIGURE 4.3   Industry Breakdown of Africa's Largest Public Companies
Source: Standard Bank

Unilever, and PZ Industries in Nigeria; Delta Corporation in Zimbabwe, Bamburl Cement in Kenya, and West African Portland Cement in Nigeria.

The locations of the top companies were also worth noting. The largest number of top-40 companies (7) were headquartered in Nigeria. Kenya had the second-largest number of top companies (6), and Mauritius had the third-

Country	Company	Sector	Rank	Value US$m
Botswana	Sechaba Breweries	Beer	15	168.7
	Barclays Bank	Finance	19	150.2
	Standard Chartered Bank	Finance	20	142.4
Ghana	Ashanti Goldfields	Mining	1	714.3
	Standard Chartered Bank	Finance	21	135.1
	Ghana Commercial Bank	Finance	26	120.0
	Social Security Bank	Finance	33	100.3
Kenya	Barclays Bank	Finance	6	256.1
	Bamburl Cement	Construction	11	178.2
	Kenya Power and Light	Utility	13	174.2
	Kenya Commercial Bank	Finance	22	134.0
	Brooke Bond	Agriculture	27	117.5
	Standard Chartered Bank	Finance	29	111.7
Malawi	Sugar Corporation of Malawi	Sugar	30	104.2
Mauritius	State bank	Finance	3	339.8
	Mauritius Commercial Bank	Finance	4	332.2
	New Mauritius Hotels	Hotels	5	260.3
	Sun Resorts	Hotels	7	221.8
	Rogers & Co	Services	16	166.6
Namibia	First National	Finance	12	175.9
	Namibian Breweries	Beer	24	121.1
Nigeria	West African Cement	Construction	9	207.0
	Nigeria Bottling	Beverages	17	154.0
	Nigeria Breweries	Beer	18	152.5
	PZ Industries	Manufacturing	25	120.7
	Nestle Foods	FoodsPortland	28	117.1
	First bank Nigeria	Finance	31	104.1
	Lever Brothers	Manufacturing	32	103.0
Zambia	ZCCM	Mining	8	211.7
Zimbabwe	Delta Corporation	Conglomerate	2	456.5
	Barclays Bank	Finance	10	204.0
	Meikles Africa	Conglomerate	14	170.6
	Innscor Africa Fast Foods	Foods	23	122.1

FIGURE 4.4   Africa's $100 Million Companies

largest group (5). However, it is noteworthy that from a capitalization stand-point, the rankings were a bit different: (1) Mauritius ($1.32 billion); (2) Ghana ($1.07 billion); (3) Kenya ($971.7 million); (4) Nigeria ($958.4 million); (5) Botswana ($461.3 million); (6) Namibia ($297.0 million); (7) Zambia ($211.7 million); and (8) Malawi ($104.2 million).

From an investor's perspective, another key point that emerges from this analysis is that notwithstanding the current political and economic challenges that exist to varying degrees in Kenya, Nigeria, and Zimbabwe, these three countries contain some of Africa's most dynamic companies (see list in Figure 4.4). Furthermore, from a historical standpoint these three countries have been (and for many corporations still are) regional hubs for multinationals in Africa. Thus, shrewd investors would be wise not to ignore these markets and their companies, as they are likely to offer liquidity and appreciation over the course of the investment holding period.

Although the Standard Bank survey just noted was insightful, it was admittedly incomplete in providing an overview of Africa's blue-chip companies as

Country	Company	Sector	Rank	Value US$m
South Africa	Billiton PLC	Basic Materials	1	8794.7
	Old Mutual	Finance	2	7028.9
	South African Breweries	Beverages/ Consumer	3	6240.4
	First Rand Limited	Finance	4	5375.9
	Anglo American Platinum Corporation	Mining	5	5375.1
	Anglogold Limited	Mining	6	5364.4
	Nedcor Limited	Finance	7	4697.7
	Standard Bank	Finance	8	4518.1
	SASOL Limited	Energy	9	4517.8
	Rembrandt Group Limited	Conglomerate	10	3830.7
Morocco	Ona SA	Conglomerate	11	2060.0
	Commercial Bank of Morocco	Finance	13	1397.0
	National Investment Company	Finance	16	1258.0
	Commerce Bank of Morocco	Finance	17	1009.6
Egypt	Helwan Cement	Construction	12	1788.2
	Kawmeya Cement	Construction	14	1390.8
	Mobinil-Egypt	Technology	15	1266.4

FIGURE 4.5 Africa's Billion Dollar Companies

it omitted coverage of the continent's largest exchanges, in South Africa and Egypt. However, an analysis of the top securities in these two markets, and those of another strong performer, Morocco, does reinforce a number of the conclusions found in the Standard Bank survey. Specifically, in these latter three markets, as in those surveyed by Standard Bank, the financial companies dominate the markets (see Figure 4.5).

One last segment of the African publicly traded securities market for investment consideration is the growing number of fast-growing South African technology companies. These firms are becoming increasingly globally focused, and a number, including Didator and Perican, have even acquired technology companies in the United States.

PART 2

Why Africa Is the Ultimate Emerging Market

In the past 10 years, African nations have been rapidly undergoing an economic and political evolution away from one-party strongman type governments to democracy and away from parastatal-led economies toward free enterprise. A number of factors have served as catalysts for this rapid and radical change in focus. Key developments that have supported Africa's growth include: (1) the end of the Cold War and its politically divisive influences, (2) the new emphasis by the Bretton Woods institutions (i.e., the International Monetary Fund and the World Bank) on private enterprise and market-led growth, and (3) the recognition by global corporations that Africa has become the world's last economic frontier. Africa represents a market of over 750 million consumers with an aggregate GDP of $536 billion. In the universe of emerging markets, Africa is arguably the last continent where first-mover advantages in terms of building brand recognition, introducing technological innovations, and creating market-leading standards still exist. African corporations are slowly starting to explore regional growth strategies and thus now afford investors greater wealth-generating opportunities through such mergers and acquisitions. Over the past five years, the World Bank and United Nations have consistently reported that the returns of foreign direct investment in Africa are the highest in the world. African public securities also can boast of some of the lowest price-to-earning (P/E) ratios in the world, offering value for access to multinationals such as Unilever, Barclays Bank, and Nestle. Furthermore, given the fact that the principal investors in Africa's public securities to date have been African institutions, African markets have been for the most part insulated from the Asian contagion–type devastation caused by wild inflows and outflows of portfolio "hot money."

In the next several chapters we discuss the various factors that make Africa the ultimate emerging market. Thus, we provide an analysis of the positive effect the end of the Cold War has had on the continent. We explore some of the general trends that have helped to improve Africa's economic and political prospects for the twenty-first century, and we look at specific examples of the successes that foreign companies are having in Africa. Lastly, we review the performance of Africa's stock markets over the past few years and present a few case studies that illustrate the wealth-creation opportunities available through participation in the African capital markets.

5

Unparalleled
Opportunity and
Potential

Notwithstanding the inherent challenges, investing in emerging markets generally, and Africa specifically, has proven to be a rewarding experience for an increasing number of investors. However, when emerging markets develop and become more popular, they invariably begin to lose the low-cost/high-growth characteristics that made them attractive to investors in the first place.

A classic case in point is Telephonos de Mexico (Telmex). In 1990, when the Mexican government began privatizing Telephonos de Mexico, little was known about the country's sole telecommunications provider. However, given the company's relatively low share cost and significant growth prospects, investors were willing to take a chance.

As Figure 5.1 indicates, in the six years since its initial public offering (IPO), the share price of TMXUS has increased over 300%.

For a large contingent of institutional investors, Telmex was their first significant emerging market foray. Subsequently the overwhelming success of Telmex contributed greatly to the investment popularity of Mexico and the investment community's overall interest in emerging market telecommunication companies. And while Telmex is arguably still a very solid investment (as of September 1999, Telmex was selling at a P/E of 11.98 versus the S&P Telecom index P/E of 49.5), with good growth potential, the company's share price is unlikely to replicate the meteoric rise that it experienced from 1993 to 1998.

The Telmex example is particularly relevant to Africa's investment prospects, as telecommunications represents an area with vast growth poten-

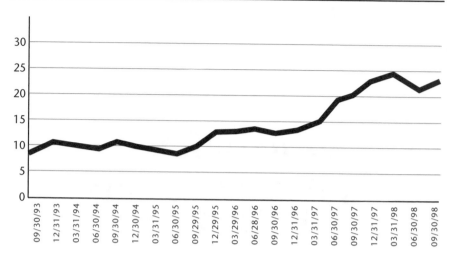

FIGURE 5.1   Telephonos de Mexico Stock Price

tial. Today, Africa's scant teledensity of 1.2 (i.e., 1.2 telephones per 100 people) means that significant capital is necessary (at least $20 billion to increase teledensity to 2) to expand teledensity. However, when one considers that there are over 45 government-owned telephone companies in Africa, it is easy to envisage the inevitability of their privatization. On a global basis, telephony is one of those sectors that has provided early stage investors with attractive return prospects. Consequently, African telecommunication opportunities have begun to attract a variety of investors.

Although Africa's potential has always been known to the emerging market investment community, it was not until the early 1990s and the convergence of four key factors (increased infrastructural development, greater political stability, natural resource depth, and investors' need for new emerging markets) that investors began exploring investment opportunities in Africa. From a pure investment standpoint, the continent still offers unique value and performance opportunities—most of which are underreported. Given the fact that most of Africa's securities are owned by Africans from the host countries where there are capital markets, there has historically been very little pressure to artificially push up share prices. This can be a good thing when it comes to finding companies that are performing well but still offer low price-to-earning values, but a bad thing when one is trying to find liquidity and undertraded markets. Nevertheless, an increasing number of African and foreign investors are finding the underpriced, unheralded publicly traded gems of corporate Africa and making a handsome profit by doing so. On a daily basis more and more information is being disseminated globally about these companies, but opportunities still remain for first-moving investors—those investors who recognize that today Africa represents the last global frontier for high-yielding, fast-growing investments.

A BUYER'S MARKET AND FINITE CHOICES

One of the tactical advantages of emerging market versus developed market investing that has proven to be a source of comfort for individual, portfolio, and direct investors is the thematic simplicity of emerging market investment. If an investor was considering telecommunications investment opportunities in a developed market like the United States there would be reams of information to analyze. Should the investor consider wireless or wired telecommunications or maybe a combination? Should the investor focus on telephony, or should paging, data, and/or Internet communication be considered? Should the investor examine regional or national opportunities? Should the investor consider large-cap, mid-cap, or small-cap telecommunications companies?

Because there are over 750 publicly traded telecommunications firms in the United States, investor prudence would demand a thorough analytical process. Still this exercise in and of itself would not necessarily guarantee a good return on investment.

However, given the relative infancy of the African capital markets, investors interested in publicly traded telecommunications opportunities as of December 1998 would have had less than 15 firms to choose from. And of the firms available for investment, investors would find that these firms enjoyed exclusive or near-exclusive operating arrangements in their countries.

Thus, an investor in Africa would only have to analyze 15 stocks (versus 750 in the United States) to pick an almost sure winner from an appreciation standpoint. This same paradigm exists for a number of other African stocks in the energy, manufacturing, mining, finance, and consumer products sectors. Thus, increasingly, many investors are finding the growth opportunities of Africa's relatively small number of blue-chip stocks quite compelling.

SHARED EXCHANGE HERITAGE—THE BRITISH FACTOR

One of the most important but least acknowledged aspects of investing in Africa is the relative similarities in structure that exist between African stock markets and those of the United Kingdom and the United States. This is directly attributable to the fact that there is a shared legacy of colonialization by England and a number of the Africa countries with exchanges. Unlike a number of other emerging "hot" markets (Latin America, Southeast Asia,

Eastern Europe, and the former Soviet Union), most of Africa at some time or another was part of the British Empire. Consequently, British culture (which ranges from the English language to the Anglo-Saxon legal and accounting system) is predominant on the African continent.

In fact, 15 of Africa's 19 stock exchanges (representing over 90% of the continent's publicly traded securities markets) are located in former British colonies. This fact has made research processes, like financial statement analysis, a relatively unencumbered process for investors familiar with the British legal and accounting system. This is not to say that Africa's various capital markets are devoid of legal, accounting, and regulatory complexities and/or deficiencies—to the contrary. However, compared to the potential difficulties encountered by investors (English-speaking or otherwise) in some of the aforementioned emerging markets or even in certain developed European capital markets, most emerging market investors find the African capital markets surprisingly user-friendly.

Investors have also found the mechanics of African investment to be quite manageable. Compared to other emerging markets, wire transfers, security settlement, custodial services (covered more extensively in the next chapter), and so forth in most African markets are very reasonable. Buoyed by the Johannesburg Stock Exchange (the world's 15th-largest), and the fact that the continent's 3 largest stock markets (in South Africa, Egypt, and Zimbabwe) have been operating for an average of 89 years, an argument can be made that the African capital markets are not so much emerging markets as they are reemerging markets.

THE VALUE PROPOSITION

Value and diversification are the two most compelling factors drawing investors into Africa today. Despite the varied concerns investors might have about Africa, on a cost-benefit basis African securities currently represent the world's best value for money investment opportunity. This fact becomes more relevant as we witness the inflationary impact that the West's recent bullish environment has had on U.S. and Western European security prices and the increasing valuations in the more established emerging markets. As the next two figures demonstrate, African securities exemplify the classic buy-low sell-high investment scenario.

In Africa, where 15 of the 19 existing stock exchanges were established in or after 1987 (3 in 1999), the markets are only now beginning to see price-stimulating trading activity. In the past, most of these exchanges were rather illiquid, and the only market participants were large financial institutions and the occasional foreign investor. Market makers trading, buying, and selling for their own account were almost unheard of. Today, as unit trusts (i.e., mutual funds) become more popular with individuals with disposable income, and investing (as opposed to saving money in the bank) is becoming more prevalent, this legacy is slowly being broken. Yet, because of the young history of most of Africa's exchanges, and the even more nascent investment culture on the continent, there has been relatively low demand for shares, and thus there are many strongly performing companies whose stock sells at undervalued prices. In this environment, great values abound for the discerning investor (see Figure 5.2).

It is noteworthy that as a result of its capacity and relative sophistication, South Africa's Johannesburg Stock Exchange is expected soon to leapfrog past other African and emerging stock exchanges. It is predicted that in the next 10 years the JSE may grow to be one of the top 10 exchanges in the world.

Some of the factors that are likely to push Africa's P/E ratios upward in the next few years include: (1) the fact that more African capital markets are likely to be added to the global emerging market indices, (2) the growing abil-

	Price/Earnings
Average of African Countries[1]	11.5x
Emerging Markets Average[2]	13.7x
MSCI World Index[3]	23.2x
S&P 500[4]	23.0x

Notes: (1) Average includes : Botswana, Egypt, Ghana, Kenya, Mauritius, Morocco, South Africa, and Zimbabwe
Sources : Standard Equities

(2) Average includes : Argentina, Brazil, Chile, Columbia, Czech Republic, Greece, Hong Kong, Hungary, India, Indonesia, Israel, Malaysia, Mexico, Philippines, Poland, Portugal, Singapore, Taiwan/China, Turkey
Source : Standard Equities

(3) Morgan Stanley Capital International World Index (1997)

(4) Standard Equities

FIGURE 5.2 Price/Earnings (P/E) Ratio Analysis

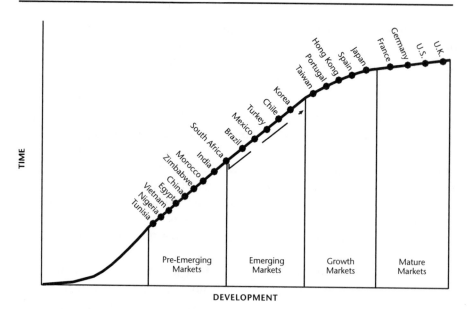

FIGURE 5.3 Africa's Emergence

ity to disseminate company-related information and country and sector research to potential investors via the Internet, and (3) the fact that African capital markets are rapidly growing and thus the values of all of the shares on the market are likely to rise.

South Africa has been the only African capital market universally included in the various emerging market benchmarking indexes that exist. This has meant that South Africa has disproportionately benefited from global investor interest in emerging markets because, by virtue of its solo stature as the Africa representative in the indices, most investors with Africa allocations have funneled their capital into the Johannesburg Stock Exchange. In the next five years it is probable that this will change and at least one (probably Egypt) to two other African exchanges will join these indices.

One of the most difficult impediments for investors seeking to invest in Africa has been the difficulty in finding up-to-date and comprehensive financial and other information about African countries, industry sectors, and companies. The reliability of the information was also often subject to question. Through Reuters and with the emergence of Bloomberg and CNN, Web sites such as Africanews.org and Africa.com, and greater analytical research being compiled by the Economist Intelligence Unit, Fleming Martin, and Standard Bank, as well as the increasing number of Africa brokerages like Databank in Ghana and Kingdom Securities in Zimbabwe, access to information is increasing.

THE GROWTH PROPOSITION

Another trend which is likely to enhance African share values in the near term is the generally rapid growth of the continent's markets. In the developed capital markets, mid- to long-term individual security price growth and performance are largely due to the fundamentals of the underlying company. This is primarily due to the width, depth, and efficiency associated with these established stock exchanges. However, like the proverbial rising tide that lifts all boats, individual security performance in less efficient emerging capital markets is more likely to be positively impacted by sheer market expansion.

Like most emerging markets, the African investment story is fundamentally a growth story. Consequently, the African capital markets provide numerous examples of companies that have experienced exponential growth. The following are examples of three such companies.

Didata Technologies in South Africa— A Market-Expansion-Led Growth Example

Didata Technologies (DDT) is South Africa's second-largest information technology (IT) company by market capitalization. Founded in 1983, the company was first listed on the Johannesburg Stock Exchange in 1987 at $.07. The group has managed to remain at the cusp of IT development in South Africa because it has been able to change with the environment. As the worldwide trend toward information management reached Africa, DDT was at the forefront.

The 1994 end of apartheid in South Africa brought with it renewed economic focus on South Africa and a wave of pro-Mandela (the country's then-president) portfolio investment capital. DDT became a beneficiary of this inflow of capital to the Johannesburg Stock Exchange. As a relative market leader in the IT sector in South Africa, DDT stood out as a relatively safe bet for foreign investors familiar with the upward global trends in the overall IT sector. However, investment in DDT (in past because of the JSE's continued rapid expansion which fueled DDT's growth) helped DDT become far more than a safe bet, and it actually became a fantastic bet for its investors.

The rapid upturn in investor interest in South Africa helped DDT form a number of important strategic alliances with major international players. These relationships, such as DDT's 1995 joint venture with EDS, allowed Didata to remain in the technological elite of South African IT companies. In 1996, the group made its first international foray by purchasing 45% of an Australian company, Com Tech. In 1997, Didata increased its Asia exposure by increasing its holding in Com Tech to 70% and by also acquiring a 55% interest in Singapore-listed Datacraft Asia. The same year, Didata also expanded into Europe by purchasing 77% of The Merchants Group, the United Kingdom's largest communication-center consultancy firm.

The result of DDT's market-driven corporate expansion for the investor has been phenomenal. A company whose market capitalization was $4.07m in 1992 has ballooned to over $2.63bn currently. More important, investors enjoyed a better than 500-fold increase in capital value during the 1990s. The price has risen from $.08 at end-September 1990 to $18.73 at end-October 1998 (prices are adjusted to reflect corporate actions). That is the equivalent of approximately 98% average annual return (including dividends) over eight years. Furthermore, the future remains bright for Didata, as the company has proven its ability to grow organically as well as to make strategic acquisitions work. Computer telephony integration, networking, and E-commerce are each on the company's near-term development horizon.

Kenya Power & Light—A Privatization-Led Growth Example

At the beginning of the 1990s Kenya Power & Light Corporation (KPLC) was Kenya's sole distributor of electricity. A public company predominantly owned by the government, KPLC supplied power bought from local bulk-supply companies, from Kenya's neighbor Uganda, and from its own generating stations.

Since its inception in 1923, KPLC had been the exclusive provider of power generation and distribution services in Kenya. Due to a chronic lack of investment capital the Kenyan government was rarely able to adequately support KPLC, and the company often failed to keep up with demand.

However, during the last four years, because of an increased focus by the government on stimulating private sector involvement within the company and within the overall energy industry, KPLC has been able to undergo a marked transformation. Management has been strengthened, and the organization has become more customer-focused. KPLC has separated generation from transmission and distribution in an effort to ease the country's power shortage and to stimulate industrial growth. The transmission and distribution functions have since been privatized, and investors are now allowed to set up designated power stations to compete with the government-owned power generation company. KPLC has embarked on an aggressive program to expand its distribution network ahead of the commissioning of new power plants, which are expected to increase the country's power supply by 60% in the year 2000.

Prior to the restructuring period, KPLC shares were trading at an almost 40% discount to book value. Investors, unfortunately, lumped the company in with Kenya's other parastatals, which were regarded, validly or not, as inefficient and often corrupt. However, since the restructuring, the privatization of both the distribution and transmission arms of the KPLC, and the promotion of private operators in the sector as a whole, the company's stock price has significantly appreciated. In the years from 1993 to 1997, KPLC's stock price had an annualized return of 135%, the best in the market.

Today, although it is estimated that Kenya's power shortfall may continue to exist until as late as 2004, KPLC's growth prospects remain high. As Kenya continues to take measures to turn around its economy, and as private power companies enter the electricity generation business in an effort to fill the demand gap, the company is on course to continue to transform itself from a government-owned to a private company. This strategy will continue to attract investors and bodes well for the company's future stock appreciation prospects.

Home Finance Company in Ghana— An Innovation-Led Growth Model

Home Finance Company (HFC) is the only dedicated mortgage finance company in Ghana. The company was formed in the late 1980s with the assistance of a transfer of International Monetary Fund–supplied hard currency. The aim of the initiative was and is to support housing development projects in Ghana.

For most of Ghana's history, the housing market has lacked long-term finance alternatives for those seeking home loans. In 1998 it was estimated that about 60% of the country's annual housing needs remained unmet, excluding accumulated backlog. Given the dearth of housing stock in Ghana, and following the very difficult decade of the 1980s, projections were that the demand for housing will continue to outstrip supply for at least the next 25 years.

In 1991, HFC became the first financial institution to take advantage of a 36-year-old law, Act 179 of the 1963 Companies Code, which introduced the concept of unit trusts, or mutual funds as they are known in the United States. At the time the law was drafted, it was even ahead of the British Companies Act.

HFC created its unit trust, principally to serve as a vehicle to assist prospective home buyers in their efforts to save the 20% down payment needed to qualify for mortgage loans. The HFC unit trust, however, remained open as an investment vehicle for corporations, groups, and individuals. Combining older traditions with newer ones, HFC's management was able to convince large numbers of "market women" (agricultural commodities traders) to invest capital saved through their traditional *Susu* or collective savings mechanism in the unit trust.

Today, the HFC unit trust has matured far beyond being merely a vehicle for saving to qualify for a mortgage, and has become a well-managed and diversified portfolio investment vehicle for a wide range of clients. In the seven and a half years since the unit trust's inception, HFC has raised more than 40 billion cedis ($20 million) for housing.

HFC's prospects in the coming years look very bright, and investors are beginning to pay closer attention to the company. Between January 1994 and November 1998, the stock price appreciated over 635%. The company has now expanded into new financial markets, developing mortgage finance products for Ghanaians who have access to dollar earnings streams, and it seems poised to take advantage of all of the relevant business opportunities in its industry.

THE PERFORMANCE PROPOSITION

Although Africa's development has historically been out of synch with the development of the world's leading economies, at the dawn of the twenty-first century this fact is likely to have a beneficial impact on the continent. In addition to the economic resurgence attributable to the post–Cold War paradigm shift, Africa will benefit from the fact that it truly is the last untapped emerging market—a reality that has forced return-driven investors and expansion-minded multinationals to explore the continent.

Figure 5.4 presents the cumulative four-year returns of the world's 25 top-performing markets. For the four-year period ending in 1997, at least one of Africa's capital markets was among the world's three top-performing markets.

Not only have African securities consistently ranked among the top performers in the emerging market universe, they have also collectively outperformed the Morgan Stanley emerging market index for the five-year period 1993 to 1998. A look at the performance of the Sub-Saharan African markets, excluding South Africa, illustrates this.

DIVERSIFICATION BENEFITS

According to the World Bank's International Finance Corporation (IFC), the globalization of the world's economies has led to an increased performance interrelation among the world's various stock markets. This fact, combined with the age-old strategy of not having all of one's betting eggs in a single basket, has prompted investors to search for truly diversified investment/portfolio options. Africa's peripheral status relative to the world's economies, coupled with the unique performance characteristics of African securities, make Africa the ideal diversification option. Figure 5.5 compares the interrelation (correlation) of some of the world's various markets.

The IFC's analysis about the relationships between stock markets is based upon the premise that the higher the correlation between two markets, the more the two move together. Using a scale of 0 to 1, the higher the fraction of 1, the closer the correlation. Thus, the United Kingdoms market has a 0.54 correlation

Country	1994 %	1995 %	1996 %	1997 %	4 Yr Cumulative %
Oman	29.1	8.2	26.1	141.7	+325.74
Trinidad & Tobago	8.1	69.5	10.9	109.3	+325.3
Iran	49.0	124.3	52.7	-17.4	+321.54
Egypt	167.2	-10.6	38.8	18.0	+291.24
New Zealand	5.8	13.1	13.5	139.1	+224.73
Ireland	11.9	23.9	28.8	76.6	+215.36
Nigeria	168.8	-26.9	55.6	-1.9	+199.93
Panama	44.1	3.1	24.9	60.5	+197.82
Morocco	40.3	5.8	38.4	37.8	+183.09
Sweden	17.3	35.0	35.4	6.5	+128.35
Finland	51.3	0.6	31.7	12.0	+124.51
Switzerland	2.4	42.9	1.2	46.3	+116.65
USA	-0.9	34.1	21.4	30.3	+110.22
Netherlands	8.9	25.7	24.5	20.7	+105.70
Brazil	67.6	-22.1	30.4	20.5	+105.15
Bangladesh	116.6	-2.5	196.0	-67.7	+101.91
Portugal	16.5	-4.1	24.9	43.6	+100.38
Namibia	-2.7	40.3	36.0	4.9	+94.75
Spain	-7.4	25.2	36.5	21.4	+92.12
Norway	22.1	8.5	26.8	13.9	+91.33
Peru	52.1	9.3	0.7	13.9	+90.68
Hungary	-17.5	-29.4	96.4	60.9	+84.06
Cote d'Ivoire	-19.7	140.8	5.3	-10.6	+82.03
Denmark	2.6	14.7	20.0	23.4	+74.26
Botswana	6.0	2.6	-20.3	99.8	+73.18

FIGURE 5.4 World Stock Market Performance, 1994–1997
Source: IFC

with the U.S. stock market, implying that share prices in London will rise 5.4% if those on the New York stock exchange increase 10%.

It follows from this logic that the lower the correlation between markets, the weaker the relationship between share price movements in different markets—and the greater the diversification benefits for investors. A negative correlation means that share price movements diverge in different markets, rising in one when they decline in another. This is the correlation between most African exchanges and those in the United States and London. For example, the Zimbabwe stock exchange has a correlation of −0.08 with the London Stock Exchange and a correlation of −0.07 with the New York Stock Exchange. Thus, American and British investors who buy the stock of companies in Zimbabwe are able to significantly diversify their risk relative to their home markets. Morocco and Nigeria, two of the other African countries analyzed by the IFC, have correlative tendencies similar to Zimbabwe. Their indices are either likely to go up when the U.S. and U.K. indices go down, or simply will not be affected by shifts in these western markets.

The one African country that does have a higher correlation with western markets—given the fact that it is more closely intertwined with the global economy—is South Africa. Overall, the minimal correlation found when African stock exchanges are compared to other western stock exchanges illustrates the potential performance autonomy of Africa's capital markets.

THE ASIAN CONNECTION

An interesting further analysis of the IFC's correlative model does, however, expose a much closer relationship between the economies of at least some of Africa's markets, particularly those in Southern Africa, and those within the IFC's Asian index. South Africa's 0.63 correlation with these countries is quite high and is illustrative of the trade dependency that the country has on exports to this region. In terms of individual countries, South Africa's highest correlative standings are with the Philippines and Malaysia—both registering at 0.55. Zimbabwe, like South Africa, also registered relatively high on the correlation index, with a 0.42 weighting for all Asian countries. Zimbabwe's individual correlations with Indonesia, Malaysia, South Korea, and Thailand all registered higher than 0.40. Nigeria and Morocco, on the other hand, maintained a much lower correlation with the Asian region, the United States, and the United Kingdom.

The strong nexus between the economies of Asia and Africa, particularly North and Southern Africa, was particularly evident during the global financial crisis triggered by Asia's financial meltdown from 1996 to 1998. In Africa, three key areas were most affected by Asia's economic problems: (1)

	U.S. S&P 500	FT Europac	IFCG Composite	IFCG Lat America	IFCG Asia	Argentina	Brazil	Chile	China	Czech Republic	Egypt	India	Indonesia	Korea	Malaysia	Mexico	Morocco	Nigeria	Phillipines	Poland	Russia	South Africa	Taiwan, China	Thailand	Turkey	Zimbabwe
U.S. S&P 500	1.00																									
FT Europac	0.40	1.00																								
IFCG Composite	0.37	0.46	1.00																							
IFCG Lat America	0.41	0.35	0.75	1.00																						
IFCG Asia	0.26	0.43	0.90	0.43	1.00																					
Argentina	0.48	0.44	0.63	0.71	0.43	1.00																				
Brazil	0.30	0.21	0.52	0.79	0.23	0.35	1.00																			
Chile	0.32	0.21	0.55	0.57	0.43	0.45	0.40	1.00																		
China	-0.05	-0.03	0.19	0.13	0.17	0.03	0.25	0.13	1.00																	
Czech Republic	-0.07	0.00	0.25	0.17	0.19	0.03	0.26	-0.09	0.09	1.00																
Egypt	0.00	0.25	0.21	0.13	0.16	0.00	0.20	0.21	-0.03	0.41	1.00															
India	0.10	0.08	0.47	0.38	0.40	0.14	0.33	0.50	0.15	0.33	0.05	1.00														
Indonesia	0.43	0.36	0.65	0.39	0.68	0.33	0.33	0.44	0.12	0.01	0.19	0.32	1.00													
Korea	0.09	0.35	0.52	0.29	0.59	0.25	0.18	0.43	0.05	0.04	0.18	0.26	0.49	1.00												
Malaysia	0.18	0.43	0.70	0.25	0.83	0.11	0.23	0.16	0.23	0.22	0.23	0.21	0.44	0.19	1.00											
Mexico	0.33	0.35	0.63	0.86	0.33	0.47	0.12	0.47	0.00	0.11	0.00	0.47	0.64	0.19	0.29	1.00										
Morocco	-0.44	-0.29	0.04	-0.18	0.04	-0.16	-0.23	0.12	0.02	0.47	0.10	0.04	0.29	0.02	0.73	0.30	1.00									
Nigeria	0.03	0.14	0.07	0.02	0.08	0.22	0.25	0.08	0.00	0.25	0.00	0.32	0.23	0.09	0.28	-0.10	-0.03	1.00								
Phillipines	0.14	0.29	0.71	0.35	0.41	0.17	0.32	0.17	0.32	0.04	0.17	0.30	0.39	0.07	0.35	-0.03	0.04	0.23	1.00							
Poland	0.12	0.35	0.39	0.28	0.29	0.32	0.44	0.29	0.10	0.37	0.23	0.23	0.29	0.20	0.39	0.04	0.15	0.19	0.71	1.00						
Russia	0.17	0.11	0.54	0.46	0.44	0.30	0.07	0.57	0.25	-0.06	0.04	0.22	0.31	0.34	0.23	0.16	-0.20	0.06	0.44	0.46	1.00					
South Africa	0.18	0.36	0.58	0.24	0.63	0.33	0.14	0.24	0.05	0.14	0.22	0.69	0.26	0.27	0.39	0.30	-0.13	0.21	0.34	0.21	0.39	1.00				
Taiwan, China	0.17	0.31	0.65	0.25	0.74	0.32	0.16	0.19	0.07	0.04	0.14	0.44	0.69	0.44	0.55	0.55	-0.09	0.19	0.08	0.06	0.30	0.55	1.00			
Thailand	0.32	0.32	0.68	0.34	0.75	0.39	0.39	0.21	0.05	0.04	0.00	0.13	0.44	0.23	0.68	0.29	0.14	0.00	0.14	0.21	0.21	0.46	0.38	1.00		
Turkey	0.09	0.07	0.30	0.18	0.20	0.16	0.09	0.22	0.18	0.11	0.18	0.27	0.23	0.08	0.44	0.13	0.27	0.14	0.18	0.18	0.27	0.12	0.07	0.07	1.00	
Zimbabwe	0.04	0.08	0.36	0.42	0.23	0.09	0.22	0.07	0.10	0.14	0.35	0.34	0.54	0.44	0.13	0.05	-0.13	0.25	0.40	0.25	0.22	0.07	0.07	0.42	-1.10	1.00

FIGURE 5.5 IFCG Total Return Correlations 1992–1997
Source: IFC Factbook 1998

African exports to Asia declined; (2) African exports of natural resource and manufactured products worldwide declined because of the flood of cheap Asian products and commodities that became available; and (3) Asian investments in Africa, particularly by the Malaysians, declined precipitously as a result of the region's declining currency values.

In 1996, Africa's exports to Asia accounted for 13% of the continent's worldwide exports. Four percent of these exports went to Japan. In terms of the more important products sold to Asia, minerals, fuels, and related products accounted for 38% of the region's exports. Food, beverages, and tobacco comprised another important contributor to Africa's export earnings from Asia, accounting for 19% of all exports. Crude materials (excluding fuels) comprised another 18% of exports to Asia.

During this period, North Africa and Southern Africa accounted for two-thirds of Africa's total exports to Asia. South Africa was the largest single exporter, accounting for 25% of exports to the Asian region. The oil exporting countries of Africa were also significant exporters to Asia. Asia imported 12% of Nigeria's oil exports, 9.7% of Algeria's exports, and 9.5% of Libya's exports. For more on African exports to Asia, see Figure 5.6.

Although Africa does not export significant quantities of agricultural products to Asia, both regions are global exporters of primary commodities such as cocoa beans, timber, rubber, coffee, and tea. Since 1970, Asia has increasingly encroached upon Africa's market share of global exports of these products. The pace of Asia's market share expansion accelerated between 1996 and 1998 as Asia's currencies depreciated and its products became even more

	1990	1996
Total Africa Exports	100.0	100.0
Mineral fuels and related materials	44.6	38.0
Food, beverages and tobacco	16.7	18.9
Crude materials (excluding fuels), oils, fats	11.7	12.6
Other manufactured goods	9.2	10.4
Machinery and transport equipment	2.5	2.3

FIGURE 5.6   Largest Export Items from Africa to Asia, 1990–1996
Source: African Development Report 1999

International Export Markets Shares						
Africa			**Asia**			
	1970	1993	Change%	1970	1993	Change%
Cocoa	80.3	60.1	-20.2	0.4	20.0	+19.6
Coffee	24.6	14.3	-10.3	4.9	10.9	+6.0
Rubber	7.4	5.6	-1.8	89.1	90.8	+1.7
Timber	13.4	7.3	-6.1	43.3	52.5	+9.2
Cotton	30.7	17.2	-13.5	16.6	35.6	+19.0

FIGURE 5.7   Competition with African Export Markets

price competitive (see Figure 5.7). Figure 5.8 lists those African export coun-tries most affected by the growth of Asia as a commodities exporter.

In the manufactured goods arena, South Africa, the continent's leading exporter by far, came under increased pressure from Asian countries such as Indonesia, Malaysia, South Korea, and Thailand.

In 1996, Africa was importing 12% of all its products from Asia. North and Southern Africa were again the main importers, purchasing 70% of all Asian imports to Africa. Key target markets for Asian goods included South Africa (24% of imports), Egypt (10%), Algeria (9.4%), Nigeria (6.8%), and Mo-

Cocoa	Coffee	Timber	Rubber	Tea
Benin	Benin	Cameroon	Cameroon	Burundi
Cameroon	Burundi	Congo (Brazzaville)	Cote d'Ivoire	Kenya
Congo (Brazzaville)	Cameroon	Cote d'Ivoire	Democratic Rep of	Malawi
Cote d'Ivoire	Congo (Brazzaville)	Democratic Rep of	Congo	
Ghana	Cote d'Ivoire	Congo		
Madagascar	Ethiopia	Gabon		
Nigeria	Gabon	Ghana		
Sierra Leone	Ghana			
Togo	Kenya			
	Malawi			
	Uganda			

FIGURE 5.8   African Commodities Producers Impacted by Asian Competition

rocco (6.5%). Although Africa benefited to some degree from being able to purchase cheaper Asian manufactured products, the sum total of price-related export losses versus price-related import gains was negative overall, and by 1998 this had helped to induce a stark decline in Africa's terms of trade (see Figure 5.9).

What the Asian economic crisis did was further depress prices in an already increasingly competitive world market for commodities. In some commodities, the cheaper Asian goods created a glut on the markets and in others they created a much softer market for all global sellers. In the oil sector, prices declined from $18.8 a barrel in 1997 to $12.7 a barrel in 1998.

Even in the face of the decision by the oil cartel OPEC to reduce world-wide production by 3.1 million barrels a day, the market remained depressed and prices fell to their lowest point since 1973. World prices of copper, timber, and rubber were also adversely affected by the dramatic currency devaluations in the ASEAN region. Economic woes in Indonesia, the Philippines, Malaysia, and Thailand, in particular, helped to depress world prices in these commodities.

On the investment front, Asia's problems shook the entire global investment community and precipitated a flight to safety/security/quality (i.e., the pulling of capital out of Asian capital markets and the reinvestment of those funds in U.S. and other more mature exchanges). In addition to further weakening the Asian economies, this capital flight led to disillusionment with all emerging

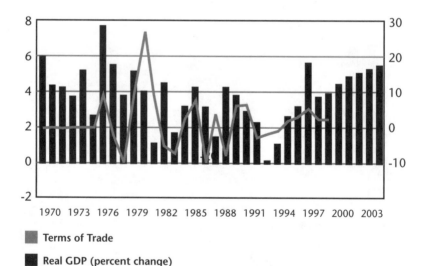

Terms of Trade

Real GDP (percent change)

FIGURE 5.9   Africa: GDP and Terms of Trade (1975–2003)
Source: African Development Report 1999

markets. Portfolio investors who had invested in emerging markets elsewhere, such as in Latin America, Eastern Europe, and Africa, followed suit and liquidated the lion's share of their investments in these markets. Of the African countries, the country most affected by this capital withdrawal was South Africa, which has the largest and most liquid market on the continent.

Yet, overall in the face of the significant capital flight that took place in most of the emerging markets, Africa's capital markets held up fairly well. Indeed, outside of South Africa, very little capital market investment outflow occurred.

In the second quarter of 1998, the Pan-African-focused Calvert New Africa Fund was ranked as the number one performing emerging market fund by the U.S. mutual fund rating index, the Lipper Index. This fact was not lost on the emerging market investment community, and thus one important positive aspect of the "emerging-market crisis" was the recognition that it was imprudent to ignore Africa's markets altogether.

In 1999 the Asian markets saw a significant return of portfolio capital, that helped to strengthen the region's collective GDP. During 1999, South Africa also saw its market benefit from returning emerging market capital.

Beyond South Africa, the overall benefit for Africa given this scenario is that Asian markets will again be interested in buying African exports and, as the Asian country currencies rise, African products will again be competitive in the global markets. Furthermore, and equally important, the Asian investment capital that was starting to flow into Africa between 1993 and 1995 should return once more.

WHY AFRICA IS NOT LIKELY TO EXPERIENCE AN ASIAN-STYLE FINANCIAL CRISIS

As a result of the 1998 Asian financial crisis, potential investors in Africa had to question the likelihood of such an event happening in Africa. However, while Africa shares many traits with the Asian Tigers (e.g., a large untapped consumer base, an emerging middle-class population, a large low-cost labor pool, etc.), there is a notable difference between the banking policies and structures of the two regions.

For the most part, Africa's banking sector can be positively described as being conservative. This condition is primarily attributable to the region's overall lack of capital and to a banking environment that has been pioneered by, and still largely consists of, conservative British financial institutions like Standard Chartered, Lloyds of London, and Barclays. As a contrast, until 1998 the banking culture within Asia's Tigers was characterized by a much more aggressive banking philosophy—a situation that resulted from the availability

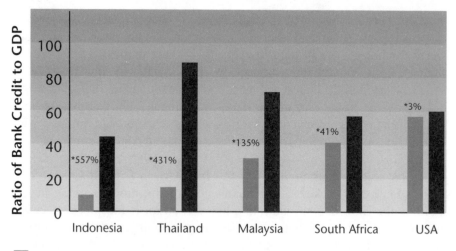

* Percentage growth of bank credit to GDP 1980-1995

FIGURE 5.10   Why Africa Is Not Likely to Experience an Asian-Style
Financial Crisis
Source: Institutional Investor, South African Reserve Bank

of capital, a rapidly expanding economy, and a relatively lax regulatory environment.

Figure 5.10 graphically illustrates the environmental contrast between
banks in Africa and Asia. Covering the 15-year period between 1980 and
1995, the chart compares South Africa's growth of bank credit to GDP ratio
with the same data for the United States, Indonesia, Thailand, and Malaysia.
South Africa's banking environment is a good proxy for the rest of Africa in
that its financial institutions are likely to share the conservative banking policy views of banks in those African countries most likely to attract investment
(e.g., Botswana, Egypt, Ghana, Côte d'Ivoire, etc.).

Although other factors contributed to the Asian financial crisis, the inabil-
ity of the region's banks to effectively manage credit was a critical element of
the problem. Notwithstanding the differences between the banking environment in Africa and Asia, the emerging market meltdown instigated by the latter has resulted in a devaluation of all emerging market assets. Focusing on
the positive aspects of this negative occurrence, this in turn has resulted in the
creation of undervalued investment opportunities for investors interested in
Africa.

6

The Economic Growth/Political Stability Factor

Political risk is probably the greatest source of concern among would-be investors in Africa. But while the reality of political risk in Africa should not be ignored, it is important that the risk be measured in the proper context. Perhaps Charles Dickens's classic quote in *A Tale of Two Cities* ("It was the best of times, it was the worst of times") offers the best description regarding the diversity of Africa's political environment. Notwithstanding the political risk quotient that should be factored into any emerging market investment decision, the list of politically sound, economically attractive African countries is steadily expanding.

From the standpoint of peace and stability, Botswana, Egypt, Ghana, South Africa, and Uganda are indicative of those African countries experiencing "the best of times," while Rwanda, Algeria, Somalia, Liberia, and Sudan represent African countries experiencing "the worst of times." The latter African nations possess economies plagued by at least one of the following four factors: high external debt, limited natural resources, externally and/or politically motivated military conflicts, and limited international business interests. For these countries, caught in the grip of a competitive and unforgiving global economy, generating attractive investment returns (and thus investor interest), while possible, is less probable.

THE CORRELATION BETWEEN ECONOMIC VIABILITY AND POLITICAL STABILITY

The new paradigm for the world's emerging economies is the quest for development/investment capital. Whether we are dealing with Thailand, Vietnam, the Commonwealth of Independent States (the former Soviet Union), South Africa, Mozambique, or Argentina, the challenge for economic development consists largely of an intense competition for highly liquid capital. The most effective barometer for assessing a country's political risk factor is an assessment of that nation's economic viability. Further, recent history has shown that the greater a country's real and/or perceived economic potential (i.e., viability), the greater the likelihood that external actors, private, commercial, and governmental, will intervene in that country's domestic affairs, financially or even militarily, to help maintain political stability.

If the last two decades of political events in emerging markets have decisively shown us anything, it's that a direct correlation exists between economic viability and political stability. Knowledge of this fact has been a key ingredient for successful investors in Africa and other emerging markets. An analysis of the recent political environment of the following emerging markets offers multiple scenarios regarding the correlation between economic viability and political stability.

Mexico

On many levels, Mexico offers the classic positive case of the direct correlation between economic viability and political stability. Mexico's geographic proximity to the largest consumer market in the world is arguably the largest contributor to its economic success. For numerous reasons related to that geographic proximity, the United States stands ready to utilize its significant global influence to ensure the economic viability of its neighbor to the South. Mexico's 1994 currency devaluation provides a clear illustration of this point. Triggered by the government's currency devaluation and the subsequent flight of capital, the Mexican peso experienced a 49% overnight decline in its exchange rate to the U.S. dollar. As a result of Mexico's status as the world's largest consumer of American goods and services, the United States had a vested interest in facilitating the swift recovery of the Mexican peso. The proverbial analogy of Mexico sneezing and the United States catching a cold represented a great economic risk to the United States. Consequently, Mexico's (U.S.-sponsored) multibillion-dollar International Monetary Fund (IMF) bailout was facilitated in record time. While President Ernesto Zedillo's administration should be applauded for its zeal in initiating harsh corrective policies to address Mexico's economic crisis, much of the country's economic recovery was actually due to the swift international response to the peso crisis.

The parallels between events in Mexico and events in African countries are many; however, Mexico's differentiating factor is its U.S.-sponsored safety net. In 1994 the Hutu president of Rwanda was assassinated. The impact of his death in that region, characterized by political instability, was still being felt in 1999. What would have happened to Mexico's economy (and thus its political stability) if the 1994 assassination of Mexico's leading presidential candidate Luis Donaldo Colosio (in Tijuana, three miles from the U.S. border) had been used as an excuse to repeal the North American Free Trade Act (NAFTA)? In 1997 Mexico was the recipient of $30 billion in foreign direct investment, more than almost any other country in the world. It is estimated that 50% of this amount is attributable to NAFTA-related investments. With labor costs that are a fraction of those in the United States and with duty-free access to the U.S. market, the Mexican economy is poised for consistent growth. With a realistically targeted annual economic growth rate of over 5%, Mexico's relative political stability is ensured by its economic viability and its value as a U.S. trading partner.

Egypt

Egypt provides another example of the symbiotic relationship between economic viability and political stability. In 1990, the Egyptian economy was burdened by a lackluster GDP and an external debt of $46 billion. The capitalization of the Cairo Stock Exchange was below $2 billion, and Islamic fundamentalist groups were continually gaining popularity among an increasing percentage of the population that felt habitually disenfranchised.

Although the Gulf War of 1991 was economically devastating to Kuwait and Iraq, it provided a much-needed spark to the Egyptian economy. Egypt was the first major Islamic nation to openly condemn the Iraqi aggression. This was a strategically critical event in that it significantly decreased Iraq's ability to transform the conflict into a united Arab Nations versus Israel and the West scenario. Additionally, when the conflict escalated from Operation Desert Shield to Operation Desert Storm status, Egypt and the United States were the cocommanders of the Allied forces. As a result of its quick and decisive actions, Egypt earned the indebtedness of the Allied forces. The United States was particularly beholden to Egypt in that an unhindered flow of oil (Kuwait) and the military security of Israel are two key U.S. foreign policy objectives. As a reward, immediately following Desert Storm's conclusion, on Egypt's behalf the United States—which controls the International Monetary Fund's greatest share of votes (22%)—facilitated a debt-relief initiative designed to boost the Egyptian economy. This initiative resulted in nearly

14% of Egypt's outstanding foreign debt being completely eliminated or attractively restructured.

Furthermore, the country moved to the top of the U.S. foreign aid list (second only to Israel) and began receiving over $2 billion a year in U.S. foreign aid. In light of its improved financial status and its commitment to embrace a World Bank/IMF–sponsored structural adjustment program (e.g., the privatization of government-owned business, the elimination of exchange controls, etc.), Egypt became an attractive destination for emerging market investors. This was so much the case that the capitalization of the Cairo Stock Exchange increased 1,080% between 1990 and 1997. A dollar invested on the Cairo Stock Exchange in 1992 would have been worth five dollars in 1997, representing a 500% increase or an annualized return of 32.2%. Investors have been rewarded by the fact that, since 1992, 118 state assets have been privatized, including the Alexandria Flour Mills; Al-Ahram Beverages; Kabo/Nasr Clothing; Misr Free Shops; Paints and Chemicals Industry; Commercial International Bank; Suez Cement Company; Egyptian Financial and Industrial Company; Starch and Glucose; Ameriya Cement; Middle Egypt Flour Mills; Middle and West Flour Mills; United Housing; and Heliopolis, for Housing and Development. Additionally, Egypt's external-debt-to-GDP ratio dropped from 96.8% in 1992 to 43.7% in 1997. Furthermore, annual inflation declined from 13.7% to 4.6% during the same period. Today, Egypt is home to the largest U.S. diplomatic services corps in the world; it is the region's undisputed military/economic leader; and it is a hub for multinational businesses seeking to penetrate Northern Africa and the Middle East. Although Egypt's political stability is still challenged by Islamic fundamentalism, the country's current economic viability keeps that challenge from becoming too great a threat.

Nigeria

There are those who would argue that sometimes the strong correlation between economic viability and political stability is not such a good thing, in that there are many instances where a thread of economic sustainability is the greatest obstacle to necessary political reform. It was this school of thought that championed economic sanctions against apartheid-era South Africa, and it is this same school of thought that more recently condemned the multinational oil companies for their economic support of the late Sani Abacha, Nigeria's then-dictator. The annual revenues received by Nigeria's state-owned oil companies are approximately $14 billion. It is said that between royalties, direct investment, and facilitated corruption, multinational oil companies wield the greatest economic influence in the country. With oil exports accounting for 95% of Nigeria's hard currency earnings, Shell and Chevron play major roles relative to the country's economy. Notwithstanding criticisms against the Abacha regime, the close alliance between Nigeria's political leaders and the multinational oil companies is an historic one. Without the oil-generated income stream to finance his political regime (much of which consisted of military salaries), it is doubtful that Abacha would have been able to retain power for as long as he did.

Consequently, Nigeria's relative state of political stability (often at the cost of true democracy) has historically been related to the stream of economic sustenance derived from its oil. The popular election of General Olusegun Obasanjo, and his stated objective of a more democratic and transparent Nigeria, earned the country a much-deserved reprieve in the minds of many would-be investors. Consequently, the country is poised to reap the economic benefits associated with being highly regarded by global political and and business leaders. Multinational oil companies argue in their defense that if they were to leave Nigeria they would be replaced by their competitors or by even less-scrupulous operators. There is a very realistic fear that a pullout (an event not likely to happen) of the multinational oil companies could cause a significant power vacuum in Nigeria. This is a particularly daunting thought when one considers the religious and tribal diversity, weapons availability (from having had military rule for over 10 years), and divergent political agendas existing in Nigeria today. With its vast population (Nigeria's 110-million-plus inhabitants make it Africa's most populous country), human resource talent (Nigeria is home to one of the continent's largest pool of professionals with graduate degrees), and its huge natural resource base, Nigeria has the economic potential to become a major global player.

South Africa

Prior to South Africa's successful democratic transition in 1994, many believed that the country was headed for disastrous civil conflict. While Nelson Mandela, and subsequently Thabo Mbeki, deserve tremendous credit for their courageous leadership and commitment to peace, the strength and international relevance of the South African economy has also played a significant role in the country's peaceful transition. As home of some of the world's most precious natural resources, the country has always had a plethora of powerful allies committed to the maintenance of political stability. For example, as the world's largest producer of platinum, South Africa plays a vital role in the production of catalytic converters and, thus, is an important supplier to the world automotive industry. Furthermore, the country is the world's fifth-largest producer of diamonds and the largest producer of gold. Additionally, South Africa represents the African gateway for numerous multinational corporations. Coca-Cola, BMW, Microsoft, Toyota, Barclays Bank, McDonald's,

Ciba Geigy, Siemens, IBM, British Petroleum, and Sony are merely a few of the multinationals which in aggregate have directly invested over $50 billion in South Africa.

South Africa is home to the world's 15th-largest stock exchange. The Johannesburg Stock Exchange has a market capitalization of approximately $220 billion, of which $100 billion is estimated to represent foreign portfolio investment, and has an economy that is equal to approximately 20% of the GDP for the entire African continent. South Africa is the 9th-largest beer market in the world, the 10th-largest soft drink market in the world (South Africa is one of Coca-Cola's 10 most profitable markets), and the largest market in the world for black hair-care products. During South Africa's democratic transition, a widely held belief was that the country's global economic relevance ensured a relatively smooth domestic political transition. For this reason, experienced Africa investors said there would be very little global tolerance for any politically motivated events that might threaten South Africa's economic viability. This same fact had undoubtedly previously contributed to the staying power of the country's apartheid regime.

Today the global impact of political instability in South Africa would be virtually untenable; a few knowledgeable investors believe that long before any civil unrest could get out of hand, foreign government and/or UN peacekeepers would be aggressively deployed in South Africa to protect international business interests in the country.

COLD WAR AFRICA

Arguably, one of the greatest fallacies in modern western education is the representation of the impact of Cold War–period hostilities on the world. Far too many western educators carelessly describe the Cold War as a war of few casualties. While it is a fact that casualties were few for the then-superpowers (and their significant allies), the toll among their less significant allies was devastating. Figure 6.1 provides a comparison of countries that had minor Cold War casualties (superpowers) and those that had major Cold War casualties (Cold War host countries).

Until the historic demolition of the Berlin Wall, predicting the Cold War's ultimate victor would have been difficult. In hindsight, however, if we trace emerging market development from 1960 to the 1990s, an interesting pattern emerges—a pattern which when considered on a regional basis presents the sequential evolution of prodemocratic capitalistic economies. In retrospect, an argument can be made that the sequential development of the world's hot emerging markets reflects a war that was won one battle at a time. The following Cold War migration graph (Figure 6.2) illustrates the correlation

Minor Casualties	Major Casualties
China	Afghanistan
England	**Angola**
France	Cambodia
Germany	El Salvador
Japan	**Ethiopia**
North Korea	Guatemala
Poland	Honduras
South Korea	**Mozambique**
USA	Nicaragua
USSR (former)	**Somalia**
	Vietnam

FIGURE 6.1   Cold War Casualties

between regions whose majority ultimately embraced procapitalist political doctrine, and the evolution of new emerging markets.

Although the demolition of the Berlin Wall signaled the cessation of Cold War hostilities, the extreme state of conflict escalation in many regions (e.g., Rwanda, Bosnia, Angola, Democratic Republic of Congo, Afghanistan, etc.) necessitated a cooling off period that defied the economic reality of the post–Cold War period.

The decade of the 1970s illustrated Africa's stark transition from a peripheral Cold War participant to a major Cold War theater. In the early to mid-1970s, Africa was the world's least militarized continent. During this period, very few African countries possessed organized military forces. In fact, until around 1975, African military spending as a percentage of GDP was one half of the entire Third World average. By the late 1970s, however, African military hardware consumption had increased significantly. In 1972, Soviet annual

PERIOD	COLD WAR FOCUS REGION	NEW EMERGING MARKETS
1960 and 1970's	Southeast Asia	NA
1970 and 1980's	Latin America	Southeast Asia
1980's	Africa	Latin America
1989	Major Cold War Funding Terminates	Eastern Europe
1990's - 2000	NA	Africa

FIGURE 6.2   Cold War Migration Process

military deliveries to Africa totaled $55 million; by 1977 that amount had increased to $2 billion. Africa's potential strategic relevance made it a top military priority for the Soviet Union. The continent went from receiving 5% of Soviet arms exported to noncommunist states, to receiving 60% of arms exported to noncommunist states. By the late 1970s, the Soviet Union supplied 75% of all weapons imported into Africa—twice as much as from France and five times as much as from the United States. An analysis of two Cold War–era African military conflicts provides a further glimpse of the Cold War's impact on Africa.

Somalia—Ethiopia

While conflict between Somalia and Ethiopia predates the Cold War by centuries, the Somalian army felt the sting of Cold War realities when (on behalf of its ethnic brethren living in the Ogaden region of Ethiopia) it attacked Ethiopia in 1975. In defense of Ethiopia, 1,000 Soviet military officers commanding 16,000 Cuban combat troops, utilizing the latest Warsaw Pact military hardware, easily repelled the Somalians.

Angola

The following quote regarding Angola's civil war, from Félix Houphouët-Boigny (the late president of Côte d'Ivoire), offers yet another example of Cold War realities: "In two years Cubans have killed thousands of Angolans, our African brothers murdered in cold blood. More victims fell in this short period, than in the 15 years of guerrilla war against the Portuguese Colonialists." During the 1980s, when the Angolan civil war was at its height, the United States provided Jonas Savimbi's UNITA (which was battling the Soviet-backed MPLA) with over $300 million worth of military hardware.

During the Cold War period, the critical need for funding by opposing domestic political factions within various countries was often the catalyst for a lethal tug of war. By succumbing to or soliciting funds from either the United States (and its allies) or the Soviet Union (or its allies), these rival factions would propel their countries directly into the center of a winner-take-all conflict between the superpowers' opposing ideologies. Although the ultimate victor was expected to proudly proclaim the virtue of capitalism (aka democracy) over communism (aka socialism) or vice versa, in most instances the primary internal motivation for conflict was the desire for domestic political dominance. In practice, this lethal game usually began with the country's top two political factions and the natural rivalry existing between them. This rivalry then would be externally exploited by superpower intervention: With the financial and strategic assistance (i.e., weapons, intelligence, military and terrorist training, etc.) of their respective superpower allies, the domestic political rivalry would escalate to confrontation then to conflict, and then to out-and-out civil war. Whether it was the North Vietnamese against the South Vietnamese in Vietnam, the FMNL Front against the National Republic Alliance in El Salvador, the Taliban against the Islamic Society in Afghanistan, or the UNITA against the MPLA in Angola, the Cold War escalation strategy remained constant.

The AK-47 assault rifle and its infamous travels during the Cold War provides a classic example of how the superpowers readily and inexpensively instigated conflict escalation. The following excerpt from *Esquire* magazine's June 1997 issue illuminates the AK-47's role in Cold War activities. "Cheap, effective and easy to use, the AK-47 has undoubtedly proven its ability to wreak havoc":

> The AK moves adroitly from hand to hand. The Soviets once supplied Kalashnikovs to the Ugandans, who supplied the Tutsi in Rwanda, who now supply Laurent Kabila's rebels in Zaire. About six million guns are in Mozambique, left behind after two decades of civil war. A similar daisy chain swirls through the Middle East. First, the Soviets built a Kalashnikov factory in Egypt and armed the Syrians, Egypt, and other Arab states.
>
> Official America loved the AK, too: In 1982, the CIA chose the Kalashnikov to arm the Mujahideen in Afghanistan, and four hundred thousand AK's were fed into the country through Pakistan. The Soviets had by then introduced light-caliber AKs with greater accuracy and range, which, since the CIA had no new stock, became trophies for the Mujahideen.

The sheer abundance of AK-47s during superpower-sponsored conflicts is reflected in Figure 6.3, which highlights the street price (informal market) of these weapons at the height of conflict.

Although it would be ludicrous to blame the former superpowers for all of the conflicts between opposing domestic political factions started between 1960 and 1989, it would be equally naive to ignore the role that Cold War hostilities played in these conflicts. As the Cold War debate was based on an ideological thesis, its related conflicts reflect this fact. As a result (with few exceptions), Cold War conflicts were more likely to be internal civil conflicts than the type of external cross-border conflicts typically known as wars of aggression (i.e., WWI, WWII, and the Gulf War).

As the Cold War's last active theater by definition, Africa would appear to be on the brink of economic development. It is a widely held belief among African economic and investment circles that the cessation of Cold War hostilities was the primary reason for much of Africa's current economic resurgence. Although the continent still is home to numerous rival political (and often tribal) and religious factions, gone is the macrostrategic incentive for third parties to foster large-scale conflict between those factions. The rapid deescalation of numerous African civil conflicts has a direct correlation with the historic dismantling of the Berlin Wall, an event that marked the end of

COUNTRY	PRICE* $	SUPERPOWER SUBSIDIZED
Angola	14.00	Yes
USA/Brooklyn, NY	600.00	No
Cambodia	10.00	Yes
Czechoslovakia	150.00	No
Afghanistan	17.00	Yes
Los Angeles	500.00	No

* Local price at the hight of civil conflict

FIGURE 6.3   The Cost of Conflict, AK-47 Prices

Cold War–inspired economic stimulus programs and the beginning of free-market-inspired economic stimulus programs.

POST–COLD WAR AFRICA

In a post–Cold War Africa, macroeconomic stimulus programs have been, for the most part, founded on the laissez-faire ideology of free market economies. Instead of soliciting funds from Cold War adversaries, African governments must now appeal to multilateral aid agencies (e.g., the United Nations, World Bank, or International Monetary Fund), multinational corporations, and portfolio investors in a three-step development process:

Step One

In exchange for embracing World Bank–sponsored structural adjustment programs (e.g., democratic principles of governance, minimal foreign exchange controls, consistent judicial and corporate governance practices, and transparency, privatization, and internationally competitive tax rates), emerging economies are rewarded by the multilateral agencies and their respective host governments, whose economic support generally takes the form of low-interest loans, debt relief, grants, economic consulting expertise, and so forth. Emerging economies are further rewarded when the world's respected economic powers (i.e., the United States, Japan, the European Union, etc.) become outspoken proponents of the virtues of the most observant subject countries (i.e., Uganda, Mexico, Poland, Singapore, Botswana, Mauritius, etc.).

Step Two

As a result of Step One (which is generally accompanied by an employer-friendly labor environment), multinational corporations seeking optimal environmental and strategic opportunities make a direct investment into the country.

Step Three

As a result of Step Two, portfolio investors (domestic and international) seeking inexpensive growth opportunities begin investing directly in businesses in the subject country, or through the local stock exchange(s) into businesses.

Thus, with the Cold War at an end, a transitional period has been embraced by the nations of Africa. Since the early 1990s, African countries have been transitioning away from past government-centered, socialist-oriented economic policies toward more private-sector-centered, free-market capitalistic economic policies. Further, the greatest overall beneficiaries of these policy shifts toward free markets have been those countries with the more viable economies (i.e., that are more richly endowed with mineral and natural wealth, large populations [a broad potential consumer base], and a comparatively strong gross domestic product vis-à-vis other countries in the same region). Nations such as South Africa, Egypt, Nigeria, Kenya, Zimbabwe, Ghana, Côte d'Ivoire, and even the Democratic Republic of Congo, notwithstanding current or prospective political challenges, are likely to continue to attract the attention of the global investment community, and also to receive external political support to help maintain relative stability in their governments.

7

Fast-Growing Sales, Improved Skills, and Abundant Services

A number of important factors are contributing to Africa's development as the ultimate emerging market. They include: (1) a rapidly growing consumer market; (2) an improving labor pool (i.e., hardworking, easily trained, eager, and comparatively inexpensive workers); (3) numerous manufacturing and marketing locations (ideal for shipment and transshipment to the global markets); and (4) an increasing availability of public- and private-funded professional service providers.

TWENTY-FIRST-CENTURY CONSUMERS

Some of the most successful businesses in the United States experienced their greatest growth during the period immediately following World War II, a period in history that marked the birth of the American middle class. From the mid-1940s to the early 1960s, the U.S. population experienced its largest migration of individuals from lower socioeconomic levels to the middle class. This population migration with its attendant impact on consumerism fueled the exponential growth of companies like Sears, McDonald's, IBM, Wal-Mart, and General Motors. The dynamic capacity of today's U.S. economy owes much of its foundation to the evolution of the American middle class.

While the economies of the United States and most western countries would be considered mature today by all definitions, the 53 independent economies in Africa measured by the same criteria would be considered as quite young and at best emerging economies. For this reason, in anticipation of significant economic growth, Africa has become a magnet for expansion-minded multinational corporations and numerous small and midsize foreign-owned businesses. Although some of these organizations have had a presence on the continent for many years, during the last five years, Africa has been inundated with new corporate arrivals (especially consumer product companies). Figure 7.1 shows a few of the multinational corporations operating in Africa today.

One of the factors that has underscored Africa's recent economic growth has been the emergence of a fast-growing consumer market. An important demographic statistic indicative of the potential for future growth in consumer demand is the fact that in most of Africa's countries 45% of the population is at or below the age of 15, while another 26% is between the ages of 15 and 30. More and more goods and service providers are realizing that with half of the continent's population younger than 20, forging brand identity now can pay significant dividends well into the future. And with economic liberal-

AIG	Johnson Publications
American Express	Kentucky Fried Chicken
AVIS	Lotus
Avon	McDonalds
Barclays Bank	Mercedes Benz
BMW	Merryl Lynch
British Petroleum	Microsoft
Budget	Mobil
Carsons	Motorolla
Chancellor Leasing	Nashua
Chrysler	Nestlé
Citibank	NIKE
Coca-Cola	Oracle
Cummings Engine	Packard-Bell
Dell	Panasonic
Domino's Pizza	Pepsi
Firestone	Reebok
Ford	Saatchi & Saatchi
General Electric	Shell
General Motors	Siemens
hertz	Silcon Graphics
Hewlett Packard	Sony
Hilton	South Western Bell
Hoechst	Subway Sandwiches
Honda	Texaco
Hyatt	Toyota
Hyundai	Xerox
IBM	
Imperial	

FIGURE 7.1   Selected Multinationals in Africa

ization increasing and private-sector-led growth playing a major catalytic role in how nations are choosing to expand, millions more who are reaching employment age each year are joining African public and private payrolls.

This growth in the number and spending power of Africa's consumers has not been missed by a number of multinational corporations around the world—including the Coca-Cola Company v. (Coke). Having determined that it can sustain double-digit growth in Africa well into the twenty-first century, Coca-Cola has designated the continent as being critically strategic. In February 1998, Coca-Cola announced a $600 million spending program for Africa. Focusing on small retailers as well as larger corporations to distribute its product, Coca-Cola is squarely targeting the growing African middle-class populations that are emerging in and around the continent's capital cities.

Coca-Cola, whose association with Africa dates back to 1939, has the distinction today of being the largest consumer products investor in Africa. The Coca-Cola Company has established 143 plants across the continent, and its Africa Group employs over 35,000 managers, technicians, and production personnel. The four top African markets for Coke are South Africa, Nigeria, Zimbabwe, and Kenya.

Underpinning the importance of Africa for Coca-Cola is the fact that of the 210 countries around the world where Coke does business, its South African operations have consistently ranked among the company's top 10 earnings contributors. Furthermore, Coca-Cola officials also see huge growth potential in the rest of Africa.

In South Africa, the most developed market in Africa, annual consumption per person of Coca-Cola is 155 units. However, per capita figures for Tanzania and Ghana, where the company is building new bottling plants, are just 14 and 7 units per person, respectively. In Ethiopia, with 55 million potential customers, annual consumption per person is just 3 units. In Kenya, a country with nearly 40 million people, per-person consumption is only 29 units. With overall annual per capita consumption of Coca-Cola in Africa at just 26 units per person, compared to America's overall annual consumption of over 370 units per person, Coca-Cola officials are very bullish about future sales prospects in Africa.

While Coca-Cola provides a vivid example of Africa's increasing consumerism, the growth of Africa's consumptive capacity is not restricted to the beverage industry. In 1998 the countries in Africa represented a total market of $553 billion. In March 1998, U.S. Commerce Department Secretary Richard Daly noted that Africa's growing focus on telecommunications infrastructure development and privatization had contributed to more than a 60% increase in the export of U.S. telecommunications equipment to Africa between 1996 and 1997. A further poignant example of Africa's telecommunication growth is the fact that since 1994 South Africa alone has become the fourth-fastest GSM market (related to cellular telephony) in the world. And it is currently estimated that that country's base of 2.75 million subscribers will grow by at least 50% during 2000–2001.

In 1998, when Canadian telecommunications multinational, Nortel, entered the South African market hoping to have the country serve as its Africa springboard, its managers were astounded by the overall opportunities they found. Nortel, which supplies the infrastructure for mobile and fixed wireless telecommunications networks, has in less that two years of activity on the continent developed eight networks in Kenya, Nigeria, Zambia, Congo, Central African Republic (where it has two networks), Gambia, and Burkina Faso. Furthermore, the company is bidding for six more networks.

According to the International Telecommunications Union, in 1998 Sub-Saharan Africa had approximately 1.20 telephones for every 100 people, and more than half of all Africans lived more than two hours' travel from the nearest telephone. Given this dearth of connectivity, the ITU predicted that more than $20 billion will be spent on telecommunications-related infrastructure before 2003, and it was further noted that plans exist already to provide facilities for 20 million mainline telephone users and 3 million cellular subscribers by the end of 2000.

In the information technology (IT) arena, global companies have also recognized the market growth potential of Africa generally, and South Africa specifically. With the intent of using South Africa as their continental hub, since 1994, virtually all of the global IT companies—Microsoft, Compaq, Oracle, Sun Microsystems, Siemens, Great Plains, Hewlett-Packard, Dell, Packard-Bell, IBM, and NEC—have established a presence on the continent. In South Africa it is estimated that there are more than 2 million personal computers, compared with fewer than 50,000 in all other African markets combined. With 80% growth in sales from mid-1998 to mid-1999, Oracle Corporation ranked its South African subsidiary as the third-fastest-growing of its 90 subsidiaries worldwide. Microsoft's South Africa subsidiary has grown 12-fold since opening in 1992 and is also ranked as an important growth contributor for the world-leading IT multinational.

In 1996, U.S. total trade with Sub-Saharan Africa grew 18.2% and outpaced America's overall growth in world trade. And between 1994 and 1997, U.S. trade with Africa grew by 32.1%, mirroring the 32.4% expansion in total U.S. trade during the same period. Along with recognizing the growth in demand for American products in Africa, U.S. companies have also been attracted to the continent's high return on foreign direct investment capital—a figure that in 1996 reflected a return of 31% as compared to 12% in Latin America, 13% in the Asia-Pacific region, and 17% in the Middle East.

It is also noteworthy to point out that as foreign direct investment on the continent grows (in pursuit of the expanding consumer markets and general opportunities there), there will also be a growing number of corporate consumers in Africa that are the subsidiaries of foreign companies. For example, U.S. corporate exports to Africa-based subsidiaries and affiliates totaled nearly $700 million in 1994.

South Africa, the unparalleled economic engine of the continent, has attracted the lion's share of FDI in Africa. Although in 1996 that nation ranked fifth in inward FDI flows to Africa, behind Nigeria, Egypt, Morocco, and Tunisia, since that year inward investment to South Africa has more than tripled, going from $683 million in 1996 to $2.4 billion in 1998 (see Figure 7.2). Illustrative, however, of the continent's further growth potential is the fact that Africa, including South Africa, only receives about 1% of the world's foreign direct investment.

According to the Washington, D.C., based Investor Responsibility Research Center (IRRC), which tracks foreign business activity in southern Africa, more than 50% of the multinational companies entering South Africa between 1994 and 1997 were from the United States. Prior to antiapartheid-driven disinvestment in the mid-1980s, U.S. firms had approximately $3 billion in assets in South Africa. At the end of 1997, however, the assets held by the roughly 300 U.S. companies in the country totalled approximately $9.5 billion and accounted for 86,000 jobs in such industries as financial services, telecommunications, information technology, food and beverages, and motor manufacturing.

Further indicative of the growing dynamism of African markets is the fact that the entire region's annual growth rate expanded from less than 2% during the period of 1990 to 1994, to 4% in the period between 1995 and 1997, with 11 countries having growth rates of 6% or greater. In some of the fastest-reforming countries, such as Uganda, growth averaged 8% between 1994 and 1997. In 1997, Ethiopia and Uganda recorded economic growth rates of 11.9 and 9.4% respectively. Malawi recorded 16.1% growth to lead the nations of Southern Africa, followed by Zimbabwe with 8.1% growth and Mozambique with 6.4% growth. In West Africa, Côte d'Ivoire grew at a 6.8% rate, and Togo grew at a 6% rate. Africa's overall fiscal deficit was cut in half, from a peak of nearly 9% of GDP in 1992 to an estimated 4.5% in 1997. During this period average annual inflation in Sub-Saharan Africa also came down, from 45% in 1994 to 15% in 1997.

AFRICA CAN COMPETE!

A second factor that has contributed to Africa's expanding ability to attract more domestic and foreign investment is an increasingly competitive labor

BUYER	TARGET	SELLER	VALUE(R-m)
Petroleum Nasional Berhad	Engen	Shareholders	2881.9
Lafarge SA	Blue Circle	Murray & Roberts Holdings	1530.0
Place Dome Inc.	Joint Venture	Western Areas Gold Mining Co	1340.0
Sudelektra Holding AG	Chrome Resources	ChromeCorp Holdings	1202.0
Sudelektra Holding AG	Consolidated Metallurgical Industries	JCI/minorities	1011.3
International Business Machines Corp.	IBM South Africa Group	Minorities	887.5
Cirio SPA	Del Monte Royal Holdings	AAC/minorities	665.0
Parmalat SPA	Bonnita Holdings	The Premier Group	404.4
DOW Chemicals	Safripol	Hoechst South Africa	400.0
Relief Support Marketing	Marketing Rights and Business	Moulded Medical Supplies	330.0
Parmalat SPA	Towerkop Business	Undisclosed	260.0
Hoechst Aktiengesellschaft	Hoechst South Africa	Minorities	209.5
HSBC Investment Bank Holdings	HSBC Simpson McKie	Undisclosed	161.0
Federal-Mogul Corporation	T&N Holdings	Minorities	110.7
Helicopter Services Group	Court Helicopters	Undisclosed	107.3

FIGURE 7.2 South Africa Inward Investment Deals Valued at More than $100 Million in 1998.
Source: Sunday Times, Business Times, September 19, 1999

pool. As Africa's governments continue to shed socialist ideology and reform former command economies in favor of free market economies, the emphasis on fostering global competitiveness has helped enhance the focus on human resource development, efficiency, and productivity.

An additional component of the development of a more competitive African labor force is the educational and training support being provided by African governments to young students and local job seekers. This emphasis on skills development has been driven by the increasing recognition by African leaders of the importance of investing in people. Notwithstanding the fact that the available amount of public funds per capita to be spent on education, health care, and the environment is much lower in Africa than in East and South Asia, according to the World Bank, African nations invest a larger portion of their public funds (4.4% of their national budgets, compared to 3.3 and 3.8%, respectively, for East Asia and South Asia) in these human resource development–related areas.

The changing face of corporate Africa and the evolving focus of public-private and labor-management-oriented partnerships has also helped to improve the continent's competitiveness as a labor market of choice. Furthermore, from a political standpoint, as more local African corporations are formed, the schism between labor and management is shrinking. Historically, management could often easily be negatively associated with foreign-owned multinational corporations that often were headquartered in countries that were former colonial powers. In today's era of increasingly local private-sector-led growth, dynamic African entrepreneurs are working more closely with their employees and introducing profit sharing, stock options, and leave incentives to foster efficiency and productivity and transform the workplace.

A classic example of this change is evident in the "new" South Africa, where labor unions that previously used strikes, work slowdowns, and other productivity-disrupting practices to destabilize the former apartheid regime are being forced to explore more globally beneficial ways to protect and promote the rights of their members. As formerly disenfranchised black South Africans take over the reins of government and strive to enter the economic arena in unprecedented numbers, the lines between labor and management are becoming blurred. With a renewed push to make South African enterprises more productive and competitive, labor and management discussions are rapidly becoming decoupled from the political realm. Both labor and management are realizing that if their products are not able to compete at home and abroad, front office and factory jobs will equally be in jeopardy, and everyone will bear some of the burden for failure.

In an ongoing study of the African private sector begun by the World Bank in the early 1990s, entitled "Africa Can Compete," the capacity and potential of the African labor market was analyzed. The study's concluding assessment was that African workers could literally compete with workers anywhere. The study focused on the garment manufacturing sector, in part because that is generally considered to be one of the starter industries for a country's industrial development. It has been shown in countries such as Bangladesh, Sri Lanka, and Mauritius that by contributing to the creation of local industrial capacity and skill formation, the garment manufacture sector is an important catalyst toward the evolution of value-added economic development. Furthermore, garment manufacture is a labor-intensive and systematic form of manufacture that is not heavily dependant on high-level operational skill or technology.

Further, given that most standardized garments are manufactured according to buyers' designs and specifications, no advanced design expertise is required locally. Thus, most standardized garments can be produced with relative ease. Buyers source standardized garments from all corners of the globe, using established purchasing criteria. The industry does not depend on heavy capital investments or long lead times to come onstream. Fabric is the largest input of the garment, representing up to 62% of the cost of the finished product (see Figure 7.3). Because of its weight and volume characteristics, fabric can be transported over long distances without a significant impact on the unit cost. For instance, using fabric imported from China to manufacture a shirt in Kenya would not add more than U.S. $0.15 to the cost of the garment. Thus, garment manufacturers can locate in Africa irrespective of whether there is a

COMPONENT	Approximate range of costs as a percentage of Total
Fabric	52-62
Direct/Indirect labour	17-18
Miscellaneous materials	12-14
Labels/Packaging	3-8
Garment washing	2
Transport (from factory to nearest port)	1

FIGURE 7.3 Components of Cost in a Man's Casual Long-Sleeved Shirt

local supply of fabric. Nor is the industry's mobility constrained by a requirement to be close to the market; by all accounts, it costs a maximum of U.S. $0.025 to transport a shirt from a port in the Far East to New York.

Of all inputs, labor is the one factor where cost differentials do matter greatly. Consequently, the cost of labor is one of the most important determinants in locating a garment factory. Countries such as Bangladesh, Sri Lanka, and Mauritius—all of which offer low-cost labor (but no significant local sources of textiles)—are far-removed from their principal markets and lack elaborate infrastructure. And yet these three countries have developed substantial export garment manufacturing industries, based primarily on labor cost advantages.

A look at a comparison of production costs for the manufacture of a man's casual long-sleeved shirt (Figure 7.4) illustrates the competitiveness of African workers in the labor-intensive field of cut-and-sew garment manufacturing.

Despite the fact that the characteristics of the garment-manufacturing sector are not necessarily universally comparable to all other sectors in Africa, the cost comparison graphic is illustrative of the fact that cheaper labor can be an incentive for greater production in Africa. Indeed, as labor costs are rising elsewhere in the world, selected African nations are becoming quite attractive as points of manufacture for both regional African markets and Western export markets. These countries include Ghana and Côte d'Ivoire in West Africa, Egypt and Morocco in North Africa, Kenya and Uganda in East Africa, and Namibia, Zimbabwe, South Africa, and Mauritius in Southern Africa.

	Zimbabwe	Kenya	Senegal	Ghana	India	United Arab Emirates
Fabric	3.28	3.00	4.31	3.18	2.90	2.95
Misc. materials	0.31	0.40	0.55	0.42	0.39	0.37
Washing	0.10	0.12	NA	0.11	0.12	6.12
Labels/Packaging	0.16	0.31	0.36	0.36	0.40	0.42
Direct/Indirect labour	0.72	1.34	2.36	1.22	1.22	1.60
Transport to port	0.18	0.20	0.15	0.05	0.15	0.17
Subtotal	5.75	5.37	7.73	5.34	5.18	5.63
Quota Cost	NA	NA	NA	NA	3.00	1.50
Total Costs	5.75	5.37	7.73	5.34	8.18	7.13

FIGURE 7.4 Cost Comparisons (U.S. Dollars) for a Man's Casual Long-Sleeved Shirt

POST–COLD WAR AFRICAN BENEFACTORS

One of the benefits of the post–Cold War era for Africa has been the evolution within the donor community away from politically oriented aid programs toward economic-development–focused programs. Private sector development-related programs have been some of the most effective initiatives launched to help African businesses to become more active in their countries' economies. Training programs in finance, entrepreneurship, export/import skills, manufacturing, management, communication, and other related areas have mushroomed across the continent over the past 10 years. Since the early 1990s, programs related to the promotion of democracy, human rights, environmental protection, and fiscal prudence, also called *structural adjustment programs,* have also been initiated (the latter albeit with mixed results).

The sum total of these programs has been that donor intervention during the 1990s has for the most part successfully helped African nations to move forward and gain greater access to the global economy. The next important challenges on the donor agenda during the twenty-first century will be the design and implementation of debt-reduction and conflict-resolution initiatives. Key participants in Africa's economic, political, and social development include the following:

Multilateral Institutions
- African Development Bank (AfDB)
- International Finance Corporation (IFC)
- International Monetary Fund (IMF)
- Islamic Development Bank
- Multilateral Investment Guarantee Agency (MIGA)
- Organization of African Unity (OAU)
- Paris Club
- United Nations (U.N.)
- U.N. Economic Commission (UNEC)
- U.N. Development Program (UNDP)
- U.N. Industrial Development Organization (UNIDO)
- U.N. Conference on Trade and Development (UNCTAD)
- World Bank

Bilateral Institutions

- Caisse Française de Developpement (CFD)

- Commonwealth Development Corporation (CDC)

- Deutsche Gesellschaft für Technische Zusammenarbeit (GTZ)

- Japan International Cooperation Agency (JICA)

- Japan International Development Organization (JAIDO)

- U.S. Agency for International Development (USAID)

- U.S. Overseas Private Investment Corporation (OPIC)

A key institution supporting the further development of Africa's human capital is the World Bank. In addition to chronicling and promoting Africa's improving labor supply, the bank uses two modern knowledge-management systems—the Live Data Base, which constitutes the largest source of data on African economies, and the Best Practice System, which shares development lessons learned—to disseminate information across the continent via the Internet. Furthermore, through a number of programs, the bank is helping African countries take advantage of the information highway in order to enhance knowledge, information exchange, and communications among African nations and between Africa and the rest of the world. An important partner of the bank in initiating these learning programs is the United Nations' Economic Commission for Africa, which has launched the African Information Society initiative. Their efforts, in large part, have led to the launch of the African Virtual University, which provides private and public institutional satellite-delivered distance education in science and engineering.

The World Bank's Economic Development Institute is also helping to strengthen the capacity and preparedness of Africa's developing labor pool through programs such as the World Links for Development program (WLD). WLD aims to connect 1,000 K-12 schools in the developed world to 1,000 schools in the developing world, with a heavy concentration on Africa. Another important initiative of the World Bank is the Internet-based master's level course on policy analysis and economic management, developed for the Africa Economic Research Consortium and targeted to students at African universities.

Other important development programs include the U.S. Agency for International Development's (USAID) Leland Initiative, which aims to provide Internet infrastructure in over 20 African nations, and the United Nations Industrial Development Organization (UNIDO) supported Alliance for

Africa's Industrialization (AAI), which seeks to promote investment and the financing of technical cooperation programs relating to small and medium-sized Africa enterprises. With such programs, the prospect for further development of Africa's labor pool and for concomitant increases in its productivity level and competitiveness are quite high.

Not all of the support for the facilitation of Africa's private sector has come from government donor agencies. Increasingly, U.S. and European management consulting firms, accounting firms, and financial institutions have set up or expanded their presence in Africa to help facilitate private enterprise focused donor-funded projects and to assist corporate Africa directly on a fee-for-service basis. Figure 7.5 lists some of the international professional service institutions on the African continent.

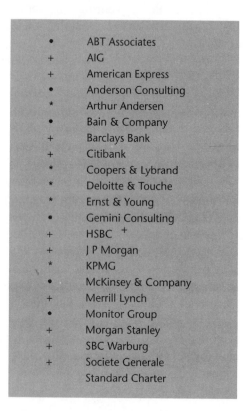

- ABT Associates
+ AIG
+ American Express
- Anderson Consulting
* Arthur Andersen
- Bain & Company
+ Barclays Bank
+ Citibank
* Coopers & Lybrand
* Deloitte & Touche
* Ernst & Young
- Gemini Consulting
+ HSBC +
+ J P Morgan
* KPMG
- McKinsey & Company
+ Merrill Lynch
- Monitor Group
+ Morgan Stanley
+ SBC Warburg
+ Societe Generale
  Standard Charter

* Accounting Firm • Consulting Firm + Financial Services

FIGURE 7.5 Selected Professional Services Providers

GREAT LOCATION FOR EUROPEAN, ASIAN, AND U.S. TRADE

Adam Smith, the Scottish political economist and philosopher who became famous for his influential book *The Wealth of Nations* (written in 1776), established what has become an often-repeated and rarely challenged assessment of the role of geography as a barometer for prospective economic growth. According to Smith, access to sea-based trade, because it is less expensive than land trade, is a key determinant of a country's and region's prospects for economic growth. In assessing the relative wealth and progress of emerging markets such as Asia and Africa, Smith wrote:

> So it is upon the seacoast and along navigable rivers, that industry . . . naturally begins to subdivide and improve itself and it is frequently not till a long time after that those improvements extend themselves to the inland part of the country. . . .
>
> All the inland parts of Africa, and all that part of Asia which lies considerably way north of the Euxine and Caspian seas seem in all of the ages of the world to have been in the same barbarous and uncivilized state in which we find them at present.

Smith further attributed England's relatively high productivity (in comparison to Asia and Africa) to the advantages of natural geography and policy. England, he explained, had fertile soil, a long coastline, and many navigable rivers. It also had secure property rights and the rule of law.

Although Smith's analysis conspicuously omits discussion and consideration of the implications of centuries of colonial exploitation on a region's development, it does accurately underscore the fact that the physical isolation of Africa's interior nations has long placed profound burdens on the region's overall development.

Yet today, African nations are more aggressively working to reverse the image of that region as the "dark continent" by focusing their resources on the development of road, rail, sea, and perhaps most important, communications infrastructure. Furthermore, by focusing heavily on capital market development, African nations have been working to improve their financial sector infrastructure and links with the global finance community.

The dynamic growth of Africa's aggregate stock market capitalization (which more than doubled in a 10-year period, from $136 billion in 1989 to nearly $300 billion in 1999) is indicative of the robust development of the continent's financial sector infrastructure. Excluding South Africa, the progress was even more striking, with Africa's stock market capitalization rising more than 10-fold, from U.S. $5 billion in 1989 to over U.S. $50 billion in 1999.

.., nowhere else in the world do investor perceptions lag behind reality more dramatically than in Africa. While it is relatively widely known that Africa contributes only a very small percentage of world GDP (3.4% in 1996) and a still smaller share of exports of goods and services (1.9%), it is less well known that Africa accounts for 8.6% of developing country GDP and 11.3% of all developing region exports. After years of stagnation and decline, the 5% GDP growth in 1996 by African nations made them the second-fastest-growing developing region in the world, behind Asia. With the recent economic troubles in Asia, it is foreseeable that in the next 10 years Africa will easily become the fastest-growing developing region in the world. Along with macroeconomic reform that has ushered in a period of declining budget deficits, slower growth in money supply, and falling inflation, increased export capacity has proven to be one of the biggest reasons for the continent's improved economic well-being.

What some African nations may lack in proximity to Adam Smith's aforementioned all important sea, they make up for in access to significant export markets in Europe and the United States. The European Community-African, Caribbean and Pacific (EC-ACP) region Convention, commonly known as the Lomé Convention, and Title V of the United States Trade Act of 1974, which established the U.S. Generalized System of Preferences (GSP), are two important treaties providing reduced rate or duty-free access of African products to the European Community and the United States, respectively.

The African Growth and Opportunity Act, or the African Trade Bill, as it is more widely known, should become law in 2000 and portends to further facilitate trade between the United States and African nations. And the South African–European Union Trade Bill should significantly improve commerce flows between South Africa and the European Union (EU).

All 48 Sub-Saharan African states are members of the Lomé Convention. The Lomé Convention has proven very important to the ACP states, with the European Union purchasing roughly 55% of the ACP countries' exports. Purchases made under the Act from 1990 to 1998 totaled more than U.S. $16 billion.

Although fewer African nations have taken advantage of the GSP, four nations that exported goods via GSP—South Africa, Angola, Zimbabwe, and Malawi—saw their exports under the program soar by 78% in 1997 to just over U.S. $1 billion (see Figure 7.6).

The leading GSP-supported export items from Africa were crude oil, ferroalloys, sugar, jewelry, vehicle parts, and tobacco. Along with selected favorable trade treaties with the United States and Europe, from a regional perspective Africa has offered domestic and multinational corporations favorable export locales through the exploitation of historic trade routes from West

COUNTRY	1997 GSP Benefits
	($ Millions)
South Africa	450.8
Angola	356.5
Zimbabwe	79.9
Malawi	28.5

FIGURE 7.6   GSP Exports from Africa

Africa to Europe; from North Africa to Europe and the Middle East; from East Africa to Europe, the Middle East, and Asia; and from Southern Africa to Europe, the Middle East, and Asia. Increasingly economic reform initiatives in Africa have also included the establishment of export processing zones designed to offer duty-free entry of manufacturing inputs, and selected tax benefits, for exporters who target 80 to 100% of their production for external sale.

PART 3

Taking the Plunge—Boldly Going Where Few Have Gone Before

Thus far, our aim has been to provide an insight into the diverse African investment universe. Our belief is that to know Africa, or at least to know about some of the more economically dynamic countries in Africa, is to begin to appreciate the tremendous emerging opportunities on the continent.

In Part Three, we begin to deal with the aspect of what *specific* opportunities exist for those interested in portfolio investment, in private equity investment, and in foreign direct investment. Furthermore, we look at some of the risks attendant to investing in Africa and provide our thoughts about how one can best get started—and what information, analytical data, and other resources are available to help investors make knowledgeable decisions when pursuing African investment opportunities.

8

The Art of the Deal— Assessing the Investment Alternatives

Once a decision has been made to explore investment in Africa, the next logical question relates to the best ways to proceed. There are, in fact, a number of ways that one can proceed. The three most common methods are stock market investment, private equity investment, and foreign direct investment.

Investors that look to invest in Africa's stock markets have traditionally been institutional investors such as insurance companies, pension funds, and transnational corporations that have publicly listed subsidiaries in Africa.

Investors in the nascent African private equity community have traditionally been the very same institutional investors, along with multinational banks such as Citibank, and increasingly multilateral institutions such as the World Bank's International Finance Corporation, the African Development Bank, and bilateral institutions such as England's Commonwealth Development Corporation.

Foreign direct investors in Africa have disproportionately been transnational corporations that are expanding into the continent. Most of the growth in this area is fueled by such entities' decisions to grow their on-the-ground marketing presence, manufacturing, and/or distribution capacity.

AFRICAN STOCK MARKET INVESTMENT— THE OPEN- AND CLOSED-END FUNDS

Today in each of the 19 markets where African securities exchanges exist, there is a growing cadre of sophisticated brokers through which foreign and

'estors can make and settle trades. Selected globally active brokerages
.... ..ave begun to facilitate trades in African securities include Fleming Martin, Inc., Standard Bank New York, Inc., Deutsche Morgan Grenfell, Merrill Lynch, ING Barings (U.S.) Securities, Inc., HSBC Securities Inc., and J.P. Morgan Securities. Given the fact that the Johannesburg Stock Exchange comprises at least 85% of the continent's capitalization, it has the most representatives within this group as members.

Although some foreign investors have the market knowledge, research capacity, and analytical resources to pick their own investments with the help of online research services such as Reuters and Bloomberg, most investors prefer to allocate portions of their portfolios to fund managers that specialize in emerging market investment. As there is a small but growing number of asset managers that focus on Africa, the typically preferred route of investment is to invest in closed-end and open-ended funds.

Most African funds are generally listed on the New York Stock Exchange or the Dublin Exchange in Ireland and incorporated in countries with preferential tax and regulatory advantages. A growing number of African countries, led by South Africa, are also raising funds through index-related "unit trusts" (i.e., mutual funds). The majority of Africa-focused fund managers are headquartered in London, England (although a growing community is emerging in Washington, D.C.), and most have significant overall emerging market investment experience. Another increasing trend is for international fund managers to partner with local African managers to provide on-the-ground advisory insight to the fund management process.

Predominantly, Africa-focused funds are targeted at high net worth individuals and international institutional investors, with minimum investment thresholds of between $50,000 and $250,000. Included in the closed-end category of such funds are the Morgan Stanley Africa Investment Fund, the Southern Africa Fund, and the Simba Limited Fund (see Figure 8.1). These funds have been targeted at more sophisticated investors and allow for the purchase of a finite number of shares by investors. However, once "closed," the shares trade at a market price set by buyers and sellers. The shares of a closed-end fund typically trade at prices different, and often higher, than the fund's net asset value (NAV—or the assets of a fund less the total of its liabilities). It is the *discount,* or the amount paid at the inception of the fund versus the appreciated share/market value, that appeals to investors. African closed-end fund managers also have for the most part reserved the right to open the funds after two to five years if a qualified majority of investors vote to do so. Today, roughly $200 million is invested in Africa through closed-end funds, most of which arrived during the heady emerging market investment period of 1995 to 1996.

Closed End Funds	US$ Mngd.	1 Month	1 Year	3 Year
Morgan Stanley Africa Investment Fund	181	-7.1	-18.7	-9.4
Simba Fund Limited	24.7	-2.9	-20	***
Southern Africa Fund	6.01		-23.88	-0.90

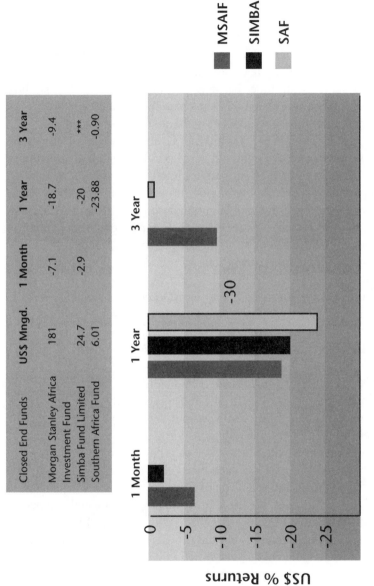

US$ percentage returns, NA V to NAV , gross income reinvested. Periods ending December 31, 1998.
All fund sizes are as at November 30, 1998 and are in US$ millions

FIGURE 8.1 Africa Closed-End Funds Chart
Source: Standard & Poor's Micropal Emerging Market Monitor, February 1999

The open-ended Africa-focused funds include the Africa Emerging Markets Fund, the Calvert New Africa Fund, the Global African Development Fund, and the GT Africa Fund (Figure 8.2). These funds allow investors to buy in at prices reflecting the current NAV on a daily basis. As they are open, there is no limit on the number of shares that can be issued, and thus no premium on the shares other than that warranted by an appreciating NAV. The fund manager can sell as many shares as requested and agrees to redeem them at the NAV per share at the time the investor wants to sell. Today, slightly more than $100 million is invested in these open-ended funds.

The combined assets of the selected closed-end and open-ended funds just described are slightly more than $300 million. Given that there are more than 2,100 available African securities worth some $280 billion, the opportunity for the increased flow of foreign investment into Africa is fairly evident. A relative comparison of developing region investment in the three other regions that have received significant attention during the 1990s—Asia, Latin America, and Eastern Europe—further illustrates the potential for growth in African investment vis-à-vis the other emerging markets (Figure 8.3).

Figure 8.3 provides a comparison of four open-ended and four closed-ended U.S. dollar-denominated funds from each region, as reviewed by the February 1999 Standard & Poor's *Micropal* Emerging Market Fund Monitor. What is evident from the chart is that Africa is significantly underweighted in the portfolios of individual and institutional investors, and as such holds the greatest opportunity for significant appreciation with the least amount of relative investment (Figure 8.4).

In terms of the preferred investment vehicles of the funds investing in Africa, most are primarily investing into listed equity stocks. Fund managers, however, are retaining the ability to invest into debt obligations and money market and related instruments, usually depending upon the attractiveness of available opportunities or where a market or other factors warrant a more defensive investment strategy. Most such funds also have reserved the right to invest up to 15% of the portfolio outside of Africa in companies which have a large share of their operations in Africa. Investment into nonlisted companies has been generally limited to newly privatized companies and to companies expected to come to the market within the near term. The last asset class to which fund managers are turning (and which will be discussed later in this chapter) is the private equity asset class.

Portfolio concentration with both closed-end and open-ended funds varies widely, with the top 10 largest investments accounting for between one-fifth and two-thirds of the total NAV of most funds. Almost all of the funds have a heavy concentration of South African securities, though some also have a strong subfocus on certain industries (e.g., financials, mining and minerals,

Open End Funds	US$ Mngd.	1 Month	1 Year	3 Year
Africa Emerging Markets Fund	97.9	-7.1	-6.10	39
Calvert New Africa Fund	8.9	-0.7	-11.6	-18.2
Global African Development Fund	5.1	-1.5	***	***
GT Africa Fund	4.11	-3.0	-13.5	-8.3

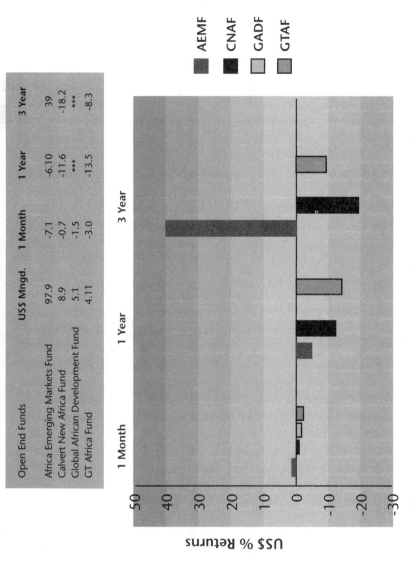

AEMF
CNAF
GADF
GTAF

US$ % Returns

1 Month   1 Year   3 Year

US$ percentage returns, NAV to NAV, gross income reinvested. Periods ending December 31, 1998.
All fund sizes are as at November 30, 1998 and are in US$ millions

FIGURE 8.2   Africa Open-End Funds Chart
Source: Standard & Poor's Micropal Emerging Market Fund Monitor, February 1999

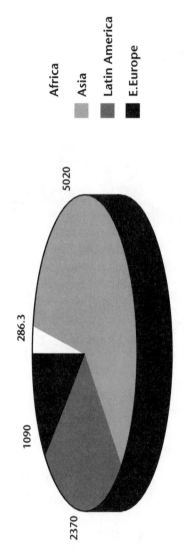

FIGURE 8.3 Dollars Invested by Region

Source: Standard & Poor's Micropal Emerging Market Fund Monitor, February 1999

All of the Regions (E.Europe, Asia and latin America) are represented by regional funds for their respective areas of investment. Africa, as a region, is represented by those Open & Closed-end Funds previously listed. All fund sizes are as at November 30, 1998 and are in US$ millions.

technology sectors). Other countries that have received significant institutional investor attention include Zimbabwe, Ghana, Côte d'Ivoire, and the new regional stock market in Côte d'Ivoire (the BRVM). Others that historically received less interest but which have been rising in focus more recently include Egypt, Morocco, and Nigeria.

From the standpoint of the stocks available for selection on Africa's exchanges, the sectoral composition reflects the overall structure of most of Africa's countries. Commodity companies (e.g., those dealing in sugar, coffee, tea, mining, and tobacco) predominate in the listings while financial institutions comprise another significant sector. Rounding out the generally available complement of securities are listings of food and industrial conglomerates, breweries, soap and consumer products, cement and construction, and cigarettes.

Although a number of countries (including Kenya, Zimbabwe, and Tanzania) still limit foreign ownership of listed companies, these prohibitions are becoming more the exception than the rule, and the number of funds investing in Africa continues to steadily rise. Equally important, the range and breadth of these funds in terms of their inclusion of stocks from a wider variety of sectors and from more and more countries outside of South Africa also continue to rise.

In many of the stock markets of Africa, prior to the mid-1990s foreign investors were prohibited from investing, and local investors were prohibited from investing offshore. This led to an environment where those shares that were carried on the stock exchanges were highly illiquid. In 1995 and 1996, when a number of the Africa stock markets began to liberalize their foreign exchange controls, interest in African securities skyrocketed. In addition to relaxing exchange control regulations that impeded market liquidity, restrictions on foreign portfolio investment levels are slowly being done away with. Historically, the African exchanges placed ceilings on the percentage of foreign ownership allowable in a given stock issue. In many instances this ceiling still persists, and it can range from anywhere between 40 and 100%, depending on the stocks. Zimbabwe, Ghana, Egypt, Kenya, and Tanzania have all had such prohibitions at varying times and to varying degrees.

Recognizing that a balance must be struck between these protectionist policies and the stimulation of growth within their capital markets, more African exchanges have focused in recent years on promoting local institutional and individual investment in the stock exchanges. Withholding a certain percentage of initial public offering (IPO) shares for local investors, promoting local savings, and providing tax and other regulatory benefits for institutional investors (i.e., local pension funds and insurance companies) to invest in securities, are just some of the ways that public equities investment is being promoted.

Region	1980	1981	1982	1983	1984	1985	1986	1987	1988	1989	1990	1991	1992	1993	1994	1995	1996	1997
East Asia & Pacific	0	0	0	0	0	44	31	202	487	2073	1053	704	2035	14619	10087	14715	14389	7936
Europe & Central Asia	0	0	0	0	0	0	0	0	0	56	185	0	65	984	2200	2728	8345	4808
Latin America & Caribbean	0	135	0	0	0	0	0	78	176	248	896	5727	8048	27185	13159	7643	13893	9947
Middle East & North Africa	0	0	0	0	0	0	0	0	0	0	0	0	0	0	106	203	1632	2259
South Asia	0	0	0	0	0	0	192	0	56	168	105	23	380	2025	6223	2340	5198	2477
Sub-Saharan Africa	0	0	0	0	0	0	0	0	0	0	0	0	144	174	860	4868	2012	1507
Low & Middle Income	0	135	0	0	0	44	223	280	719	2545	2239	6454	10672	44987	32636	32498	45470	28934
South Africa	-	-	-	-	-	-	-	-	-	-	-	-	-	-	219	4571	1759	1393

Note : - = data not available

FIGURE 8.4 Portfolio Investment Activity, 1980–1997
Source: World Bank, Global Development Finance, 1999

118

Allowing foreign brokerages to join African exchanges and deregulating brokerage activities is another way in which efforts have been undertaken to stimulate increased investment and trading activity within the African exchanges. Efforts to launch educational campaigns to explain the benefits of listing via IPOs, and the introduction of stock option plans and other employee share plans within African-listed companies, are also starting to help create liquidity and greater dynamism in the securities markets.

With the arrival of the new millennium, technology is also being more rapidly integrated into Africa's stock exchanges. The Casablanca exchange in Morocco, the new regional exchange in Côte d'Ivoire (the BRVM), and the Johannesburg Stock Exchange all have modern clearing and settling systems. A growing number of exchanges are also establishing central depository systems to improve transparency, and some, such as the BRVM, also are electronic. Pan-African associations such as the African Capital Markets Forum based in Accra, Ghana, and the African Stock Exchange Association based in Johannesburg, South Africa, have been active in promoting automation and improved transparency among the member exchanges.

In terms of tracking the performance of African stock markets generally, and the performance of African funds specifically, there are a number of indices that are monitored by active investors and serve as benchmarks for the fund managers. The Morgan Stanley index, the Fleming Martin index, and the International Finance Corporation's Emerging Market index are three of the most widely accepted and quoted indices against which African stock market performance is compared. *The Wall Street Journal, The New York Times,* the *International Herald Tribune,* and the *Financial Times* are but a few of the journals published in global financial market capitals which disseminate this information.

All of the standard performance evaluation indicators, such as price-to-earnings (P/E) and price-over-book (P/B) ratios (historical and expected), earnings per share (EPS), and earnings before income tax, depreciation, and amortization (EBITDA), are actively calculated and relied upon by African fund managers and individual investors assessing the universe of African securities. Standard and Poor's *Micropal* Emerging Market Fund Monitor is one of the most widely referenced and quoted research and analysis benchmarks against which to compare the performance of African funds. On a market-by-market basis, Fleming Martin, Merrill Lynch, and Standard Bank are three of the internationally recognized producers of market research. Increasingly this information is also becoming available through the time- and space-condensing medium of the Internet via online research portals.

INVESTMENT IN AFRICAN GOVERNMENT SECURITIES

As is the case with most emerging economies, the evolution of Africa's government securities market has lagged behind the evolution of the continent's various publicly traded securities markets. This fact reflects the interrelationship between a country's level of economic development and political stability, which in turn influences the success of its government securities offerings. However, to the extent that liquid, efficient, and diverse treasury markets foster investor confidence, the development of Africa's government securities market has been increasingly recognized as a necessity.

More and more, as international fixed-income consumers have become more globalized and sophisticated, they are becoming attracted by the return potential of government securities in Africa. Where the variety of government-backed securities in more developed capital markets covers a range of sectors, risk, and maturity, options in African government securities are less diverse. In fact, approximately 95% of securities issued by African governments are issued by the government treasury, versus government agencies, and have maturities of less than one year. This situation is primarily attributable to the volatility (or the perception thereof) of emerging economies and the impact such volatility may have on a government's perceived ability to meet its payment obligations.

While long-term, low-interest debt obligations would theoretically translate into a minimal economic drain on African governments, the market reality demands a premium for longevity. Thus, in an environment where short-term interest rates are between 15 and 25%, the 10 to 15 point premium (which would mean interest rates of 25 to 40%) necessary for a successful three- to five-year government debt offering has thus far proved to be prohibitive. As a result of the higher interest rates, payment guarantees, and the extensive credit analysis that would be required (with the exception of a few special circumstances) to sustain long-term African government debt offerings, long-term African government debt is rare. Figure 8.5 highlights rare examples of African governments that have successfully issued long-term debt and describes the unique characteristics that made this possible.

LIBOR (London Interbank Offering Rate) is the most popular performance benchmark for African government-issued securities, and they are usually quoted as offering an interest rate-related return of LIBOR plus. The use of LIBOR-linked quotes is also due to the relatively high participation of global banks (especially European-based banks) in the consumption of African government debt offerings.

An analysis of Côte d'Ivoire and its government debt offering in 1996 provides a good example of the type of macroeconomic trends that attracts

Botswana : Boasts the continent's strongest macro Economic Fundamentals (3 to 4 year import cover reserves) and arguably Africa's most politically stable government.

Morocco : Low external debt, stable and consistent economic growth. The country established multi-lateral, donor and investor credibility by its aggressive approach to structural adjustment.

Nigeria : Brady Bonds. Continent's most populous country and major provider of petroleum products to the United States. Brady Bonds are sovereign bonds issued by developing countries that are backed by a US government sponsored program designed to provide credit enhancement as a reward for certain structural reforms.

South Africa : With an annual GDP of over $120 billion, South Africa is Africa's largest economy producing 60% of the continent's combined GDP. Additionally a relatively prudent fiscal policy and a smooth political transition have earned good will and credibility.

FIGURE 8.5 Africa's Long-Term Government Debt Issuers

investors. Like much of Africa during the post–Cold War period of the early 1990s, the future of Côte d'Ivoire's economy represented a bit of a question mark to both local and foreign investors. Côte d'Ivoire's strong ties with France and its long standing as one of the political and economic hubs of West Africa, particularly francophone West Africa, intimated that a certain minimal level of economic growth would be obtainable. What remained to be seen, however, was whether the country's economic and political leaders would embrace the austerity program required to fulfill the International Monetary Fund's (IMF) structural adjustment program(s). To their credit, during this period Côte d'Ivoire's leaders pursued the often difficult initiatives prescribed and diligently adhered to the initiatives designed by the IMF to provide economic stimulus. Democratic elections, exchange control reform, an aggressive privatization effort, and a reduction in trade barriers were some of the key factors that prompted the investment community to reevaluate Côte d'Ivoire's sovereign risk. Subsequently the improved confidence level (and hence the improved perception of Côte d'Ivoire's creditworthiness) translated into an appreciation in value for the country's government-issued debt—an event that rewarded the forward-thinking investors who had anticipated the country's economic turnaround.

Overall, for institutional and individual investors that have a higher tolerance for risk, buying certain African government securities at the right time has produced attractive returns. By successfully identifying turn-around economies, these investors have acquired government securities on a deeply discounted basis (sometimes for literally pennies on the dollar) and have been able to sell them for attractive returns when market sentiment becomes positive.

During the early to mid-1990s, Ethiopia, Ghana, Uganda, and Mozambique all offered investors scenarios where investment in government-issued securities yielded equity-like annualized returns of 40% or better. While local brokers are still the best source for government-issued securities, an increasing amount of African government securities trading activity is being facilitated and monitored by the same major international brokerage firms (e.g., Morgan Stanley, J. P. Morgan, Fleming Martin, Merrill Lynch) that are developing a presence to trade African corporate securities.

VENTURE CAPITAL AND PRIVATE EQUITY INVESTMENT

In the early 1990s, a number of bilateral and multilateral donor institutions, including the World Bank's International Finance Corporation (IFC), the Commonwealth Development Corporation of England (CDC), and the U.S. Agency for International Development (USAID), identified the lack of equity capital—particularly within the entrepreneurial business class—as an impediment to the growth of the continent's private sector. To provide a spark to help mobilize such capital, a number of venture capital (VC) development-oriented projects were launched, resulting in the establishment of some of Africa's first VC funds.

The premise of these initiatives was to create an asset class of "patient" risk capital in Africa, which could be used to support start-up and early stage businesses. The financiers of venture capital firms typically are willing to forgo dividend or interest payments during the life of their investment in exchange for a higher yielding (40 to 60%) return when the portfolio companies go public or are sold to other corporations.

In the United States and Europe, the VC market includes the merchant banking subsidiaries of large institutions such as investment banks, bank holding companies, insurance companies, and industrial companies. In Africa, a number of special purpose investment vehicles have been created to raise and invest venture capital.

In the early 1990s, publicly supported VC funds such as those developed by USAID, the European Union (EU), and CDC were often capitalized by the donor and managed by individuals hired to oversee the investment process. These initiatives were most often treated as an extension of the donor's development mission and managed as a private-sector development-oriented project. The most relevant distinction between these funds and private venture capital funds was the fact that the management of the public funds did not share in the attendant risk or reward of the investments made during the life of the fund. Many of these types of funds were established as country- or region-specific funds. A number of these funds have been established by the Commonwealth Development Corporation, including the Development Finance Company of Uganda, the Ghana Venture Capital Fund, the Tanzania Venture Capital Fund, and the Commonwealth Africa Investment Fund. The USAID-supported Southern African Development Community focused Southern Africa Enterprise and Development Fund is another such fund, as is the Cauris Investment fund in French-speaking West Africa, which was established by the West African Economic and Monetary Union (UEMOA).

During the latter half of the 1990s, the predominant structure of VC funds shifted toward the establishment of "private" VC funds, which entailed the fund manager raising the fund capital from a limited number of sophisticated investors in a private placement and also agreeing to invest principal capital in the fund itself. In this way, the fund manager shares in the risk and reward of the investments.

Typical private VC funds have a life of about 10 to 12 years, and the investor base is comprised of pension plans, insurance companies, wealthy individuals, bank holding companies, multinational corporations, endowments, and foreign investors. Through this model, VC fund managers receive income from two sources—(1) an annual management fee during the life of the fund, and (2) a profit, "carry" allocation. The fund's primary source of income is a capital gain from the sale of stock of the companies in which the fund has invested (the portfolio companies) after a three- to five-year period from the time of investment. The fund-managing general partner typically receives a *carried interest* in the fund equal to 20% of the profits, and the limited partner(s) that provide the fund's capital receive 80% of the profits. Private equity funds are in fact a subset of the VC asset class which is focused on second-stage, rapidly growing and expanding companies, as opposed to the entrepreneurial start-ups typically targeted by VC funds. An early example of these types of funds was the Africa Growth Fund, established by HSBC Equator Bank in the late 1980s–early 1990s.

One of the key catalysts for the establishment of more Africa-focused venture capital/private equity funds has been the U.S. government's Overseas Private Investment Corporation (OPIC). This government agency's mission is to facilitate, support, and promote U.S. investment in the emerging market regions of Asia, Latin America, Eastern Europe, and Africa. The key funds that have been supported by OPIC include the $120 million, southern-Africa-focused New Africa Opportunity Fund (NAOF); the $150 million, Sub-Saharan Africa (excluding South Africa) focused Modern Africa Growth and Investment Company (MAGIC) Fund; and the forthcoming $350 million Sub-Saharan Africa infrastructure project focused, New Africa Infrastructure Fund (NAIF).

Other significant funds that have been established in the latter part of the 1990s include the African Development Bank–supported South Africa Infrastructure Fund, and the International Finance Corporation and American Insurance Group supported $500 million Africa Infrastructure Fund. In recognition of former militarily ruled Nigeria's strides toward democracy, the International Finance Corporation also recently approved the capitalization of a $30 million private equity fund for that country.

By December 2000 more than $1 billion of private capital will have been targeted toward African businesses. If past performance serves as an indicator, these funds will not only help leverage additional investment in Africa but will also create thousands of jobs on the continent and significantly help expand the revenues of the companies in which they are invested. The New Africa Infrastructure Fund alone is expected to leverage an additional $2 billion of investment in Sub-Saharan Africa, create roughly 6,800 jobs, and generate almost $50 million in annual revenues for the projected portfolio companies and their suppliers. In addition, according to OPIC, the fund will also generate an expected $350 million in American exports.

For prospective investors interested in private equity opportunities in Africa, the important thing to remember is that the existing funds have only scratched the surface of the capital need faced by the continent. According to numerous sources, including the World Bank, over the next 20 years Africa's infrastructure investment needs alone are expected to exceed $100 billion.

THE ROLE OF PRIVATIZATION

One of the most influential developments during the past decade in terms of stimulating stock market interest, investment, and trading activity in Africa has been the growing number of privatizations underway on the continent.

To a large extent, the privatization wave on the African continent is a 180-degree reversal of nationalistic initiatives begun during the 1960s and 1970s, when the influence of socialism was at its height. However, at that time, Africa was only one of many developing regions engaged in a North-South battle against "imperialism" and threatened by the seeming omnipotence of western multinational corporations.

During this period, with the implicit intent of saving national assets from harmful foreign control, governments in many of the world's developing countries seized control of (nationalized) domestic goods and service providers. Southeast Asia, Latin America, and Africa became engaged in massive nationalization efforts, which included, but were not limited to, programs to bring under government control all operations involving telecommunications, banking, mining, manufacturing, health care, bottling, and tourism.

However, while nationalization effectively minimized the fear of "capitalist exploitation," the practice was not without its own deficiencies. On the average, most state-controlled providers of goods and services were (and many still are) plagued by structural inefficiencies that rendered them overly bureaucratic, technologically without innovation, bloated, and financially unsound.

During the late 1980s and 1990s, however, as the global influence of free-enterprise–oriented economic policies spread, developing nations in Africa and globally began to seek to bring more private entrepreneurs and corporations into effective control and management of previously privatized enterprises. As privatization became an integral component of World Bank and International Monetary Fund prescriptions for economic development, privatizing state industries also increasingly brought additional benefits—such as balance of payment support, debt relief, and project finance—to Africa's governments.

Notwithstanding the often much publicized examples of privatization-related success, such as the Ashanti Goldfields deal in Ghana, the Mobilnil deal in Egypt, and the Sonatel deal in Senegal, privatization in Africa is still in its infancy. Conversely, in the world's other emerging markets thousands of privatizations have taken place during the last 15 years. As the world's last emerging market, Africa is easily a decade behind Southeast Asia and Latin America relative to privatization. And although the pace of African privatizations increased between 1992 and 1997, in 1998 the asset value of the 6,000+ African government-controlled enterprises still eligible and scheduled for privatization exceeded $200 billion.

However, notwithstanding the relatively slow process of privatization in Africa to date, a 1997 International Finance Corporation discussion paper entitled "Trends in Private Investment in Developing Countries, Statistics for 1970–95," which reviewed data from the World Bank Privatization Database, confirmed that privatization in Africa has indeed had a positive impact on the overall flow of investment (particularly foreign direct investment) in Africa over the past 20+ years. The report points out that the state-owned enterprise (SOE) sales that took place in Africa have been primarily in the sectors of petroleum and mining, with the sale of two assets—Nigeria's NNPC oil field and Ghana's Ashanti Goldfields—accounting for nearly 40% of total privatization revenues.

Figure 8.6 provides an overview of the pace of privatization in selected African countries from 1988 to 1995. Overall foreign direct investment (FDI) from privatization in Africa during this period accounted for slightly less than 20% of total FDI received. Although this was less than the percentages recorded by Europe and Central Asia (40%), and Latin America and the Caribbean, (21%), Sub-Sahara Africa's percentage of privatization-related FDI was higher than that of South Asia (14%), East Asia and the Pacific (5%), and the Middle East and North Africa (4%).

Overall, between 1984 to 1995 2,700 privatizations were completed in Sub-Saharan Africa, with a total value of $2.8 billion. However, the average transaction was less than $1 million, and a number of liquidations were valued at zero. In terms of assessing which countries were in the forefront of privatization activity, Mozambique, Angola, Tanzania, Ghana, Zambia, Kenya, and Guinea led the African continent.

African countries that have embarked upon privatization programs can be divided into two groups: first, according to the degree of privatization—major, modest, as well as minimal privatizers; and second, according to when countries embarked upon their privatization programs—early starters, not-so-early starters, and late starters.

Major privatizers are those where the majority of state enterprises have been divested. These countries include Benin, Guinea, and Mali. Modest pri-

Country	Privatization Revenues (US$ Millions)	Number of Privatization	FDI from Privatization (US$ Millions)
Benin	54	12	44
Burkina Faso	0	1	0
Burundi	4	8	0
Cape Verde	0	1	0
Cote d'Ivoire	154	24	26
Egypt	679	23	214
Ghana	619	52	451
Guinea-Bissau	1	3	0
Kenya	95	52	38
Morocco	860	45	247
Mozambique	52	113	21
Nigeria	763	58	500
Sao Tome & Principe	0	1	0
South Africa	637	3	0
Tanzania	111	41	97
Togo	28	7	28
Tunisia	132	32	23
Uganda	101	34	64
Zambia	71	10	52
Zimbabwe	307	3	246
Total:	4668	523	2051
Emerging markets Overall:	131048	3793	47456

FIGURE 8.6 Selected African Countries Privatization Summary, 1988–1995

vatizers are those where less than 10% of the total value of public assets has been sold. Those countries include: Burkina Faso, Côte d'Ivoire, Gambia, Ghana, Kenya, Madagascar, Mozambique, Niger, Nigeria, Senegal, Tanzania, Togo, Uganda, and Zambia. The rest of the countries within Africa can be considered minimal privatizers.

Early privatizers are those countries that began their programs in the late 1970s through the mid-1980s. They include the countries of Benin, Guinea, Niger, Senegal, and Togo. The not-so-early privatizers are those that began their programs in the late 1980s. They include Côte d'Ivoire, Ghana, Kenya, Mozambique, Nigeria, and Uganda. The late starters, which did not begin privatization programs until the 1990s, include Burkina Faso, Cameroon, Ethiopia, Sierra Leone, South Africa, Tanzania, Zambia, and Zimbabwe.

An important by-product of the privatization programs has been the focus on developing capital markets. Recognizing that a successful privatization program depends in large part on the extent of domestic savings and the investment behavior of the private sector, since the late 1980s African nations have been establishing capital markets to help facilitate the flow of domestic savings toward the purchase of public enterprises.

The stock exchanges have also been developed to help ensure that there are sufficient savings in aggregate to absorb state assets and to help the private sector readily switch its investment from liquid low-risk money market instruments into less liquid, more profitable, publicly funded securities. Along with influencing the availability of capital and the investment processes, the structure and function of African capital markets has also influenced the ways in which business managers who approach investors project the current performance and future potential of their enterprises.

The stock exchanges of Dar es Salaam in Tanzania and Lusaka in Zambia are two examples of the direct effect of privatization on capital markets. The Dar es Salaam Stock Exchange Ltd. (DSE) was incorporated in September 1996, and its management is vested in a council whose role is to provide an organic link between the Capital Markets and Securities Act (CMSA) and the DSE.

The CMSA was established in 1994, with the task of promoting and developing capital market institutions and raising the awareness of market players to opportunities in the domestic market. Likewise in Zambia, the Lusaka Stock Exchange (LUSE) was launched in February 1994, but it only became active in 1996 when market turnover jumped to $2.6 billion from the $300,000 averaged in 1994 to 1995. Foreign participation increased considerably in 1996 when some 48 foreign investors acquired more than 40% of the Zambian sugar share issue, buying shares worth $1.4 million. In secondary market trading, foreigners accounted for 90% of business during 1996, with trades valued at around $2.4 million.

In terms of the methods of privatization chosen by African countries, there have been five principal methods of public asset sales: open tenders, deferred public offerings, preemptive sales, public flotations, and auctions of assets. Different nations have chosen different strategies. In Zambia there have been a comparatively large number of management and employee buyouts, up to 17 by 1995. In Ghana, Nigeria, and Zambia, deferred public offerings (where after a stipulated period the sole purchaser is expected to sell a certain percentage of shares to the general public) have been preferred. The public auctioning of shares prevails in Uganda, and the preemptive sales practice is most common in Kenya. Figure 8.7 lists the number of sales by type between 1988 and 1995.

In assessing the key sectors in which privatizations took place in Sub-Saharan Africa between 1988 and 1995, it was noted that overall the manufacturing sector (value-added production of agricultural, mineral, and petroleum products primarily) was the key sector of interest to investors (see Figure 8.8).

Tender	844
Liquidation	458
Competitive Asset Sale	421
Direct Sale of Shares	291
Lease Concession	187

FIGURE 8.7 Sales of Shares by Type 1988–1995

In the past five years a number of successful efforts have been undertaken across the continent to improve infrastructure-related services by placing the management reins in private hands through leases, concessions, and other methods short of the full sale of assets. From a sectoral standpoint, these initiatives have impacted the water, seaport/airport, railway, telecommunications, and electricity sectors.

Privatization of the Water Sector

Control of water distribution and treatment has long been perceived as exclusively within the public realm. Before the late 1990s, in most African countries the state operated a monopoly over the water system and justified the exclusion of the private sector from the sector as a means of protecting the public consumer. However, given the relatively poor state of the water systems in the majority of Africa's countries, more recently several countries have recognized the need for more effective water management and have begun to address such critical issues as cost recovery, water misuse, and waterborne disease prevention.

Increasingly lease-and-operate contracts are being entered into with private companies, which has helped to commercialize operations and to produce more efficient distribution and management of the countries' water resources. An example where this model has been very successful is in Mali, where in 1995 the government-controlled power and water company, EDM,

Sector	Sales		Liquidations		Other		Total	
	No.	%	No.	%	No.	%	No.	%
Agriculture	96	10.7	19	11.8	12	12.9	127	11.0
Forestry	1	0.1	0	0	1	1.1	2	0.2
Fishing	15	1.7	0	0	0	0	15	1.3
Mining	13	1.5	3	1.9	3	3.2	19	1.6
Manufacturing	466	52.1	42	26.1	30	31.9	538	46.5
Utilities	7	0.8	1	0.6	6	6.3	14	1.2
Construction	16	1.8	3	1.9	1	1.1	20	1.7
Trade	47	5.3	17	10.6	2	2.1	66	5.7
Hotels and Tourism	57	6.4	3	1.9	17	18.0	77	6.7
Transport and Storage	35	3.9	17	10.6	13	13.8	65	5.6
Real Estate	6	0.7	3	1.9	1	1.1	10	0.9
Other Services	17	1.9	3	1.9	1	1.1	20	1.7
Financial	47	5.3	7	4.3	0	0	54	4.7
Not Specified	72	8.0	43	26.7	8	8.5	121	10.7
TOTAL	895	100.2	161	100.2	94	99.9	1150	99.5

FIGURE 8.8 Preferred Types of Privatized Asset Disposition

brought in outside management. Within three years the new team was able to improve net production by 24%, billings by 37%, and new customers by 60%, while only increasing the cost to consumers by 5%.

Privatization of Airports and Ports

Given the landlocked nature of many of the countries of Africa, improving the capacity and efficiency of the continent's airports and seaports has become a major priority among export-competitiveness-minded African governments. Notwithstanding the relatively new emergence of private participation in port management even in more industrialized countries, a growing number of African nations have begun to restructure their airports and seaports through the unbundling of services, rehabilitation and modernization of equipment, and hiring of private managers through management contracts, concessions, and various forms of leases. Although there have been aggressive efforts of privatization (e.g., seaports in Cameroon and airports in Côte d'Ivoire and Togo), in most countries a gradual process has emerged which commences with the implementation of management contracts and progresses to higher levels of control through build-operate-transfer (BOT) contracts.

In addition to initiatives launched in relation to airport management, more and more countries are considering bringing in private management to help run the national airlines. Kenya Airways in 1996 was the first African carrier to be privatized; and in 1999, when South Africa Airways sold a stake in its carrier to a European consortium, the transaction became one of the continent's most prominent privatizations. Other carriers that are at least partially privatized include Royal Air Maroc (the Moroccan national airline) and Air Tunisia of Tunisia. Private carriers also exist in South Africa, Zambia, and Zimbabwe, but Nigeria is where private ownership in this sector has flourished the most: Today 22 private carriers are licensed, of which 14 provide scheduled passenger service and 8 offer charter flights. Today, national carrier Nigeria Airways and the West African regional carrier Air Afrique are being prepared for privatization.

Privatization of Railway Systems

Like transport by sea and via water, rail transport has been identified as an important sector in terms of trade and in-country commerce stimulation. Given the variation in road quality in many of Africa's landlocked countries, rail transport is the principal means of receiving imports and transporting exports. The principal private-sector-related interventions that have been implemented have involved the contracting out of management and operations systems among the national railways. Within the last few years, further unbundling and restructuring has begun with railways divesting themselves of noncore services and granting concessions where it is deemed that private operators can perform more efficiently than the state.

In Mali, Kenya, and Senegal, the rail systems have been partially privatized through the implementation of management contracts and leases. In 1998 a concession agreement in Cameroon was signed by a French–South African joint venture to invest $80 million in the railway system with the proviso that afterward competitive cost recovery rates will be able to be charged. Other countries that have engaged in contracts that involve private companies for the first time include Côte d'Ivoire and Burkina Faso, which have allowed a private company to manage the key route between Abidjan and Ouagadougou and Tanzania, which has divested itself of noncore operations and hired private sector management. Tunisia is an additional country which has undertaken a modernization project en route to identifying private management.

Privatization in the Telecommunications Sector

The telecommunications sector has historically been and continues to be one of the most lucrative infrastructure sectors in Africa. This has also been one of the most heavily regulated and protected of all of the sectors still controlled primarily by the governments. For the most part, privatization in this sector has taken place at a very gradual pace. Commercialization through the unbundling of post, telecommunications, and broadcast functions is most often a step which precedes a sale of interest in the telecommunications industry. Management contracts are often the next step en route to more active private participation. This has typically come through one of two routes—the opening of the sector to private participation (Ghana and Uganda), or the acquisition of a strategic investor with management capacity to take over network management responsibilities (South Africa).

Private participation in cellular telephony has in recent years become a third critical way of stimulating private involvement in this sector. It is critical to note, however, that in most instances the aim of African governments in granting cellular licenses is to expand telephone coverage, and not necessarily to promote competition. As the cellular lines have often had to run on the state's existing network, this has undermined the efficiency and effectiveness of a number of emergent cellular systems. However, this too is changing with the growing penetration of satellite telephony.

Private participation in the construction and installation of new facilities has also contributed to the improvement and expansion of services in this sector. The greatest challenge in the telecommunications sector for African nations will be catching up with demand, as the International Telecommunications Union has predicted that between 3 and 6 million mainlines will be needed to meet pent-up demand just through the year 2000. This is, and for the near term will continue to be, one of the continent's fastest-growing infra-structure sectors.

Privatization of the Power Sector

Supporting power generation in Africa has been one of the principal areas of activity of multilateral institutions such as the World Bank and the African Development Bank. The introduction of management contracts, leases, demonopolization, and build-own-operate contracts have all been key cata-lysts for the privatization/commercialization of this sector.

The governments of Sierra Leone, Rwanda, Mali, Guinea, Ghana, and the Gambia have all entered into power generation management contracts with private companies. Thus far, given the significant capital requirements for operations in this industry, the only segment that has been opened up beyond the management segment has been the generation segment.

2000–2001 OPPORTUNITIES

In assessing investment opportunities over the next 10 years in Africa, it will be important to recognize the importance of privatization on the conti-nent as a catalyst for the development of the capital markets in the region. Key privatization-linked sectors that have yielded and will continue to yield significant returns will include those related to manufacturing, commodity exports from the region, and telecommunications.

Along with African brokerage firms and investment promotion agencies, interested investors will find the World Bank to be a useful source of information about the status of selected privatization programs. The bank's Internet-based privatization information service for international investors, www.privatizationlink.com, provides online access to business profiles of state-owned companies and assets currently for sale, along with details of rel-evant laws, regulations, and procedures governing those transactions. With a growing number of African countries getting credit ratings from globally rec-ognized agencies such as Standard & Poor's and Moody's, it is also likely that opportunities to invest in African bonds will increase.

Overall, the next 10 years should witness a significant proliferation in the number and variety of investment vehicles for local and foreign investors interested in Africa.

9
"Buyer Beware"—
The Risks of Investing
in Africa

Having insight about investment opportunities without an appreciation of the possible risks associated with such investment always leads to an incomplete analysis. No discussion about emerging market investment opportunities in Africa would be complete without addressing possible associated risks. Given the media propensity to often focus on "problems in Africa" (war, political instability, poverty, debt, etc.), we would be remiss if we did not address some of the challenges associated with investment on the African continent.

The following information is put forth with the intent that by providing the reader with a balanced perspective when considering investment opportunities in Africa, he or she will be able to take steps which mitigate, if not eliminate, risks associated with doing business on the continent. If the risks within each deal or investment initiative can be anticipated and quantified, we believe that the possible return threshholds will continue to make the region an attractive investment destination where the benefits far outweigh the risks.

POLITICAL RISK

Notwithstanding the fact that the African continent is home to 53 countries, which on the face of things means that there could be 53 target investment destinations, many of Africa's markets are far too small or too poor to present significant attractive opportunities. Africa has more than a dozen countries with populations of less than 2 million people (e.g., Togo, Benin, Comoro

Islands, Guinea-Bissau, Eritrea, Cape Verde, Equatorial Guinea, Lesotho, Botswana, Burundi, Rwanda, São Tomé & Principe, and Seychelles). The economic development of at least 10 others is hampered by desert conditions, by being landlocked, or by being isolated because the country is an island, or in a poor location otherwise (e.g., the Central African Republic, Djibouti, Malawi, Chad, Niger, Mauritania, Sudan, Burkina Faso, Rwanda, Burundi, Madagascar, and Somalia).

According to the World Bank and the United Nations, more than 25 of Africa's nations are among the poorest and least-developed countries in the world. These are often the same ones that make global news because of political instability. It must be understood that such instability is often the result of the populace or military tiring of poverty and thinking that a change in government can somehow improve the poor economic hand the country was dealt when Europe carved up the continent at the onset of colonization in the 1800s. In most instances, the successor government has not had any greater success than the previous ones, because there is not much to work with in terms of creating an economically self-sufficient nation state. From the standpoints of human resources, mineral and natural resources, or strategic location (e.g., not having a port), these countries have found it hard to compete in the global business environment.

In these countries the political risk is heightened considerably, making the quantification and mitigation of risk, or the perception thereof, very difficult. This can have a tremendous impact on the valuation and/or the performance of an investment. The extent of this impact can range from the devaluation associated with investments that are located in areas of perceived political instability (i.e., Angola, Liberia, Democratic Republic of Congo, Sudan), to the complete loss of an investment due to destruction, appropriation, or theft. Although there are a myriad of political risk indicators and measurement tools, the ability to effectively assess political risk is as much an art as it is a science. Consequently, investors seeking to assess African political risk should be cognizant of the emerging market investor's golden rule that:

"There is a direct correlation between economic viability and political stability!"

Based on this rule, investors seeking to minimize exposure to political instability and the attendant risks should concentrate on those countries that are more economically viable. Thus, investors interested in Africa would favor, for instance, South Africa, Botswana, Ghana, and Morocco over Rwanda, Somalia, Algeria, or Niger.

The caveat to this admonition is that political risk can also be present in African countries where there is potential economic viability, but where the country is in conflict, being poorly run, or otherwise is economically retarded or operating at less than optimal capacity because of poor governance. This is the case with a number of potentially dynamic African economies such as Angola, the Democratic Republic of Congo, Cameroon, Ethiopia, Kenya, and Zimbabwe. Prudent investors would have these countries on a watch list for signs of governmental changes (which does not always entail a change in the head of state)—which may in turn lead to changes in political leadership or economic policies—and thus in investment prospects. In these cases, an assessment of the underlying wealth/assets of the country can help such shrewd investors figure out where the next great investment opportunities in Africa will lie, and thereby get a step up on others also looking at those markets.

The difference that a governmental change can make is clearly apparent when one considers Nigeria. For over 20 years, until early in 1999, Nigeria's economy, one of the wealthiest on the continent because of the country's large population and significant oil reserves, had been run into the ground by successive military juntas. By the time Nigeria's last military leader, Sani Abacha, died unexpectedly of a heart attack in 1998, that nation's infrastructure had become decrepit, fraud and corruption were rampant, and the country was ostracized from the world economy. The United States and other nations that were dependent on Nigerian crude oil (Nigeria is one of the top exports of petroleum to the United States) were constantly in a quandary about political engagement with that country because of the tyranny of its military leadership.

Fast-forward to early 2000—and Nigeria, notwithstanding many challenges that still persist, is becoming attractive to the global investment community with interest in Africa. Under the helm of democratically elected President Olusegun Obasanjo, the country is reaping a significant democracy dividend for ending military rule. And at the forefront of the effort to help Nigeria transition back into the global economic community is the U.S. government. Those who recognized that even during the past regimes patient money in the form of direct foreign investment had continued to flow into Nigeria are now finding themselves strategically positioned to benefit from the opportunities existent in the continent's most populous nation.

Political Risk Mitigation Strategy

The best way to avoid making investments in politically unstable countries is to improve one's capacity to analyze the economic prospects of a selected country (i.e., its economic viability) and to gather information about its political environment. Fortunately, today there a number of printed and electronic sources of information about the economic and political status of Africa's countries. Some of the more well-known information sources include the

Economist Intelligence Unit's quarterly and annual reports on the African nations, *Africa Confidential* (a fortnightly political journal), and the Africanews.org Web site, which provides African news as presented by 34 African journals and newspapers.

U.S. government reports from the State Department and Department of Commerce also provide valuable insight and analysis for review when considering the political status of African countries and identifying/analyzing potential macroeconomic risks for new investors to the market.

To protect investors against politically related risks such as expropriation, inconvertability of the local currency, and the loss of assets due to armed conflict, the World Bank created the Multilateral Investment Guarantee Agency (MIGA), through which insurance policies covering these and related issues can be purchased by investors. The U.S. Overseas Private Investment Corporation provides similar insurance.

COUNTRY RISK—ASSESSING LEGAL AND REGULATORY, MARKET INFRASTRUCTURE, CURRENCY, AND CORRUPTION-RELATED RISK

Legal and Regulatory Risk

In a 1998 presentation entitled "Credit Ratings Foster African Development," prepared for guests of the Washington, D.C., based Center for Strategic and International Studies, former U.S. Secretary of the Treasury Robert Rubin put forth a number of important ingredients to Africa's being able to develop the momentum to successfully stimulate sustainable economic growth. Among the issues that Rubin mentioned were a sound domestic banking system, and a predictable and fair legal system.

When considering investment in Africa, the lack of any one of these ingredients can represent a significant risk. Within the banking sector, the existence of privately owned, competitive banks, operating within a regulatory framework established by supervisory and regulatory bodies that have set standards that approach international standards is very important. Additional important components to look for within this regulatory framework would be updated property, securities, and banking laws.

In Africa today, most countries are in the process of implementing legal and regulatory reforms. Institutions such as the World Bank's Finance and Investment Advisory Service (FIAS) have provided legal and regulatory experts to help Africa's nations promulgate comprehensive, clear, and transparent commercial laws. FIAS and other donor-supported legal reform programs have also sought to update Africa's laws (many of which have remained on the books since the independence years of the 1960s), to expand them to include environmental protections and arbitration clauses, and to account for the many intellectual property-right-related issues that impact business in the Information Age. The end goal of these initiatives has consistently been to help African nations develop investor-friendly legal environments.

One relative advantage that all African nations have (in terms of the ease with which foreign and institutional investors can grasp relevant business-related legal and regulatory concepts) is the fact that the legal and regulatory framework of the continent is predominately based on British common law. And where a given country's legal system is not based on British laws, it is generally patterned after the French Napoleonic Code, or in a few cases, after Portuguese law. An easy way to determine which country is governed by which system is through an assessment of the official language spoken in the country, which almost invariably is one of these three Western European languages. South Africa, which boasts the continent's most sophisticated legal and regulatory system, developed its judicial framework from Dutch-Roman law.

In West and Central Africa, one particularly important initiative in the area of strengthening the legal and regulatory environment has been the development of OHADA or, in English, the Harmonized Code of Business Laws of Africa. Promulgated by the French-speaking countries in these regions, OHADA was created to support regionalization in West and Central Africa by standardizing and harmonizing the business-related legal and regulatory environment in these two regions. The administrative office and supreme court of OHADA is headquartered in Abidjan, Côte d'Ivoire. The OHADA initiative received its initial assistance from France and the World Bank, and more recently has been supported by institutions such as the American Bar Association.

Legal and Regulatory Risk Mitigation Strategy

Investors interested in Africa are encouraged to become familiar with the legal and regulatory environment of the African countries in which they are considering investment through the engagement of local legal counsel. While fund, stock exchange, and government securities investors can be somewhat insulated (by their fund manager and/or stock broker) from needing to have specific knowledge of legal and regulatory risk (other than knowing that it might exist), direct and individual private equity/venture capital (PE/VC) investors are well advised to have a working knowledge of the legal and regulatory risks of particular countries of interest. Fortunately, with the growth of the Internet as an information dissemination tool it is getting much easier to find African laws and regulations via the MIGA-sponsored Web site www.ipanet.net, through contact with each country's Investment Promotion Agency (a complete list of which is found in the Appendix), and through contact with the legal department of multilateral institutions such as the World

Bank (www.worldbank.org), the International Monetary Fund (www.imf.org), and the African Development Bank (www.afdb.org).

For direct investors, private equity investors, and venture capital investors, it is recommended that local legal counsel be retained. The American (or British, Japanese, etc.) Embassy in a respective host country, and/or the respective African country's embassy in America (or England, Japan, etc.) are good starting points for such references. The legal departments of large multinational banks in target investment countries are also generally knowledgeable about and willing to suggest capable local counsel.

Market Infrastructure Risk

One set of underappreciated risks that can often impede and erode investor confidence among portfolio investors interested in Africa stock exchanges are infrastructural inadequacies in the country's ability to provide (1) global custodial services, (2) automated trading procedures to clear and settle transactions, and (3) reliable voice and data communications systems. Lost share certificates, lengthy settlement procedures, illiquidity, and poor communications systems are definite deterrents to a country's ability to attract domestic and/or foreign investment.

South Africa's Johannesburg Stock Exchange launched an automated trading system in 1996 and in 1999 introduced STRATE, an automated clearing and settlement system intended to increase efficiency in that market. In late 1998, the BRVM, a regional stock exchange whose members are West African French-speaking countries, also launched a comparatively sophisticated trading and clearing and settlement system. Kenya, Mauritius, Namibia, and Botswana are other exchanges on the path toward improving their securities-exchange–related infrastructure. In Africa's other exchanges, the level of sophistication and automation of the trading, clearing, and settling systems varies. However, almost all of the continent's stock exchange management offices recognize that over the next 10 years their ability to effectively attract investment, particularly foreign investment, will to some degree be dependent on having globally competitive market infrastructure.

Market Infrastructure Risk Mitigation Strategy

Novice foreign securities investors must extend their analysis beyond the particular company or security they are interested in and seek information about the overall securities trading environment in that country. Large foreign brokers active in African markets, such as Merrill Lynch, Fleming Martin, and Standard Bank, produce useful quarterly and industry-related reports on Africa's stock exchanges and provide periodic updates on issues related to market infrastructure and other exchange improvement-related developments as they occur.

Currency Risk

Of all the risk types associated with emerging market investment generally, and Africa-related investment specifically, currency risk presents the least amount of specific predictability. The reasons for this are the multitude of variables—such as political stability or lack thereof, inflation, labor unrest, commodity prices, and global and local market perceptions—that can affect currency valuation. As it is difficult to predict when and how these factors can be influenced by external regional and global factors, forecasting how, when, and to what extent they will affect a country's world currency valuation can be quite difficult.

Currency Risk Mitigation Strategy

Emerging market investors utilize the following tools to effectively manage currency risk:

- *Return Horizon/Expectations.* While the specific extent of currency risk cannot be determined, the individual variables that contribute to currency risk are quantifiable, a fact that will allow for the identification and monitoring of currency trends. It is important that investors in Africa be sure that the return expectations of a particular investment correlate with their perception of the investment's currency risk. Additionally, investors in Africa should be prepared to hold on to an investment for a minimum of three to five years, a decision that would force the investor to take a stance on the three- to five-year prospects of the investment's economic environment. The logic of this process is that if the investor believes that the three- to five-year return potential of a particular investment (taking into account the country's economic environment) is positive, then the strength of the investment's returns should mitigate whatever negative effects that may be caused by currency devaluation.

- *Diversification/Hedging.* With the exception of certain special situations (which generally relate to locking in long-term gains or exploiting specific short-term time windows), the prevailing wisdom is that the best investment hedge for long-term investors is a well-diversified portfolio. As a rule, the cyclicality of capital markets is dictated by their interrelation and the law of averages. Thus, by simple definition, when the value of one currency is up the value of some other currency is down—and the more diverse one's portfolio is the less the chance of currency depreciation in one market negatively impacting the total portfolio value. Hence the justification for establishing a portfolio with currency diversity.

- *Forward Cover.* For those investors who want to limit specific currency exposure, currency risk hedges or *forward cover* is available. Like an insurance policy, this hedging strategy allows an investor to pay a premium to a third party in exchange for a contractual commitment that allows the investor to acquire the hedged currency for an agreed-upon price, or exchange rate, irrespective of the value of that currency in the open market at that time. While this concept is quite logical in theory, in practice the premiums associated with buying forward cover in most African markets have proven to be prohibitively expensive.

Corruption-Related Risk

In 1993, Transparency International, an NGO set up to combat corruption, was created. The international NGO sponsors anticorruption conferences every two years to promote good governance and to encourage world governments to take harder stances against those who request *and* give bribes. Since 1996, corruption, which had historically been played down as a major impediment to increased investment in emerging markets, has been targeted for corrective intervention by institutions such as the Organization for Economic Cooperation & Development (OECD) and the World Bank. An illustrative example of the negative impacts of corruption was presented by the Asian Development Bank:

Why Corruption Matters

Direct costs are high . . .

- Over the past 20 years, one east Asian country is reckoned to have lost $48 billion through corruption, surpassing its debt of $40.6 billion.
- In another Asian country, a government found that over the past decade State assets have fallen by more than $50 billion, because they have been undervalued by corrupt officials.
- In yet another Asian country, recent government reports show that $50 million daily is misappropriated.
- Several Asian countries have paid from 20 to 100% more on goods than their market value.

And they are not restricted only to emerging markets . . .

- In one North American city, businesses cut $330 million from an annual waste disposal bill of $1.5 billion by ending domination of regulatory bodies by organized crime.
- In one European city, anticorruption initiatives have reduced the cost of infrastructure by 35 to 40%.

Wherever existent, the indirect costs are high . . .

- Lower investment productivity.
- Quality is compromised and public safety endangered.
- Civil service morale is eroded.
- Poverty reduction is thwarted.
- Foreign and domestic investment is redirected.
- Stability is threatened.

In African nations, the "dash," or small gift/grease payment, has been around since before the colonial period. At the first Transparency International forum held in Africa, convened in Durban, South Africa, in October 1999, Wangari Maathai, a Kenyan human rights activist, allocated some of the blame for the introduction of the dash to the arrival of colonial powers and missionaries. "They gave gifts, mild forms of bribes and kickbacks to persuade the natives to bend their code of conduct." Recognizing that the people who accepted the bribes were also at fault, she pointed out that these people "agreed partly because they were greedy and selfish, but also because they knew they would face no risks because they had the protection of the newcomers." Yet, unfortunately, she continues, the problem did not end with the end of colonialism, because by this time the targets of corruption were quite successful and had achieved the status of model citizens in the community. "At independence, with perhaps a few exceptions like Jomo Kenyatta, it was collaborators who inherited economic and political power. Many freedom fighters still live in poverty and obscurity; the message to the next generation is clear [going along helps one to get along]."

During the 1970s and 1980s, when African government-led economic strategies were at their height and huge donor-funded projects were being developed almost everywhere, grease payment graft reached its highest point. During the 1990s, efforts to end these practices were slowly and then more emphatically introduced. Most recently, attention has also turned toward cracking down on those giving the bribes (most often businesses/investors from developed countries) as well as those who have been taking them. The United States, with the Foreign Corrupt Practices Act, which makes it illegal to give bribes as well as to receive them, has long been a proponent of stiffer global anticorruption laws. The United States has long argued that other competitors from Europe and Asia have been able to unfairly gain market share in Africa because of having fewer legal prohibitions and negative ramifications about paying to play, and otherwise indirectly working to influence government business decisions through promises of individual gain made to key decision makers.

Today, corruption within the global business community generally, and in Africa particularly, is enemy number one. That does not mean that corruption has now ceased to exist on the continent. However, it does mean that efforts to promote transparency are being implemented at an unprecedented rate; that the legal penalties for bribery are being stiffened; and that general sanctions, particularly within multilateral agencies, for those that are implicated in a corruption scandal, are becoming more severe.

Corruption Risk Mitigation Strategy

The popular antidrug slogan "Just Say No," is one response to the query regarding what one should do when facing a bribe/corruption-related proposition. Ideally, however, the aim is to again analyze the broader business environment before getting close to making an investment decision, and thereby determine if the country/region is one in which corruption is a significant factor in the business/deal process. Sometimes one will have to walk away from opportunities.

In the long run, most corruption-garnered gains are short-lived, and the risks of getting caught far outweigh any perceived financial benefits. "When in Rome," one should *not* always "do as the Romans do," because most often one will not fully understand the rules, and thus will be far more likely to be out of his/her money, without the deal desired, and with no one to complain to.

Risk mitigation in this area should begin with a probing evaluation of the overall market. In terms of helpful resources for evaluating environments, there is an annual country ranking prepared by Transparency International (*http://www.TI.org*) that can be referenced. Another useful reference, entitled the *Index of Economic Freedom,* is published annually by the Washington, D.C.–based Heritage Foundation. Along with ranking over 100 countries on the overall level of openness and transparency in each market, this reference also grades countries based upon the level of illegal activity in the market. The *Index* also grades countries based upon such criteria as the existing trade policy, taxation levels, degree of government consumption of economic output, monetary policy, capital flows and foreign investment, banking environment, existence of wage and price controls, the existence and protection of property rights, and the regulatory environment.

Along with trying to determine which countries to avoid, it is important to recognize that countries where great opportunities lie may also be ones in which various levels of bribes, dashes, or kickbacks may be requested. Using bank references, U.S. Embassy references, local counsel, and other on-the-ground intelligence to get a sense of the type of business person/organization that one is dealing with is a very good way to undertake a reference check on a potential investment partner/project.

Increasingly, institutions such as Dun & Bradstreet are able to provide credit ratings on larger African companies, and these references can serve as a barometer of the type of institution with which one is considering investing. South Africa and Egypt are the only countries in Africa that hold sovereign credit ratings, but today more African nations are recognizing that such ratings help improve the sense of security which investors desire when making investments in emerging markets generally, and less well-known African markets specifically.

The African Association of Stock Markets has within the past year made the issue of sovereign ratings a key agenda item for the organization. Furthermore, Standard and Poor's announced in 1998 that it would begin an outreach and awareness campaign for African nations, designed to show that sovereign ratings do not require a prior borrowing history and can be used as an important assessment and investment attraction tool. These ratings score countries on the likelihood that they will repay loans and bonds strictly according to the agreed terms and are based on an array of political and economic factors that might affect a country's financial health. Thus, along with on-the-ground intelligence via U.S. and other foreign government agencies, local legal counsel, accounting firms and banks, Dun & Bradstreet and Standard and Poor's may also provide insightful information useful in avoiding direct and indirect corrupt practices.

SCAMS

Scams have been around since the beginning of time, and while their sophistication level varies greatly, the one thing that successful scams seem to have in common is their ability to disguise the perception of risk. One of the first lessons all successful investors learn is that if something sounds too good to be true, it probably is. Yet despite the reality of this statement, far too many investors are tempted by or succumb to investment scams.

The most common forms of these fraudulent business proposals comprise six main categories:

1. Disbursement of money from wills

2. Contract fraud (C.O.D. of goods and services)

3. Purchase of real estate

4. Conversion of hard currency

5. Transfer of funds from overinvoiced contracts

6. Sales of crude oil below market prices

The 4-1-9 Scam

The most prevalent and successful type of advance fee fraud is the 4-1-9 scam, most often associated with Nigeria and involving fund transfer fraud. The 4-1-9 scam is named after Section 419 of the Nigerian Criminal Code, which forbids fraudulent and illegal activities involving government agencies. In response to the growing prevalence of these scams, the U.S. Secret Service established Operation 4-1-9, designed to target Nigerian advance fee fraud on an international basis. In 1998, the Financial Crimes Division of the Secret Service was receiving 100 telephone calls and 300 to 500 pieces of correspondence per day from victims and potential victims.

In such schemes, a company or individual will typically receive an unsolicited letter by mail, most often from a Nigerian addressee claiming to be a civil servant. In the letter, the addressee will inform the recipient that he is seeking a reputable foreign company or individual into whose account he can deposit funds that the Nigerian government overpaid on some procurement contract.

Would-be fraud perpetrators obtain the names of potential victims from a variety of sources, including trade journals, professional directories, newspapers, and commercial libraries. Con artists do not target a single company, but rather send out scam mailings en masse. The letters refer to investigations of previous contracts awarded by prior regimes alleging that many contracts were overinvoiced by corrupt ministries. Rather than return the money to the government, they desire to transfer the money to a foreign account. The sums to be transferred are generally within the $10 to $60 million threshold, and the foreign request recipient is offered a commission of up to 30% for assisting in the transfer. An example of such a letter might read as follows:

Dear Sir,
I am sure you will be surprised to read this from me not having met me before. Actually, I made up my mind to contact you after concluding that there is no other way to reach somebody of your status for the project for which we desperately need a partner. Eventually, I got your company's name from a personal friend at the Foreign Affairs Office in Lagos.

I am the Director of Contract Approvals & Appraisals. I have been privileged to head the Contract Award Committee of the Nigeria National Petroleum Corporation for the past 5 years. Myself and a few other colleagues, including the chief accountant and the computer analyst, due for retirement soon, have carefully mapped out the sum of $28,500,000.00 (TWENTY EIGHT POINT FIVE MILLION US DOLLARS ONLY) to enable us to go into a lucrative business venture with your company, or for the importation of some of your products into the Nigerian market. This amount was accrued from over invoiced contracts and commissions received for awarding various contracts to foreign firms over this past 5 years.

Now all these contracts have been fully executed and full payment has been made to the contractors. These over invoiced/commissions of ours are presently in a floating account of the Central Bank of Nigeria. Together with some top officials of the bank, we have decided to seek a reliable partner to whom we can forward this sum. We will remit these funds into your foreign account and later share it in a ratio of 60% for us, 35% for you, while 5% is reserved to offset any expenses incurred during this transaction.

To effectively and officially get these funds transferred into your company's or your personal account, we shall need from you (2) blank copies each of your company's letter headed papers and invoice sheet duly signed and stamped below by you. Also include your full banking particulars, where this money will be wired into. With these blank documents, we shall transcribe on them the actual contract specification and put up claims and demand for official approval of these funds under your name. The invoice will be used to demonstrate the contract and supply valued at $28.5 MILLION DOLLARS.

Please get in touch with me immediately on my fax number 234-1-862599 in receipt of your fax message and the required documents. Immediate action will commence and hopefully we must get this fund into your account within a few working days. Please call/fax me immediately as we cannot afford to waste much time in this transaction. This is to comply with the present Provisional Ruling Council (P.R.C.) Government in Nigeria that has instructed and asked us to pay immediately all debts and outstanding payments to all foreign firms.

Thanking you for your co-operation, while waiting anxiously for your reply in case you require further details from me.

YOURS FAITHFULLY,

Another variation on the 4-1-9 scam involves a request for the issuance of a letter of credit.

Dear XXX,
LETTER OF URGENT REQUEST FOR $200 MILLION U.S. DOLLARS BANK GUARANTEE FOR OUR OVERSEAS LENDERS/FINANCIERS: XXXXXXXXXXXXX

With reference to our previous communication and subsequent discussion with your good bank in the States; we hereby request as a matter of urgency your establishing an irrevocable confirmed U.S. dollars bank guarantee for USD $200 MILLION U.S. DOLLARS in favor of our overseas lenders/financiers; XXXXXXXXXXXXXXX, through their designated overseas bank; to enable them to fund our capital development sustainable projects in Sub-Saharan West-Africa with special emphasis in the Republic of Benin, Equatorial Guinea and Ghana.

We have concluded arrangements with U.S. plants and equipment suppliers to supply the required technologies coupled with technical and production management agreements.

However, they can not commence delivery of the said plants and equipments to our project sites in West-Africa without their receiving payment for their said goods from us.

Therefore, we would highly appreciate your establishing the said bank guarantee in favour of our said lenders; XXXXXXXXXXXXXX; who will then pay directly to our U.S. bank; Bank of America for onward draw down and disembursement.

In view of the above, we hereby attach sample copies of their required bank guarantee as a text of what they required. It might also be of interest to your bank to know that the said funds are not meant for the Nigerian economy, as Nigeria presently is still under economic and political sanctions from the United States. As such we are concentrating all our efforts and resources in other parts of West-Africa excluding Nigeria hence our incorporation of our company in Ghana as a resident company.

Finally, Sir, we will be more than glad if you reply us through our Lagos/ Nigerian office fax/phone-. XXXXXXXXXXXXXX and/or our Nigerian address soonest.

We will stop our efforts to seek another partner, while we look forward to working with your good selves. Thanks in advance for your cooperation.

Yours Sincerely,

Initially, the intended victim is instructed to provide company letterhead and pro forma invoicing which will be used to show completion of the contract. One of the reasons is to utilize the victim's letterhead to forge letters of recommendation to other victim firms and to seek out a travel visa from the U.S. embassy in Nigeria. The victim is told that the completed contracts will be submitted for approval to the Central Bank of Nigeria. Upon approval, the funds will be remitted to an account supplied by the intended victim.

The goal of the schemer is to delude the target into thinking that he or she is being drawn into a very lucrative, albeit questionable, transaction. Victims are often convinced of the authenticity of advance fee fraud schemes by forged or false documents bearing apparently official Nigerian government letterhead and seals, as well as false letters of credit, payment schedules and bank drafts.

The fraudster may establish the credibility of his contracts, and thereby his influence, by arranging a meeting between the victim and "government officials" in real or fake government offices. The intended victim must be reassured and confident of the potential success of the deal, since he will become the primary supporter of the scheme and must willingly contribute a large amount of money when the deal is threatened. The term "when" is used because the con-within-the-con is that the scheme will be threatened in order to persuade the victim to provide a large sum of money to save the venture.

The letter, while appearing transparent and even ridiculous to most, unfortunately is growing in its effectiveness. It sets the stage and is the opening round of a two-layered scheme or scheme within a scheme. The fraudster will eventually reach someone who, while skeptical, desperately wants the deal to be genuine.

The second phase of the scheme involves the victim being invited to travel to Nigeria or a border country to complete the transaction. Individuals are often told that a visa will not be necessary to enter the country. The con artists may then bribe airport officials to pass the victims through Immigration and Customs. Because it is a serious offense in Nigeria to enter without a valid visa, the victim's illegal entry into the country may be used by the schemer to coerce him into releasing funds. Violence and threats of physical harm may also be employed to further pressure victims.

While admittedly the new democratically elected Nigerian government has taken significant steps to curb corruption in Nigeria, imposing harsh jail sentences on criminals convicted of perpetrating 4-1-9 scams, such scams still persist and more recently have been recorded coming from other African countries. Thus, our aim in presenting this background information is not be to be disparaging about business and investment opportunities in Nigeria. Quite the contrary, we hope to keep honest and respectable potential investors interested in Nigeria and other countries in Africa from falling prey to unscrupulous criminals.

Scam Risk Mitigation Strategy

Experienced Africa investors rely on three tests to avoid business/investment scams when evaluating an investment's authenticity: the Common Sense Test, the Time Test, and the Expert Opinion Test.

- *The Common Sense Test.* If one begins each deal analysis with a healthy bit of skepticism, this test becomes a fairly straightforward one. If the opportunity looks too good to be true, then it probably is. Also, if one does not have a good reason to justify "why me" when a scheme is presented, it is best to not get involved.

- *The Time Test.* This test is useful in two ways when evaluating the validity of an investment. Because most scam artists use a quick hit-and-run approach, the bogus opportunities they present are generally presented or offered as being time-sensitive. For this reason, inexperienced

Africa investors should be wary of any trade or investment opportunity that the sponsor claims is "only going to be available for a short while." Time will also give the investor the chance to thoroughly research and analyze the opportunity. While some scams may get past the common sense test, they are more apt to unravel during the time test.

- *The Expert Opinion Test.* Given the vast array of African investment/ business opportunities, investors will invariably encounter opportunities in areas that are unfamiliar to them. Ostrich farming, diamond mining, smart-card banking, cellular telephony, distance learning, and cobalt processing are examples of the diverse array of African investment opportunities that might represent areas of unfamiliarity for investors. When successful Africa investors are confronted with these situations they do not hesitate to solicit consultation from industry experts.

The methodology of using an expert opinion test can in practice often lead to a face-to-face meeting between the industry expert and the investment sponsor of questionable repute. The economic logic behind the expert opinion test is that the returns on a good investment, or the money saved by not making a bad investment, will more than make up for the costs of the expert opinion.

PORTFOLIO RISK

Not everyone interested in investing in Africa will want to do so by directly entering into deals with local businesses and governments. Many prospective investors may choose to enter the African market initially via the continent's stock markets. For these investors, managing portfolio risk (i.e., the risk that the share price of the stock they buy will not have appreciated, or will have depreciated, at the time they want to sell it in the market) will be their biggest challenge. For these investors, timing, diversification, and market segmentation will be necessary to adroitly navigate Africa's listed security environment.

Once an investor has determined which country he or she is interested in, has become comfortable with the macroeconomic environment there, and has decided to invest in the capital markets, a logical question is, "Where does Africa fit in my portfolio?"

The two most important decisions that have to be made by an investor when constructing a portfolio in the African market is the determination of risk tolerance and time horizon. For this reason, prudence dictates that an investor's portfolio exposure to Africa be appropriately allocated. Despite the tremendous upside potential of African securities, it is important that investors appreciate their risk. African capital markets (like all emerging markets) can be volatile, illiquid, and subject to currency fluctuations and business practices atypical to developed capital markets.

Figure 9.1 demonstrates the typical asset allocation classification investors might use to categorize portfolio investment-related risk.

Although it would probably be imprudent for African securities to represent one's core portfolio holdings, an argument could be made that it is equally imprudent for a well-diversified portfolio not to have any exposure to Africa.

Portfolio Risk Mitigation Strategy

Investors wanting to quantify the risks associated with various African investment opportunities are encouraged to utilize *performance benchmarks*. For instance, some investors in Africa divide the continent into separate risk categories, assigning specific return expectations to respective categories. For example, using a risk scale of 1 to 3 (1 representing the lowest risk and 3 representing the highest risk) an investor can establish return expectations for Africa's various countries. If the Lipper Emerging Market Index (a recognized emerging market index) was the performance threshold for an African country with a risk level of 1, then countries with risk levels of 2 and 3 would have to demonstrate a return potential of 1 plus a proportionately higher risk premium. If the risk premium were, say, 5 basis points per risk level, then a Botswana (arguably Africa's most politically stable country)-based investment with a 25% return expectation would be more attractive on a risk-adjusted basis than a Nigeria-based investment with a 25% return expectation.

The Case for Funds   Given the potential complexity of investment in Africa's listed securities, potential investors are advised to establish a relative comfort level before diving in too deep. For this reason investment funds (closed-end and open-ended) versus individual stock purchase transactions are the recommended investment vehicle of choice for most foreign investors in Africa. In addition to the portfolio benefits of security diversification, the fund approach offers the advantage of professional management expertise. The fund approach can also be a useful tool for new investors ultimately interested in pursuing individual transactions, as fund participation will provide (in the form of quarterly performance reports) a useful quarterly flow of relevant African investment information. This information will thus provide a solid foundation for the establishment of the investor's research library for use in analyzing individual stock picks.

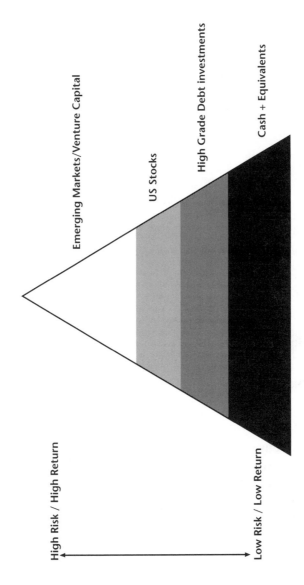

FIGURE 9.1 Asset Risk Allocation Pyramid

PRIVATE EQUITY/VENTURE CAPITAL (PE/VC) RISK

Although Africa's publicly traded securities markets are the primary focus of this book, it should be noted that PE/VC investment opportunities represent the continent's highest return potential. Notwithstanding this fact, however, African PE/VC investment opportunities (like PE/VC investment opportunities everywhere) also have the highest risk of failure/100% loss of investment principal. While this risk is generally manageable, it must be fully appreciated by potential investors.

Thus, the three greatest risks associated with African PE/VC investment are as follows:

- *Limited disclosure.* While publicly traded capital markets all over the world have minimum managerial and financial disclosure requirements, companies that are not traded publicly do not have to pass the same level of disclosure scrutiny. Consequently, PE/VC investment decisions require a greater amount of preinvestment due-diligence and postinvestment monitoring.

- *Illiquidity.* Unlike publicly traded securities, which theoretically offer an immediate market valuation and a pool of interested buyers, valuation and liquidity options for PE/VC investments are inherently less tangible, as there is no formalized market through which buyers and sellers can convene. Subsequently (while most PE/VC investors seek 3- to 5-year holding periods and most PE/VC funds have 10-year life cycles), PE/VC holding periods *can* be indefinite.

- *Management.* The aforementioned reasons, coupled with the generally less developed nature of privately held companies, dictate that investors be active in the management of these companies. Whereas the investment performance of publicly traded securities during times of crisis can be protected by shareholder loyalty, market perception, and management depth, the investment performance of privately held securities is more susceptible to negative events. Historically, the most successful PE/VC investments have been made by direct investors or fund managers—a fact that is directly attributable to the active management role associated with these two types of investors. Despite the inherent risks, African PE/VC investments have mirrored the global PE/VC trend of increasing investor appetite. The primary reason for this is the potential for superior investment returns. Many African PE/VC investments have delivered $U.S. dollar-denominated annual growth rates of over 40%, and a healthy number of these investments have generated annual growth rates of over 100%. Diversification is also a contributing factor in the decision to make an African PE/VC investment. If Africa is considered the last untapped emerging market, then African PE/VC represents the last untapped investment category in the last emerging market.

An analysis of South Africa's PE/VC market provides a vivid illustration of this point. As of the fourth quarter of 1998, the aggregate value of companies listed on the Johannesburg Stock Exchange (which represent delisting and/or LBO candidates for PE/VC investors), the country's 500 largest privately owned businesses, South Africa's foreign-owned corporations, and government-owned business available for privatization exceeded $650 billion.

As of this same period, the aggregate value of all of the South African–based PE/VC funds was less than $4 billion—which translated into a potential transaction-to-investable dollar ratio of over 40 to 1. Compared to other countries with similar publicly traded capital market capacity, South Africa arguably offers the world's most attractive potential transaction-to-investable dollar ratio. The most conservative estimates suggested that South Africa could have easily accommodated 10 times as much PE/VC as was available in the fourth quarter of 1998. Whereas many U.S.-based PE/VC funds are happy to conclude 1 to 4 transactions a year, most South Africa–based PE/VC funds can conclude 4 to 10 transactions per year.

Although no other African country can compare to the sheer PE/VC capacity of South Africa, all of the other countries in Africa offer attractive potential transaction-to-investable dollar ratios, a fact that illustrates the vast potential for PE/VC investors on the continent.

PE/VC Risk Mitigation Strategy

As has been previously discussed, emerging markets have more political risk than their developed market counterparts. This is reflective of the environment in Africa as well. Consequently, similar to those investors creating listed security portfolios, many PE/VC investors utilize the technique known as *benchmarking* to establish return expectations commensurate with the risks associated with a particular investment. Many African PE/VC investors also utilize the Lipper Emerging Market Index as a performance benchmark for their emerging market investments. The index (though not a direct replica of any specific emerging market) offers investors a relative base reference case for emerging market performance comparisons.

Direct private equity and venture capital investors also utilize various emerging market indexes as performance thresholds. For instance, if the Johannesburg Stock Exchange (JSE) All Share Index projected a five-year annualized investment return of 20%, then utilizing the JSE as a comparison performance benchmark, PE/VC investors would establish a performance threshold expectation. As an example, it would not be unreasonable for these investors to determine that their direct, private equity or venture capital returns should exceed the JSE's performance by 10 to 20%, given the higher risk of such investments.

In addition to the risk mitigation options just mentioned, African PE/VC investors also have the option of purchasing political risk insurance. Although such protection was once a rarity, the availability of political risk insurance has expanded to accommodate increasing investor interest in emerging markets. And while most large insurance carriers have the capability of providing political risk insurance, three groups in particular—the Overseas Private Investment Corporation (OPIC), the American International Group (AIG), and the World Bank's Multilateral Insurance Guarantee Agency—have committed significant resources to becoming the leaders of this growing niche market. Such insurance, among other things, protects emerging market investors from the risk of:

- Inconvertibility of local currency
- Asset appropriation by government
- Loss from civil strife and/or war

Investment in Africa offers significant rewards, but it is important to acknowledge the attendant risks. For both portfolio investors and those interested in private equity (PE, VC, and foreign direct investors considering joint ventures, acquisitions, or mergers), to be forewarned and prepared is to be well-equipped to assess investment opportunities on the continent. From our vantage point, although there may be risks that we have not addressed, the areas covered in this chapter do represent the more frequent risks that serious prospective investors should account for, aim to quantify, and work to mitigate.

10
Are You Ready?
Get Set, Go!!!!

Relatively speaking, the easiest part of investing in Africa is gathering information for the assignment. The part which is much harder is making the definitive decision to invest and then deciding upon what steps to take to actually put one's money to work on the continent.

In the universe we operate in there are three principal types of investors: corporate investors, institutional investors, and individual investors.

Corporate investors are generally export-oriented companies (service providers as well as manufacturers) seeking to establish a presence in a new market that has been identified as one in which the company's products/services are in high demand and are price/quality competitive. This type of investor would principally be interested in establishing a joint venture or subsidiary, or in making an acquisition. This is typically known as making a *foreign direct investment.* In Africa, the principal participants in this type of investing are relatively large multinationals such as automobile manufacturer Ford, breakfast cereal producer Kellogg's, automobile rental agency Avis, computer manufacturer Compaq, and software services company Oracle. In Africa, corporate investors also include multinationals involved in the mining industries that extract natural resources from the continent for processing abroad. Global oil, precious metals, gold, and other mining companies are included among this category of investors.

Institutional investors generally include insurance companies, financial institutions, public and private pension funds, private equity funds, and large companies with treasury departments. These investors usually are seeking to establish diversified investment portfolios and thus are willing to make investment allocations in a relatively wide spectrum of investment vehicles, depending upon their short-term, medium-term, and long-term return goals. In Africa, participants in this type of investing include institutions such as the American Insurance Group (AIG), and the pension funds of U.S. *Fortune* 500 companies General Electric and U.S. West.

The last group of investors increasingly targeting Africa are individual investors. For these investors (and for investors from the other two groups as well) the key discriminator between successful investments and those that are less successful is access to and use of information. Those that have thoroughly researched an investment prospect/project are likely to receive higher returns almost every time. Thus, having the ability to get timely and comprehensive information is critical in developing the capacity to garner above-average investment returns. In the rest of this chapter we will present a few steps that if followed should help Africa-focused investors to find and consummate lucrative investment transactions on the continent. Step 1 provides an overview on how to access the array of investment information (that is, becoming more and more available); Step 2 discusses ways in which portfolio investors can identify a broker; and Step 3 provides useful information to institutional investors about how to find an investment adviser.

STEP 1: FINDING INVESTMENT INFORMATION

Historically, it has been rather difficult for would-be investors in Africa to gather and maintain an up-to-date and accurate picture regarding the opportunities and trends within African economies. Finding company-specific information was almost impossible, unless you were an insider or knew one. In a few countries with larger exchanges, such as South Africa, Egypt, and Nigeria, there were some exceptions, but for the most part the performance of private companies was known to only their bankers and accountants.

Multilateral Institutions

During the decade of the 1990s, the World Bank and the International Monetary Fund in particular encouraged, supported, and in some cases demanded that African private sectors be afforded a greater role in the development strategies of the continent's economies. These Bretton Woods institutions have also played an important role in promoting the use of globally recognized accounting standards, have supported the development of bankable business plans and feasibility studies by public and private African companies seeking foreign investment, and have begun to gather and disseminate information about Africa's private sector economic growth.

Key among the institutions that disseminate information about the African private sector, industry trends, and country-specific economic trends are the International Monetary Fund; the World Bank sister institutions (1) the IBRD Fund, (2) the International Finance Corporation, and (3) the Multilateral Investment Guarantee Agency; the African Development Bank; the United Nations Development Program; and the United Nations Industrial Development Organization.

For both savvy investors knowledgeable about Africa and those new to this vast emerging market, these institutions provide excellent sources of macroeconomic and, at times, microeconomic information about African investment opportunities. From an investment resource standpoint, the two most important multilateral institutions are the World Bank Group and the African Development Bank Group.

The World Bank Group. The World Bank Group is made up of five institutions: the International Bank for Reconstruction and Development (IBRD), the International Development Association (IDA), the International Finance Corporation (IFC), the Multilateral Investment Guarantee Agency (MIGA), and the International Center for the Settlement of Investment Disputes (ICSID).

Established in 1944, the International Bank for Reconstruction and Development is the largest of the World Bank Group organizations and was established to lend to developing countries with comparatively higher per capita incomes. IBRD loans are used principally to finance infrastructure projects such as highways, hospitals, and schools, and to meet balance of payment obligations of nations in the process of reengineering their economies (i.e., undergoing structural adjustment).

Established in 1960, the International Development Association is the World Bank Group's concessional lending window. It provides longer-term, zero interest loans to the poorest of the developing nations. The aims of IDA include reducing poverty and fostering sustainable and broad-based development and economic growth. IDA lends to those countries that have per capita income of less than U.S. $905 and lack the financial capacity to borrow from IBRD at market rates. Currently, 80 countries are eligible to borrow from IDA.

African nations are the largest beneficiaries of IDA funds, receiving more than half of those funds. IDA funding for Africa principally is focused on supporting nutrition and health, education, energy, and infrastructure.

The International Finance Corporation was established in 1956 to support the growth of the private sector in developing countries. The IFC lends directly to private companies (while the IBRD and IDA lend to governments). The IFC aids the private sector by providing long-term loans, equity investments, guarantees and standby financing, risk management services, and quasi-equity instruments such as preferred stock, subordinated loans, and income notes. The three primary services of the IFC are: (1) debt and equity for financing private sector projects; (2) helping companies in the developing world to mobilize financing in the international capital markets; and (3) providing advice and assistance to businesses and governments.

The IFC itself includes two additional noteworthy institutions, the Africa Enterprise Fund (AEF) and the Africa Project Development Facility (APDF).

The Africa Enterprise Fund was established in 1989 to provide debt and equity financing to small and medium-sized enterprises. Funded project costs range in size from U.S. $250,000 to $5 million, and typical financing ranges between U.S. $100,000 and $1.5 million. The fund finances new businesses as well as expansion, modernization, and diversification of existing businesses. AEF can provide up to 40% of project finance, and usually this is in the form of a loan or equity investment or a combination of the two. The AEF usually cofinances projects with a local investment partner, such as a commercial bank, investment bank, or development agency with a strong local presence and experience in corporate finance. AEF officers are seated in the headquarters and regional offices of the IFC and work in cooperation with the previously mentioned local investment partners in appraising projects, assessing sponsors, and monitoring companies.

The Africa Project Development Facility was established in 1986 as a joint venture between the African Development Bank and the United Nations Development Program to support African entrepreneurs in preparing project proposals for presentations to banks and other finance institutions. The APDF also assists promoters with project implementation. A common source of funding for companies receiving APDF assistance has been the African Enterprise Fund. Projects with costs from U.S. $250,000 to $7 million are eligible for APDF services, and under certain conditions smaller projects will also be considered. APDF project officers are seated in the previously noted field offices of the IFC. The APDF headquarters office is in Washington, D.C.

The Multilateral Investment Guarantee Agency was established in 1989 to encourage the flow of foreign direct investment to its developing member countries in support of economic development and private sector growth. MIGA provides investment guarantees against risks of currency transfer, expropriation, and war and civil disturbance (political risk). Through the Investment Promotion Agency Network it also provides governments with advice on improving the climate for foreign investment. The IPA Network facilitates information exchange for international investors and another MIGA service, the PrivatizationLink, via the Internet. It also provides online access to business profiles of state-owned companies and assets currently for sale, along with details of relevant laws, regulations, and procedures governing these transactions.

The International Center for the Settlement of Investment Disputes was established in 1966 to promote increased flows of international investment by providing facilities for the conciliation and arbitration of disputes between governments and foreign investors. The ICSID also provides advice, carries out research, and produces publications in the area of foreign investment law. ICSID is an excellent resource to use for foreign direct investors considering an investment in Africa. Understanding a country's legal environment is an important aspect of evaluating new markets.

The African Development Bank Group (AfDB). The African Development Bank Group was established in 1963 to promote the economic and social development of its 53 African member countries. Founded with initial capital resources of U.S. $250 million, the Bank's authorized capital in 1997 was U.S. $23 billion. The AfDB includes the African Development Bank (ADB); its concessionary loan affiliate, the African Development Fund (ADF); and the Nigeria Trust Fund (NTF). The African Development Bank Group also includes the more recently established Private Sector Department (PSD).

The African Development Bank makes market rate loans to African governments to finance economic and social development on the continent. Historically, the ADB has financed the establishment of infrastructure projects and also funded technical assistance and institutional development projects. The ADB has also assisted regional member countries in mobilizing external sources of investment in Africa.

The African Development Fund is similar to the IDA of the World Bank Group and provides finance on concessional terms to the poorer of the regional member countries. It also fosters and supports regional and sub-regional cooperation, trade, and joint projects among member countries. The fund is normally replenished on a three-year basis.

The Nigeria Trust Fund was established in 1976 by the Government of Nigeria to assist the development of the poorest regional members of the AfDB Group. The NTF extends loans to qualifying countries on the most concessional terms of the affiliated financial institutions of the AfDB Group.

The Private Sector Department was initially established in 1991 as the Private Sector Development Unit (PSDU). Commencing with a capital base of U.S. $200 million, PSD was conceived to provide debt and equity finance for new and expanding private sector projects in Africa. In 1997, the AfDB enhanced and reorganized the PSDU and upgraded it to the PSD. Although the actual investment and/or debt ceiling for PSD financing is determined on a case-by-case basis, the bank's equity participation in a project cannot exceed 25% of the value of the project.

African Investment Agencies

During the past 10 years an integral component of the effort to stimulate private sector growth in Africa has been the twin push to (1) have countries privatize government-owned parastatal companies, so as to improve their productivity and profitability, and to (2) create a business environment that would be attractive to both foreign and domestic investors and lead to a greater flow of investment capital into the private sector.

To spearhead these efforts, key institutions (divestiture agencies and investment promotion agencies) were established to promote investment and privatization at the national level. These agencies have become central repositories for information about current and planned privatization initiatives (i.e., government sales of assets). Along with ministries of finance, they have also become the principal disseminators of information about special tax and other investment attraction incentive programs promulgated to support economic growth in targeted priority sectors in each country. Lastly, these agencies have begun to identify local businesses—both public and private—that are best prepared for growth through the receipt of foreign direct and portfolio investment. These agencies have become important promoters of the African private sector.

Bilateral Information Sources

In the United States, the four-year bipartisan effort in Congress to develop and pass the Africa Growth and Opportunity Act–an unprecedented trade bill for Africa designed in large part to open up the U.S. market to products made in Africa—has ushered in a new era of foreign policy with the continent. In 1996, responding to the bill, President Bill Clinton initiated his own Africa trade and investment initiative, which among other things led to the creation of a new Africa Trade Representative Office in the Office of the U.S. Trade Representative. As a result, Africa seats were added to the boards of the Overseas Private Investment Corporation and the Export-Import Bank of the United States. Led by President Clinton's historic visit to Africa, between 1996 and 1998 more U.S. cabinet members traveled to Africa than at any previous time in history. During this period, U.S. Treasury Secretary Rubin, Secretary of Transportation Slater, and Secretary of Commerce Daley all made multicountry visits to Africa. In addition, the U.S. Trade and Development Agency deployed an Africa regional manager in Southern Africa to report on opportunities available for U.S. businesses. And in an unprecedented demonstration of the U.S. government's commitment, the Overseas Private Investment Corporation committed nearly a billion dollars to African private sector investment projects.

The result of this activity, from the standpoint of U.S. investors, was the start of the information engine of the U.S. government in developing, gathering, and disseminating information about Africa at a prolific rate. The Trade Promotion Coordinating Committee of the Administration, which includes representatives from 18 agencies, has been very active in expanding the wealth of information available about the continent. Two of the most important U.S. government agencies in terms of investment promotion in Africa are the Overseas Private Investment Corporation (OPIC) and the the U.S. Trade and Development Agency (TDA).

The Overseas Private Investment Corporation is a self-sustaining U.S. government agency that assists U.S. investors through activities designed to promote overseas investment and reduce related risks. The four programs offered by OPIC include: (1) debt, equity, and guarantee finance; (2) guaranteeing private equity funds which provide capital to U.S. companies investing in overseas projects; (3) insuring investments against a broad range of political risks; and (4) facilitating outreach and promotional activities designed to inform U.S. companies about overseas investment opportunities. OPIC's programs are available for most but not all of the countries in Sub-Saharan and North Africa.

The U.S. Trade and Development Agency promotes economic development by funding feasibility studies and consultancies, reverse trade missions, specialized training grants, business workshops, and various forms of technical assistance. The TDA seeks to help U.S. firms undertake the feasibility and planning phases of major international infrastructure projects in middle-income and developing countries, including the countries of Africa. TDA focuses on providing assistance in the development of projects that have significant business potential for U.S. exporters and investors, typically in the following sectors: energy and power, manufacturing, agriculture, health care, mining and mineral exploration, environmental services, transportation, and telecommunications. The TDA has two regular publications: *TDA Pipeline,* which provides biweekly information on agency-supported projects, and *TDA Update,* published quarterly, which highlights TDA's programs.

Business Associations

Although a growing number of chambers of commerce and other business associations are devoted to expanding Africa's private sector, seven institutions are particularly noteworthy: the Corporate Council on Africa (CCA), the African Business Roundtable (ABR), the Committee of French Investors in Africa (CIAN), Business Council Europe-Africa-Mediterranean (BCEAM), the West African Enterprise Network, the East African Enterprise Network, and the Southern African Enterprise Network (SAEN).

Established in 1992, the Corporate Council on Africa is a nonpartisan, tax-exempt membership organization of corporations and individuals dedicated to strengthening and facilitating business relationships between Africa and American individuals and organizations by creating educational, cultural, and investment exchange opportunities.

Established in 1989 and reorganized in 1995, the African Business Round-table is a continent-wide organization of Africa's most prominent businessmen and women. The ABR aims to have its members serve as emissaries to the global business community as advocates for business opportunities in Africa. Additionally the organization seeks to facilitate intra-African trade and investment.

The Committee of French Investors in Africa is the largest organization of French institutional and individual investors on the continent. Both a lobbying and business facilitating organization, the CIAN annually publishes a special report known as the "Rapport Jean-Pierre Proteau," which gives information on the activities, investments, and profits of French companies operating in Africa.

The Business Council Europe-Africa-Mediterranean was established in 1973 by seven European nations (Germany, Italy, Great Britain, Belgium, France, Portugal, and The Netherlands) and seven associations similar to the French-based CIAN. The BCEAM currently represents more than 1,500 European Union firms with interests in North and Sub-Saharan Africa. The aim of the BCEAM is to bring together European investors and other operators engaged in economic activity in African countries and to work for closer cooperation between the European private sector and African countries.

The three existing regional "Enterprise Networks" in Africa are based on the unique model of creating national grassroots enterprise networks comprised predominantly of dynamic entrepreneurs and indigenous corporations that feed into regional associations. Seeking to attract new-generation African entrepreneurs, the networks recruit on a selective basis individuals "interested in playing a strategic role in bringing the African private sector into the global economy and preparing it for the new millennium." The first network established was the West African Enterprise Network, founded in 1993 and administratively based in Accra, Ghana. Since its inception the organization has grown from the 35 founding members to a membership of over 350 business owners and executives, and spread from 7 countries to 13 countries. In July 1998, the East African Enterprise Network was established. The 30 founding members came from Ethiopia, Kenya, Tanzania, and Uganda. Administratively based in Uganda, the organization welcomed 100 participants to its first regional conference held in February 1999. The Southern African Enterprise Network is the most recently initiated of the three organizations, being launched in September 1998. However, it has grown rapidly from a membership of 25 entrepreneurs from 5 countries, to over 100 members from 11 countries. SAEN is administratively based in South Africa.

Publications

The increase in investment interest in Africa has been accompanied by significant growth in the depth, sophistication, and number of publications relating to African business and investment. Longtime publications include the reference compendiums *Africa South of the Sahara* and *Africa North of the Sahara*, monthly and quarterly reports such as the *Economist* Intelligence Unit country reports, and magazines such as *Jeune Afrique Economie, Africa Confidential, West Africa*, and *African Business*. Newer publications such as the *African Business Handbook*, the *African Stock Exchanges Handbook, Business in Africa, African Financing Review*, and *African Review of Business and Technology* have added to the growing body of information available to investors seeking up-to-date information about African economies and companies.

Investment Reference Books

For the portfolio investor, a number of useful resources have also been published in recent years. In addition to broker-produced analytical research, the following publications are useful to consult when considering investing in securities available via Africa's stock exchanges:

African Stock Exchanges Handbook. Provides an overview of Africa's capital markets, complete with contact information for selected brokerage firms.

Emerging Stock Markets Factbook. An IFC compendium that provides an overview and comparison of the world's stock exchanges, including those in Africa.

Finance Africa. A monthly magazine focused on investment and banking in Africa.

Emerging Markets Africa. A fortnightly report on African capital markets.

Africa Financing Review. A bimonthly publication that provides insight, analysis, and "unbiased opinion" on issues related to finance in Africa, particularly Africa's capital markets.

Locate Africa. The newsletter of the African Investment Promotion Agency Network.

Southern African Investor. A monthly investor periodical that discusses recent and projected investment projects in the Southern Africa region.

The Internet

Perhaps more than any other medium, the Internet has emerged as the most important catalyst in expanding the flow of investment-related information into and out of Africa. In the five-year period between 1993 and 1998, Internet connectivity has enabled investment promoters on the continent to promote countries and companies in a way previously unimaginable. Today, news about Africa's markets is available when it happens from online services such as the Africa News Service Online, and other news providers such as MSNBC and CNN. African search engines and sites proliferate daily, and ISP companies such as Africa Online are making rapid strides to allow more and more businesses and agencies to reach the world through telephony.

Given the rapidity with which new sites are emerging within the Internet, it would be difficult to provide a comprehensive list of every site that contains useful information about investing in Africa, but here are a few key sites that can help a new investor get his or her bearings:

- *African Stock Exchanges Association.*   An Association of African capital markets (www.jse.co.za/thejse/asea.htm)

- *Africa Business Network.*   IFC-sponsored to promote African business development (www.ifc.org/abn)

- *IPAnet.*   Investment Promotion Agency Network (www.ipanet.net)

- *Finix.*   Links to 145 stock exchanges worldwide (www.finix.at/fin/ selinks.html)

- *Mbendi.*   African business encyclopedia (www.mbendi.co.za)

- *Privatization Link.*   Privatization opportunities in emerging countries (www.ipanet.net)

- *Afrika.Com.*   "The largest Internet site on Afrocentric business and information" (www.afrika.com)

- *Africa News Service.*   Online distribution of over 40 African periodicals (www.africanews.org)

- *Africa Online.*   Largest pan-African ISP provider, with some regional information (www.africaonline.com)

- *One World News.*   Global provider on news, with good coverage of Africa (www.oneworld.org/news/africa)

- *CNN–Africa.*   Online CNN presence (www.cnn.com/WORLD/africa/ index.html)

- *World Bank.*   World Bank's Web site (www.worldbank.org)

- *African Development Bank.* African Development Bank's Web site (*www.afdb.org*)

- *Africa.com.* A comprehensive "all things related to Africa" portal with access to numerous other Web sites, Africa-related suites including online securites trading (*www.africa.com*)

STEP 2: FINDING A BROKER

For many potential African investors, having reliable information will only provide part of the solution. Not wanting to take their first venture into the African investment arena without professional assistance, they will seek to find a knowledgeable broker to help them structure their portfolio. Thus, finding such a broker becomes a crucial part of their investment strategy.

If one is interested in identifying brokers on the African continent, the best way to obtain a list of possible candidates is to contact the securities exchange in the target country. They will be able to mail, fax, and in most cases, e-mail a list of the exchange members to prospective investors.

The challenge can often be in picking one specific broker over another, with limited (often no) discriminating information to use to make a choice. This is where a request for references is quite useful. Finding out if the broker has any foreign customers and obtaining contact information for those customers can help significantly enhance the broker interview process.

Also, increasingly, larger U.S. brokerages such as Merrill Lynch, Alliance Capital, and Morgan Stanley are entering the African markets and can offer brokerage services to new investors. Larger African brokerages that are affiliated with European Banks can also be helpful. These institutions include Standard Bank and HSBC.

Lastly, there are also a few African brokerages, primarily in South Africa, that have established offices in New York and England so as to be able to serve their clients in Africa and to identify prospective investors in the United States and United Kingdom.

For those investors who are even more prudent and would prefer to have the additional diversity that mutual funds (also known as unit trusts) provide, finding a fund manager is an even more suitable next step than simply finding a broker.

Micropal (www.micropal.com), the Standard and Poor's company that provides online information about 38,000 funds, is an excellent research resource to consult for up-to-date performance information about funds with exposure in Africa.

Although the following list is not comprehensive, the universe of existing funds with exposure to Africa includes: the Morgan Stanley South Africa

Fund, the Calvert New Africa Fund, the Alliance Capital Southern Africa Fund, the Simba Fund, and the Merrill Lynch Middle East/North Africa funds.

STEP 3: FINDING AN ADVISER

For institutional investors seeking to identify an asset manager that specializes in Africa, the number of Africa-savvy investment advisers continues to grow. For the past 10 years the World Bank's International Finance Corporation has been supporting the establishment of regional and country-specific African venture capital and private equity funds. In addition, during the later 1990s the U.S. Overseas Private Investment Corporation has been actively supporting the establishments of venture capital/private equity funds that are focused on Africa.

The importance of these two institutions is that through contact with them an investor can get useful recommendations about the opportunities, risks, and prospects related to investment in Africa via a fund manager. And equally important, they have a fairly good handle on who is who in the African fund management universe.

Although a look at selected asset managers in Africa today presents more well-known firms such as Citibank, AIG, Framington Capital, Merrill Lynch, Alliance Capital, Morgan Stanley, and New Africa Advisers, there is a rapidly growing pool of new advisers who are actively encouraging investors to explore opportunities in Africa. A disproportionate number of these fund managers operate out of Washington, D.C. and London, England—arguably the site of the world's largest aggregation of Africa-related portfolio investment information.

Another phenomenon worth noting is that more and more global fund managers are beginning to provide Africa exposure. These advisers select stocks from a global basket and in this way seek to allocate risk across countries and continents as well as industries. Two useful tools to use to identify players in this market include the online research providers Bloomberg and Reuters, as both are continuing to expand their coverage and information offering related to Africa.

PARTING COUNSEL

As is the case with all investments, it is important to truly understand that all African investments do not appreciate; a good number depreciate. However, if investors have patience and can stay in the market for at least three to five years, we have no doubt that they will be successful if they choose to invest in

Africa. The world's final investment frontier is entering the new millennium with a lot of momentum. Those that investigate the premises we have made in this book are sure to find that the dynamism we have discussed exists. We just hope that those who concur with our views and who have found what we have, will pass it on!!! And for those who have completed this book, we want to offer you hearty congratulations! Having made it to this point, you now join an elite and expanding group of individuals who are conscientiously developing their knowledge of African investment. They will have the opportunity and capacity to reap the full reward of investing in the ultimate emerging market—Africa.

The only thing left to do now is to dive in, so study the options closely, take a deep breath, and go for it.

Good Luck!

Epilogue

THE ONLINE REVOLUTION IS COMING—AFRICAN INVESTMENT IN THE INTERNET AGE

Just as it has in every other facet of life today, the Internet is having an enormous impact on investment and investing in Africa. Everything from research to analysis, to trading and settlement, to mutual fund investment is rapidly moving online on the continent.

A particularly interesting prospective entrant into the African online trading universe is E*Trade, the maverick American retail online brokerage firm. E*Trade's South African partners have garnered the rights to E*Trade Africa and plan to aggressively develop E*Trade's platform continent-wide and provide a vehicle for Internet users worldwide to invest in Africa's stock markets. Furthermore, discussions are underway to use this electronic backbone to help institutional investors invest in Africa—creating an Instinet or Bloomberg Tradebook type institutional trading facility. And lastly, through Africa.com, an African securities trading platform is being developed to provide potential African investors with greater access to private placements and initial public offerings. Along with hosting investor relations sites that will provide information about the host countries, streaming visual images (and audio) of the companies, their management, and their customers, the initiative will offer virtual road shows and bring African investment opportunities to the desktops of global investors—one desktop at a time.

The greatest activity involving online trading in Africa is occurring in South Africa, where there are more than 10 online brokers, and where one of the country's largest banks has announced plans to establish a virtual bank. E-commerce in South Africa in general is also expected to grow by 38% in

2000, 31% in 2001, and 28% in 2002. From 1998 to 1999, online consumer spending grew 140% and is projected to grow by another 125% in 1999.

Continent-wide, in the world of research, the proliferation of Bloomberg and the expansion of Reuters in Africa are making it increasingly easy and cost effective to undertake research on African public securities. As the number of public companies grows, and the level of the sophistication of the research continues to increase, it will become easier and easier to analyze African publicly traded securities.

Increased ability to communicate cost effectively via the Internet has helped the fledgling exchange associations get off the ground—and is helping their members to pursue collaborative ventures. As they compare notes and assess the growing impact of globalization, African exchanges are recognizing that the rapid consolidation of businesses worldwide is affecting the viability of each African country having an individual exchange. With many countries having fewer than 100 companies on their exchanges, it will soon be impractical to expect multibillion-dollar pension funds to consider investing in these markets. There would be no liquidity, and the universe of offerings would be too limited.

However, the message that it will be important in the next 10 years to consider the combining of African exchanges into regionally oriented exchanges—and potentially a continent-wide exchange—is taking hold. West Africa has already created the continent's first truly regional exchange in Côte D'Ivoire, and this has spurred discussions in East and Southern Africa. Furthermore, two of the continent's largest economies, Nigeria and South Africa, have concluded a pact to allow companies to crosslist on each exchange. Soon the online brokerages will be able to trade in both markets—melting away the geographical boundaries.

In the next five years it is highly likely that investors interested in Africa will be able to invest there through one—or a number—of online pan-African electronic stock exchanges. As more and more research on these offerings is moved online, and more and more industry publications go online, Africa will become a plugged-in continent and offer even more attractive opportunities to prospective investors.

With the information age sure to continue revolutionizing the investment universe globally and in Africa, the best in African investment is truly yet to come. Very soon more and better information, larger and higher-yielding opportunities, with greater and greater transparency, will be available. However, the greatest returns will—as always—go to those who prudently move most swiftly into the space. Africa's investment frontier awaits! Bonne Chance Encore!!!

Appendix A

FIGURE A.1 African Stock Exchanges

AFRICAN STOCK EXCHANGES

Botswana

Name and address:	Botswana Stock Exchange
	Fourth Floor, Finance House
	Gaborone, Botswana
	Private Bag 00417
	Gaborone, Botswana
	Tel: [267] 374-078/305-190
	Fax: [267] 374-079
	E-mail: bse@info.bw
History:	The Botswana Stock Exchange was established in 1989 as the Botswana Share Market. It assumed its present name in 1995. The Botswana Stock Exchange is governed by the Botswana Stock Exchange Act of 1994 and regulations promulgated thereunder in 1995. The Ministry of Finance has appointed a Botswana Stock Exchange Committee which is responsible for the management of the stock exchange. There are two stockbrokers, and dual listings were approved in 1996. Companies listed on the Botswana stock exchange are in the banking, insurance, real estate, distribution, tourism, and brewery sectors. At present, investors do not have direct exposure to the Botswana diamond industry, the source of much of Botswana's growth and foreign exchange earnings. In U.S. dollar terms, the Botswana stock exchange has been one of the better emerging market exchanges. Domestic and foreign stocks is $16 billion. Domestic only is $800 million.
Market capitalization	U.S. $1.74 billion
Trading days:	Monday–Friday
Trading hours:	9:00–4:00 Monday–Thursday; 9:00–12:00 Friday (Two callovers, at 9:00 A.M. & 3:00 P.M., for 20 minutes each)
Settlement:	Trade date + 7 (5 working days)
Currency:	Pula
Capital gains tax:	None
Dividends tax:	15%
Stamp duty:	None
Foreign ownership limits:	No individual foreign investor may hold more than 5% of a listed security, and foreign

investors, in the aggregate, may not own more than 49% of a listed security.

Regulation on capital repatriation: Residents only–100% of annual net income

Penalty on currency conversion:　None

Number of listed companies:　13 domestic
　　　　　　　　　　　　　　9 dual listed

Number of listed fixed instruments: 2

Number of stockbrokers:　2

Names and addresses of selected stockbrokers:

> Stock Brokers Botswana
> Private Bag 00113
> Gaborone, Botswana
> Tel: [267] 357-900
> Fax: [267] 357-901

> Investec Securities
> P.O. Box 49
> Gaborone, Botswana
> Tel: [267] 580-800
> Fax: [267] 580-888

Côte d'Ivoire

Name and address:　Abidjan Stock Exchange
　　　　　　　　　Avenue Joseph Anoma
　　　　　　　　　Immercible
　　　　　　　　　BVA DIBP
　　　　　　　　　Abidjan, Côte d'Ivoire
　　　　　　　　　01 B.P. 1878
　　　　　　　　　Abidjan 01, Côte d'Ivoire
　　　　　　　　　Tel: [225] (22) 21-57-42
　　　　　　　　　Fax: [225] (22) 22-16-57
　　　　　　　　　E-mail: brvm@brvm.org

History:　The Abidjan Stock Exchange was created in 1974. However, in 1988 it was transformed into a regional stock exchange for the West African states that are members of the West African Monetary Union (all countries using the CFA franc as legal tender). Consequently, the stock exchange activities for the countries in the West African Monetary Union (Côte d'Ivoire, Senegal, Cameroon, Togo, Burkina Faso, Gabon, Guinea, Mali, and Niger) are now centralized in Abidjan.

Market capitalization (6/30/99):　U.S. $1.5 billion

Trading days:	Monday, Wednesday, and Friday for equities and Tuesday and Thursday for bonds
Trading hours:	9:30–10:30
Settlement:	By account, on a cash basis
Currency:	CFA franc
Capital gains tax:	None
Dividends tax:	None
Stamp duty:	Yes (265 basis points)
Foreign ownership limits:	None
Regulation on capital repatriation:	None
Penalty on currency conversion:	None
Number of listed companies:	36
Number of listed fixed instruments:	13
Number of stockbrokers:	6

Names and addresses of selected stockbrokers:

BIAO
01 BP 1724
Abidjan 01, Côte d'Ivoire
Tel: [225] (22) 20-07-20
Fax: [225] (22) 20-07-00

Citibank
01 BP 3698
Abidjan 01, Côte d'Ivoire
Tel: [225] (22) 21-46-10
Fax: [225] (22) 21-76-85

SGBCI
01 BP 1355
Abidjan 01, Côte d'Ivoire
Tel: [225] (22) 20-12-34
Fax: [225] (22) 20-14-82

BICICI
01 BP 1298
Abidjan 01, Côte d'Ivoire
Tel: [225] (22) 22-03-79
Fax: [225] (22) 20-17-00

Ecobank
01 BP 4107
Abidjan 01, Côte d'Ivoire
Tel: [225] (22) 21-10-41
Fax: [225] (22) 21-88-16

SIB
01 BP 1300
Abidjan 01, Côte d'Ivoire
Tel: (225) 20-00-00
Fax: (225) 21-97-41

Egypt

Names and addresses:	Cairo Stock Exchange
	4A El Sherifein Street
	Cairo, Egypt
	Tel: [20] (2) 392-1447/8968/1402
	Fax: [20] (2) 395-9200/392-8526
	E-mail: www.egyptse.com
	Web: info@egyptse.com
	Alexandria Stock Exchange
	11 Talat Harb Street
	El Manshia
	Alexandria, Egypt
	Tel: [20] (3) 484-3600/1/2/3
	Fax: [20] (3) 484-3604
History:	The Alexandria Stock Exchange is the oldest stock exchange in Africa. It was established in 1883. The Cairo Stock Exchange was created in 1903. The Cairo and the Alexandria stock exchanges grew in importance until 1959 when, as a group, they constituted the fifth-largest stock exchange in the world. However, with the nationalization program of President Nasser in the 1960s, the Egyptian stock exchanges declined in value until 1992, when the Egyptian government enacted a capital markets law to liberalize the two exchanges. Since then, the Egyptian stock exchanges have performed well in the emerging markets universe of stock exchanges.
Market capitalization (6/30/99):	U.S. $27 billion
Trading days:	Sunday–Thursday
Trading hours:	11:30–3:30
Settlement:	Physical trade +3–4 days
Currency:	Egyptian pound
Capital gains tax:	None
Dividends tax:	None

Stamp duty: None
Foreign ownership limits: None
Regulation on capital repatriation: None
Penalty on currency conversion: None
Number of listed companies: 918
Number of listed fixed instruments: 28
Number of stockbrokers: 140
Names and addresses of selected stockbrokers:

> Al Ahram Co. for Securities Brokerage
> 4 Al Shawarby Street
> Cairo, Egypt
> Tel: [20] (2) 393-3543/392-4494
> Fax: [20] (2) 390-6579
>
> Baraka Co. for Securities
> 1 Nasit Al Kady Al Fadel
> Cairo, Egypt
> Tel: [20] (2) 392-3588/392-1478
> Fax: [20] (2) 390-6579
>
> El Alameya Co. for Securities Brokerage
> Emobelia Building
> 26 Sherif Street, Flat No. 544
> Cairo, Egypt
> Tel: [20] (2) 393-5874
> Fax: [20] (2) 393-1434
>
> El Rashad Securities Brokerage
> El-Bostan Commercial Centre
> El-Bostan Street
> Cairo, Egypt
> Tel: [20] (2) 393-7580/7581
> Fax: [20] (2) 393-7586
>
> Elahram Co. for Securities Brokerage
> 4 Shawarbi Street, Flat No. 23
> Cairo, Egypt
> Tel: [20] (2) 392-4494
> Fax: [20] (2) 390-6579
>
> Elgiza for Brokerage
> 26 Elmahatta Street
> Giza, Egypt
> Tel: [20] (2) 571-3179
> Fax: [20] (2) 571-3179

Elsalam Co. for Securities Intermediation
44 Abdel-Khalek Street
Cairo, Egypt
Tel: [20] (2) 391-3186
Fax: [20] (2) 392-8162

EFG
55 Charles de Gaulle Street
Giza, Egypt
Tel: [20] (2) 571-7846/7/8
Fax: [20] (2) 571-6121

Megavest Int. Co. for Securities Brokerage
1191 Cornesh El Nile Street
Cairo, Egypt
Tel: [20] (2) 574-9662/9663/9664
Fax: [20] (2) 574-9664

Misr Co. for Securities Brokerage
6 El Bostan Street
El-Tahrir Square
Cairo, Egypt
Tel: [20] (2) 574-9195
Fax: [20] (2) 574-9663

Okaz Co. for Financial Intermediation & Investment
35 Emad El Din Street
Cairo, Egypt
Tel: [20] (2) 393-7580/7581
Fax: [20] (2) 589-1499

Triple A Securities
45 A Champollion Street
Kasr El-Nil
Cairo 11121, Egypt
Tel: [20] (2) 578-1302/3
Fax: [20] (2) 578-1301

Ghana

Name and address:

Ghana Stock Exchange
Fifth Floor Cedihouse
Liberia Road
P.O. Box 1849
Accra, Ghana
Tel: [233] (21) 669-908/914/935
Fax: [233] (21) 669-913
E-mail: stockex@ncs.com.sh
Web: ourworld.compuserve.com/homepages/
Khaganu/stockex.htm

History: The Ghana Stock Exchange opened in 1990. However, the formal establishment of the exchange was preceded by several years of over-the-counter trading of Ghanaian company shares. Sectors which are represented on the exchange include beverages, tobacco, import trading, automobile dealership, banking, insurance, some light manufacturing, and real estate and property development. Typically, companies listed on the Ghana Stock Exchange have multinational partners and are leaders in their sectors. However, except for Ashanti Goldfields Company Ltd., most of the securities on the Ghana Stock Exchange do not provide an investor with exposure to the hard currency earning sectors of the Ghanaian economy, such as gold and other forms of mining, cocoa trading, timber harvesting and processing, and electric power generation.

Market capitalization (6/30/99):   U.S. $1 billion

Trading days: Monday, Wednesday, Friday

Trading hours: 10:00–12:00

Settlement: Trade date +5

Currency: Cedi

Capital gains tax: Beginning year 2000

Dividends tax: 10% withholding

Stamp duty: None

Foreign ownership limits: No foreign investor may hold more than 10% of a listed security, and foreign investors, in the aggregate, may not own more than 74% of a listed security.

Regulation on capital repatriation: None

Penalty on currency conversion: None

Number of listed companies: 21

Number of listed fixed instruments: 2

Number of stockbrokers: 12

Names and addresses of selected stockbrokers:

CAL Brokerage Limited
P.O. Box 14596
45 Independence Avenue
Accra, Ghana
Tel: [233] (21) 231-102/221-056/221-087
Fax: [233] (21) 231-104/668-657
E-mail: calbank@ncs.com.gh

CDH Securities
P.O. Box 14911
SSNIT Tower Block, Third Floor
Accra, Ghana
Tel: [233] (21) 667-425/667-193
Fax: [233] (21) 662-167
E-mail: cdh2encs.com.gh

Consodiscount Asset Management Co. Ltd.
P.O. Box 14911
SSNIT Tower Block, Third Floor
Accra-North, Ghana
Tel: [233] (21) 667-425/668-437
Fax: [233] (21) 662-167
E-mail: cdh2@ncs.com.gh

Databank Brokerage Limited
Private Mail Bag, Ministries Post Office
SSNIT Tower Block, Fifth Floor
Accra, Ghana
Tel: [233] (21) 669-110/667-088/666-909
Fax: [233] (21) 669-100/775-743
E-mail: databank@africaonline.com.gh

EBG Stockbrokers Limited
P.O. Box 16746
19 Seventeenth Avenue, Ridge (West)
Accra-North, Ghana
Tel: [233] (21) 231-931/932
Fax: [233] (21) 231-934
E-mail: ecobank@ncs.com.gh

First Atlantic Brokers Ltd.
P.O. Box 5188
No. 1 Seventh Avenue
Accra-North, Ghana
Tel: [233] (21) 667-088/666-909
Fax: [233] (21) 775-743

Goldkoast Securities Ltd.
P.O. Box 17187
350 Nima Avenue
Accra, Ghana
Tel: [233] (21) 225-155/226-310/229-892
Fax: [233] (21) 233-050/777-380
E-mail: gcs@goldcoas.com

Merban Stockbrokers Ltd.
P.O. Box 401
Merban House, 44 Kwame Nkrumah Avenue
Accra, Ghana
Tel: [233] (21) 666-331/332/333
Fax: [233] (21) 667-305
E-mail: merban-services@ghmail.com

National Trust Holding Co. Ltd.
P.O. Box 9563
DTSM House, Rwane Nbsunal Avenue
Airport-Accra, Ghana
Tel: [233] (21) 229-664/106
Fax: [233] (21) 229-975

New World Investments Ltd.
P.O. Box 16452
Mobil House, Liberia Road
Airport-Accra, Ghana
Tel: [233] (21) 660-163
Fax: [233] (21) 228-610

SDC Brokerage Services Ltd.
P.O. Box 14198
Second Floor, City Building, Post Office Square, High Street
Accra, Ghana
Tel: [233] (21) 669-372/373/374/375
Fax: [233] (21) 669-371
E-mail: sdc@africaonline.com.gh

Strategic African Securities Ltd.
P.O. Box 16446
228 Ring Road Central
Airport-Accra, Ghana
Tel: [233] (21) 231-386/233-777
Fax: [233] (21) 229-816
E-mail: sasltd@ncs.com.gh

United Securities Trust Ltd.
Enterprise House, High Street
Accra, Ghana
Tel: [233] (21) 669-501/664-423/667-513
Fax: [233] (21) 667-395
E-mail: ustivsb@africaonline.com.gh

Kenya

Name and address:	Nairobi Stock Exchange First Floor, Nation Center Kimathi Street P.O. Box 43633 Nairobi, Kenya Tel: [254] (2) 230-692 Fax: [254] (2) 221-200
History:	Over-the-counter trading in shares has been conducted in Kenya since the early 1920s. The Nairobi Stock Exchange was created in 1954. Originally, this exchange was recognized by the London Stock Exchange as an overseas stock exchange. However, under colonial law, participation on the exchange was limited to residents of European origin. Since the early 1990s, the performance of the Nairobi Stock Exchange has been volatile. In 1994, Kenya was proclaimed "the world's best performing stock market," ahead of 67 other stock markets. Its price index rose 174% in U.S. dollar terms. The food, beverage (including brewing), and tobacco sectors are important on the Nairobi stock exchange. Banks, nonbank finance houses, and insurance companies are also represented. A noteworthy aspect of the Nairobi stock exchange is the significant number of government-affiliated listed companies in the energy, banking, and transportation sectors.
Market capitalization (6/30/99):	U.S. $1.6 billion
Trading days:	Monday–Friday
Trading hours:	10:00–12:00
Settlement:	Trade date + 7
Currency:	Kenyan shilling
Capital gains tax:	None
Dividends tax:	5% resident withholding tax; 10% nonresident withholding tax
Stamp duty:	None
Foreign ownership limits:	No foreign investor may hold more than 5% of a listed security, and foreign investors, in the aggregate, may not own more than 40% of a listed security.
Regulation on capital repatriation:	None
Penalty on currency conversion:	None
Number of listed companies:	58

Number of listed fixed income instruments: 24
Number of stockbrokers: 20
Names and addresses of stockbrokers:

> Ashbhu Securities
> P.O. Box 41684
> Ambank House, 21st Floor
> Nairobi, Kenya
> Tel: [254] (2) 715-411/210-167
> Fax: [254] (2) 210-500
>
> Crossfield Securities Ltd.
> P.O. Box 34137
> Kalyan House, Second Floor, Tubman Road
> Nairobi, Kenya
> Tel: [254] (2) 229-444
> Fax: [254] (2) 222-148
>
> Discount Securities
> P.O. Box 42489
> Phoenix House, Second Floor
> Kenyatta House
> Nairobi, Kenya
> Tel: [254] (2) 219-538
> Fax: [254] (2) 336-553
>
> Dyer & Blair Ltd.
> P.O. Box 45396
> Reinsurance Plaza, Ninth Floor
> Taifa Road
> Nairobi, Kenya
> Tel: [254] (2) 227-803
> Fax: [254] (2) 218-633
>
> Equity Stockbrokers Ltd.
> P.O. Box 47198
> Queensway House, Third Floor
> Nairobi, Kenya
> Tel: [254] (2) 221-452
> Fax: [254] (2) 221-672
>
> Faida Securities
> P.O. Box 45236
> Nanati House, Kimathi Street
> Nairobi, Kenya
> Tel: [254] (2) 243-811
> Fax: [254] (2) 243-814

Francis Drummond & Company Ltd.
P.O. Box 45465
Queensway House, Third Floor
Nairobi, Kenya
Tel: [254] (2) 334-533
Fax: [254] (2) 223-061

Kenya Wide Securities
P.O. Box 43858
Kimathi House, Second Floor
Nairobi, Kenya
Tel: [254] (2) 251-001
Fax: [254] (2) 246-197

Kestrel Capital (EA) Ltd.
P.O. Box 40005
Hughes Building, Seventh Floor
Nairobi, Kenya
Tel: [254] (2) 251-759/815/893
Fax: [254] (2) 243-264

Ngenye Kariuki & Co. Ltd.
P.O. Box 12185
Travel (UTC) House, Fifth Floor
Nairobi, Kenya
Tel: [254] (2) 224-333/220-052
Fax: [254] (2) 217-199

Reliable Securities Ltd.
P.O. Box 50338
Beagle House, Sixth Floor
Kimathi Street
Nairobi, Kenya
Tel: [254] (2) 241-350
Fax: [254] (2) 241-392

Shah Munge & Partners Ltd.
P.O. Box 14686
Nation Center, Twelfth Floor
Nairobi, Kenya
Tel: [254] (2) 227-300/230-672
Fax: [254] (2) 213-024

Sterling Securities, Ltd.
P.O. Box 45213
Bruce House, Fourteenth Floor
Standard Street
Nairobi, Kenya
Tel: [254] (2) 213-914
Fax: [254] (2) 218-261

Suntra Stocks Ltd.
P.O. Box 74016
Commonwealth House, Fifth Floor
Moi Avenue
Nairobi, Kenya
Tel: [254] (2) 337-220
Fax: [254] (2) 224-327

Town & Country Securities Ltd.
P.O. Box 122518
Hazina Towers, Eleventh Floor
Loita Street
Nairobi, Kenya
Tel: [254] (2) 244-739
Fax: [254] (2) 240-706

Malawi

Name and address:

Malawi Stock Exchange
Ground Floor, Able House
Cnr Hannover Avenue/Chilembwe Rd.
Blantyre, Malawi
P.O. Box 2598
Blantyre, Malawi
Tel: [265] 622-803/627-817/824-327
Fax: (265) 62-4353
E-mail: sml@malawi.net

History:

The Malawi Stock Exchange was created in November 1996. From 1992 until its establishment, capital market activities were under the aegis of the Reserve Bank of Malawi, which was responsible for the establishment of the stock exchange. The first few years of the exchange's trading activities were characterized by modest returns in U.S. dollars. By 1998, the Exchange had 3 securities and a market capitalization of U.S. $165 million. Sectors represented on the exchange are tourism, sugar, and insurance. Currently, two of the three securities (tourism and sugar) provide an investor with exposure to the hard currency earning sectors of Malawi.

Market capitalization (6/30/99)　　U.S. $165 Million

Trading days:　　Monday–Friday

Trading hours:　　9:00 A.M.–Midday, Monday–Friday

Settlement:　　Trade date + 7

Currency:　　Malawian kwacha

Capital gains tax:　　Taxed at the marginal tax rate if shares sold within one year of purchase, but the first 10,000 Malawian kwachas are exempt from tax.

Dividends tax:　　None

Stamp duty:　　None

Foreign ownership limits:　　No foreign investor may hold more than 5% of a listed security, and foreign investors, in the aggregate, may not own more than 49% of a listed security.

Regulation on capital repatriation:　　None so long as foreign investor registers with the Reserve Bank of Malawi

Penalty on currency conversion:　　None

Number of listed companies:　　6

Number of listed fixed instruments:　2

Number of stockbrokers:　　1

Name and address of stockbroker:

> Stockbrokers Malawi Limited
> P.O. Box 2598
> Blantyre, Malawi
> Tel: [265] 622-803/824-327
> Fax: [265] 624-353
> E-mail: SML@malawi.net

Mauritius

Name and address:　　Stock Exchange of Mauritius
Ground Floor, Si Com Building
Celi Court, Antelne Street
Port Louis, Mauritius
Tel: [230] 212-9541/9542/9543
Fax: [230] 208-8409
E-mail: stockex@bow.intnet.mu

History:　　The Stock Exchange of Mauritius was created in 1988. The exchange operates in two markets—the official list for listed companies, and the over-the-counter market for unlisted companies.

The market is unique in that it represents a gateway to Africa for Asian investors. The stock exchange of Mauritius has been one of the most consistent performers in Africa.

Market capitalization (6/30/99):	U.S. $1.5 billion
Trading days:	Monday to Friday
Trading hours:	10:00–11:00 (Monday, Wednesday, Friday), (over the counter 1:30–2:30 P.M. Tuesday and Thursday)
Settlement:	Trade date + 5
Currency:	Mauritian rupee
Capital gains tax:	None
Dividends tax:	None
Stamp duty:	None
Foreign ownership limits:	Prior consent of the Stock Exchange Commission (S.E.C.) is required for foreign investment of 15% or more of the voting capital of a Mauritian sugar company.
Regulation on capital repatriation:	None
Penalty on currency conversion:	None
Number of listed companies:	45
Number of listed fixed instruments:	2
Number of stockbrokers:	11

Names and addresses of selected stockbrokers:

Asmo Securities & Investments Ltd.
43 Sir William Newton Street
Port Louis, Mauritius
Tel: [230] 212-9863/4/5/212-1269/212-0697
Fax: [230] 208-8508
E-mail: asmo@bow.intnet.mu

Associated Brokers Ltd.
10 Sir William Newton Street
Port Louis, Mauritius
Tel: [230] 212-3038
Fax: [230] 212-6690
E-mail: abl@bow.intnet.mu

Capital Markets Brokers Ltd.
Third Floor, Moorgate House
29 Sir William Newton Street
Port Louis, Mauritius
Tel: [230] 212-1336
Fax: [230] 212-8238
E-mail: cmb@bow.intnet.mu

Cavell Securities Ltd.
Hare Mallac Building
18 Edith Cavell Street
Port Louis, Mauritius
Tel: [230] 208-0808
Fax: [230] 208-8798
E-mail: alh@hm.intnet.mu

Compagnie des Agents de Change Ltee
Ninth Floor, Stratton Court
Poudriere Street
Port Louis, Mauritius
Tel: [230] 212-2578
Fax: [230] 208-3455
E-mail: cac@intnet.mu

First Brokers Ltd.
Fourth Floor, R. Li Wan Po Building
12 Remy Ollier Street
Port Louis, Mauritius
Tel: [230] 211-0582
Fax: [230] 211-0584

General Brokerage Ltd.
Eighth Floor, Les Cascades Building, 33 Bis
Edith Cavell Street
Port Louis, Mauritius
Tel: [230] 212-9863
Fax: [230] 212-9867

MCB Stockbrokers Ltd.
Raymond Lamusse Building, MCB Head Office
Sir William Newton Street
Port Louis, Mauritius
Tel: [230] 208-2801
Fax: [230] 208-9210
E-mail: mcb.sb@intnet.mu

Ramet & Associes Ltee
16 Queen Street
Port Louis, Mauritius
Tel: [230] 212-3535
Fax: [230] 208-6294

SBM-HG Asia Ltd.
Level 6 State Bank Tower, 1 Queen Elizabeth II Avenue
Port Louis, Mauritius
Tel: [230] 202-1437
Fax: [230] 202-1234
E-mail: dussoye.rd@sbm.intnet.mu

Newton Securities Ltd.
Level 8 Happy World House
Sir William Newton Street
Port Louis, Mauritius
Tel: [230] 208-8626
Fax: [230] 208-8749
E-mail: newton@bow.intnet.mu

Morocco

Name and address:	Casablanca Stock Exchange Avenue de l'Armée Royale Casablanca, Morocco Tel: [212] (2) 452-626 Fax: [212] (2) 452-625
History:	The Casablanca Stock Exchange was created in 1929. However, it underwent reforms in 1948, 1967, and 1993. From 1990 until the end of 1995, returns from equities handily outperformed Moroccan treasury bill returns and surpassed inflation. Sectors represented on the exchange are banking, finance, investment, distribution, and manufacturing. Morocco is noted as having one of Africa's most successful privatization programs. As such, the stock exchange has been well-received by the emerging market investment community.
Market capitalization (6/30/99):	U.S. $15 billion
Trading days:	Monday–Friday
Trading hours:	9:00–1:00
Settlement:	Physical, trade date + 3
Currency:	Dirham
Capital gains tax:	None
Dividends tax:	10%
Stamp duty:	None
Foreign ownership limits:	No exchange control restrictions on foreign investors
Regulation on capital repatriation:	None
Penalty on currency conversion:	None

Number of listed companies: 53
Number of listed fixed instruments: 85
Number of stockbrokers: 15
Names and addresses of selected stockbrokers:

ABN AMRO Securities
47 Rue Allah Ben Abdellah
Casablanca, Morocco
Tel: [212] (2) 29-59-59
Fax: [212] (2) 20-86-78

Attijari Intermediation
2 bd Moulaqy Youssef
Casablanca, Morocco
Tel: [212] (2) 29-39-91
Fax: [212] (2) 47-64-32

BMCI Bourse
26 Place des Nations-Unies
Casablanca, Morocco
Tel: [212] (2) 46-15-80
Fax: [212] (2) 47-64-32

Casablanca Finance Intermediation
57 Rue Ibn Toufail, Quartier Palmier
Casablanca, Morocco
Tel: [212] (2) 25-01-01/441-244
Fax: [212] (2) 98-11-12/441-240

CityBourse
34 avenue Hassan Sephir
Casablanca, Morocco
Tel: [212] (2) 45-21-09
Fax: [212] (2) 45-21-10

Credit du Maroc Capital
20 bd Zerktouni
Casablanca, Morocco
Tel: [212] (2) 94-07-44
Fax: [212] (2) 94-07-66

EuroBourse
Iman Center, Rue Mohamed Errachid
No. 1-Floor 10
Casablanca, Morocco
Tel: [212] (2) 54-15-54
Fax: [212] (2) 54-14-45

ICF Al Wassit
Espace Porte d'Anfa
29 Rue Bab el Mansour
Casablanca, Morocco
Tel: [212] (2) 36-93-83
Fax: [212] (2) 36-93-81

Maroc Inter-Titres
Tour Bemcom, rond-point
Hassan II, Berne et.
Casablanca, Morocco
Tel: [212] (2) 48-10-01
Fax: [212] (2) 48-09-52

SogeBourse
Angle rues Dubreuil et Bournazel
Residence Ezzahra
Quart. des Hôpitaux
Casablanca, Morocco
Tel: [212] (2) 48-73-32
Fax: [212] (2) 49-28-57

Mozambique

Name and address:	Maputo Stock Exchange Avenida 25 de setemtro Maputo, Mozambique Tel: [258] (1) 308-826/308/828 Fax: [258] (1) 310-559
History:	Started operating in October 1999 with the support of the Lisbon Stock Exchange and World Bank.
Market capitalization (6/30/99):	So far only treasury bonds with face value of U.S. $5 million
Trading days:	TBD
Trading hours:	TBD
Settlement:	TBD
Currency:	Mozambiquan Metical
Capital gains tax:	18%
Dividends tax:	18%
Stamp duty:	None
Foreign ownership limits:	TBD
Regulation on capital repatriation:	Need approval by the Central Bank
Penalty on currency conversion:	Need approval by the Central Bank
Number of listed companies:	None
Number of listed fixed instruments:	None

Number of stockbrokers: N/A
Names and addresses of stockbrokers: None

Namibia

Name and address: Namibian Stock Exchange
                                           Shop 11 Ground Floor
                                           Kaiserkrone Centre
                                           P.O. Box 2401
                                           Windhoek, Namibia
                                           Tel: [264] (61) 227-647
                                           Fax: [264] (61) 248-531

History: The original Namibian stock exchange was
                                           started in the early 1900s. The current stock
                                           exchange was launched in 1992. The first list-
                                           ings on this exchange were dual listings of com-
                                           panies already listed on the Johannesburg Stock
                                           Exchange. Single listings (of companies which
                                           are listed on the Namibian Stock Exchange with-
                                           out a listing on the Johannesburg Stock Ex-
                                           change) commenced in 1994. Bonds have also
                                           been issued on the Namibian Stock Exchange.
                                           Sectors represented on the exchange include dia-
                                           monds, fishing, tourism, breweries, and banking.
                                           Investors have obtained good U.S. dollar returns
                                           on the Namibian stock exchange.

Market capitalization (6/30/99):   U.S. $716 million
Trading Days: Monday–Friday
Trading Hours: 10:00–12:00, 2:00–4:00
Settlement: Physically
Currency: Namibian dollar
Capital gains tax: None.
Dividends tax: 10% on nonresidents
Stamp duty: None on Namibian Stock Exchange transac-
                                           tions.
Foreign ownership limits: None; however, South African Common Mone-
                                           tary Area exchange controls exist. Also, a bank
                                           may not be acquired without the approval of the
                                           Central Bank.
Regulation on capital repatriation: None
Penalty on currency conversion: None
Number of listed companies: 15 local, 25 dual listed
Number of listed fixed instruments: 2
Number of stockbrokers: 6
Names and addresses of selected stockbrokers:

ABN-AMRO/Huysamer Stals
P.O. Box 196
Eighth Floor, Southern Life Building
Post Street Mall
Windhoek, Namibia 9000
Tel: [264] (61) 237-477
Fax: [264] (61) 227-321

BOB Securities (Pty) Ltd.
P.O. Box 27
First Floor, City Center Building
Leviason Arcade
Windhoek, Namibia
Tel: [264] (61) 256-666
Fax: [264] (61) 256-789

Fleming Martin Securities Ltd.
P.O. Box 3970
Fifth Floor, Frans Indongo Gardens
19 Bulow Street
Windhoek, Namibia
Tel: [264] (61) 254-194
Fax: [264] (61) 254-193

HSBC Simpson McKie
P.O. Box 1272
Windhoek, Namibia 9000
Tel: [264] (61) 239-708
Fax: [264] (61) 232-513

Investec Securities
P.O. Box 24142
Seventh Floor, Frans Indongo Gardens
19 Bulow Street
Windhoek, Namibia
Tel: [264] (61) 238-823
Fax: [264] (61) 238-864

Jolyon Irwin
P.O. Box 186
Eleventh Floor, Sanlam Center
Independence Avenue
Windhoek, Namibia
Tel: [264] (61) 238-899
Fax: [264] (61) 238-936

Nigeria

Name and address:	Nigerian Stock Exchange
	P.O. Box 2457
	Stock Exchange House
	2–4 Customs Street
	Lagos, Nigeria
	Tel: [234] (1) 266-0287/266-0305
	Fax: [234] (1) 266-8724/266-8281

History: The Nigerian Stock Exchange was founded in 1961. It comprises a first-tier board for established companies and a second-tier board for small and medium-sized companies. The second-tier securities market was launched in 1985 for medium-sized and small companies that did not meet the listing requirements of the first-tier market of the stock exchange. Although Nigeria earns most of its foreign exchange earnings from the export of petroleum, there are no listed petroleum companies that enable an investor to benefit from those foreign exchange earnings.

Market capitalization (6/30/99):	U.S. $2.9 billion
Trading days:	Monday–Friday
Trading hours:	11:00–1:30
Settlement:	Trade date + 5
Currency:	Naira
Capital gains tax:	10%
Dividends tax:	10%
Stamp duty:	None
Foreign ownership limits:	None
Regulation on capital repatriation:	Foreign investors are permitted to repatriate dividends, royalties, fees, and capital.
Penalty on currency conversion:	None
Number of listed companies:	172 first tier
	16 second tier
Number of listed fixed instruments:	74
Number of stockbrokers:	12 often used by foreign investors

Names and addresses of selected stockbrokers:

BGL Securities Ltd.
Plot 1061b Abagbon Close
Off Ologun Agbaje Street
Victoria Island, Nigeria
Tel: [234] (1) 262-3141
Fax: [234] (1) 262-3258

Capital Bancorp Ltd.
P.O. Box 1362
Eleganza Building, Eleventh Floor
15b Wesley Joseph Street
Lagos, Nigeria
Tel: [234] (1) 263-0118
Fax: [234] (1) 263-1238

CSL Stockbrokers Limited
P.O. Box 9117
Fifth Floor, Primrose Tower
17A Tinubu Street
Lagos, Nigeria
Tel: [234] (1) 266-5944

Denham Management Ltd.
P.O. Box 4454
New Africa House, 31 Marina
Lagos, Nigeria
Tel: [234] (1) 266-1763/266-4445
Fax: [234] (1) 266-1763
E-mail: denham@infoweb.abs.net

Empire Securities, Ltd.
Plot 1115A
Adeola Odeku Street
Victoria Island
Lagos, Nigeria
Tel: [234] (1) 262-0505
Fax: [234] (1) 617-803

Enterprise Stockbrokers Plc
85 Ogunlana Drive
Surulere
Lagos, Nigeria
Tel: [234] (1) 835285
Fax: [234] (1) 585-1173

F&C Securities, Ltd.
17b Bishop Aboyede Cole
Victoria Island
Lagos, Nigeria
Tel: [234] (1) 262-0772/1307
Fax: [234] (1) 262-0839

Icon Stockbrokers Ltd.
PMB 12689
NIDH House (8th Floor)
63/71 Broad Street
Lagos, Nigeria
Tel: [234] (1) 266-3293
Fax: [234] (1) 266-0067

International Standard Securities Ltd.
144A, Association Road
Dolphin Scheme
Lagos, Nigeria
Tel: [234] (1) 269-4832

Interstate Securities Limited
P.O. Box 71040
Clergy House, Ground Floor
14 Catholic Mission Street
Lagos, Nigeria
Tel: [234] (1) 263-1600

Securities Transactions and Trust Company Ltd.
P.O. Box 51045
2A Osborne Road, Foreshore Towers
Lagos, Nigeria
Tel: [234] (1) 269-0861
Fax: [234] (1) 269-4392

South Africa

Name and address:

Johannesburg Stock Exchange
17 Diagonal Street
Johannesburg 2000, South Africa
Tel: [27] (11) 377-2200
Fax: [27] (11) 838-7106
Web: www.jse.co.za.

History:

The Johannesburg Stock Exchange was founded in 1887. Initially, the purpose of the exchange was to provide a marketplace for the numerous mining and financial houses formed shortly after the Witwatersrand goldfields were discovered in 1886. In 1995, the exchange opened its membership to corporations and foreigners and moved to an automated electronic trading system. Although mining-related companies represent the Johannesburg Stock Exchange's largest sector, the exchange offers a diverse array of investment sectors. Due to its sophistication and capacity, the market represents the primary gateway to Africa's capital markets for U.S. investors. The Johannesburg Stock Exchange is one of the 12 largest stock exchanges in the world.

Market capitalization (6/30/99):	U.S. $218 billion
Trading days:	Monday–Friday
Trading hours:	9:30–16:00
Settlement:	Physically, in weekly account
Currency:	Rand
Capital gains tax:	To be introduced in 2001
Dividends tax:	None, although a special formula is applied to mining companies.
Stamp duty:	0.25% payable by the buyer/new owner where no marketable securities tax has been paid. A marketable securities tax of 0.25% is payable on purchases executed on the Johannesburg Stock Exchange.
Foreign ownership limits:	None
Regulation on capital repatriation:	None
Penalty on currency conversion:	None
Number of listed companies:	890
Type of traded instruments:	Equities, preference shares, corporate debentures, traditional options on debentures.
Number of stockbrokers:	164 (top 10 listed here)

Names and addresses of selected stockbrokers:

ABN AMRO Securities South Africa Ltd.
1st Floor, JSE Annexe, 1 Kerk Street
Johannesburg 2001, South Africa
P.O. Box 11461
Johannesburg 2000, South Africa
Tel: [27] (11) 240-3500
Fax: [27] (11) 836-5811

ABSA Securities (PTY) Ltd.
24th Floor, Sanlam Centre, Jeppe Street
Johannesburg 2001, South Africa
P.O. Box 1190
Johannesburg 2000, South Africa
Tel: [27] (11) 330-4813
Fax: [27] (11) 333-9293

AMB-DLJ Securities (PTY) Ltd.
Rosebank Office Park, 181 Jan Smuts Avenue
Rosebank 2196, South Africa
P.O. Box 1773
Parklands 2121, South Africa
Tel: [27] (11) 343-2200
Fax: [27] (11) 343-2234

Deutsche Morgan Grenfell
9th Floor, Shell House, 9 Riebeck Street
Cape Town 8001, South Africa
P.O. Box 601
Cape Town 8000, South Africa
Tel: [27] (21) 419-4235
Fax: [27] (21) 419-5935

Fleming Martin Securities Ltd.
1016 The Stock Exchange, 17 Diagonal Street
Johannesburg 2001, South Africa
P.O. Box 934
Johannesburg 2000, South Africa
Tel: [27] (11) 240-2400
Fax: [27] (11) 838-2344

Investec Securities Ltd.
946 The Stock Exchange, 17 Diagonal Street
Johannesburg 2001, South Africa
P.O. Box 691
Johannesburg 2000, South Africa
Tel: [27] (11) 833-5740
Fax: [27] (11) 836-0007

Merrill Lynch South Africa Ltd.
10th Floor, AA Life Building, 27 Diagonal Street
Johannesburg 2000, South Africa
Tel: [27] (11) 498-6000
Fax: [27] (11) 833-1967

NIB Securities (PTY) Ltd.
3rd Floor, Syfrets Centre
140 St. George's Mall
Cape Town 8001, South Africa
P.O. Box 138
Cape Town 8000, South Africa
Tel: [27] (21) 488-1166
Fax: [27] (21) 488-1100

SG Frankel Pollack Securities (PTY) Ltd.
Suite 1902, General Building, Cnr Smith & Fields Street
Durban 4001, South Africa
P.O. Box 1558
Durban 4000, South Africa
Tel: [27] (31) 301-9724
Fax: [27] (31) 301-0566

Standard Equities (PTY) Ltd.
Entrance No. 6, 4th Floor
3 Simmonds Street
Johannesburg 2001, South Africa
P.O. Box 61309
Marshalltown 2107, South Africa
Tel: [27] (11) 636-0100
Fax: [27] (11) 636-0512

Sudan

Name and address:	Khartoum Stock Exchange
	P.O. Box 10830
	Al Barka Road, Fifth Floor
	Khartoum, Sudan
	Tel: [249] (11) 776-322/782-450
	Fax: [249] (11) 782-225
History:	In 1962, the first governmental discussions about launching a stock exchange were held. However, it was another 30 years before these discussions, and subsequent legislative actions, led to the establishment of the Khartoum Stock Exchange in 1994. Indeed, although the market opened in October of 1994, it was not until 1995 that active trading commenced. Today, the Khartoum Stock Exchange, despite the civil unrest in Sudan, is quite active with 42 listed companies.
Market capitalization (6/30/99):	N/A
Trading days:	Sunday–Thursday
Trading hours:	8:00 A.M.–2:00 P.M.
Settlement:	Physical
Currency:	Sudanese dinar
Capital gains tax:	Yes
Dividends tax:	Yes
Stamp duty:	No
Foreign ownership limits:	Yes
Regulation on capital repatriation:	Yes

Penalty on currency conversion: No
Number of listed companies: 42
Number of listed fixed instruments: None
Number of stockbrokers: 11
Names and addresses of stockbrokers: N/A

Swaziland

Name of the stock exchange: Swaziland Stockbrokers Ltd.
Address: c/o Swaziland Stock Brokers Ltd.
Suite 205, Dhalanudeka House
Walker Street
P.O. Box 2818
Mbabane, Swaziland
Tel: [268] 204-6163
Fax: [268] 204-4132

History: This stock exchange was created in July 1990 by Sibusiso Dlamini, a former World Bank executive who became Swaziland's prime minister. Currently, the exchange has 6 securities and a market capitalization of U.S. $87 million. All listings are included in the only index, the SSM Index, which is unweighted. Sectors represented on the exchange are banking and manufacturing.

Market capitalization (6/30/99):   U.S. $87 million
Trading days: Monday–Friday
Trading hours: 10:00–12:00
Settlement: Physical
Currency: Lilangeni
Capital gains tax: None
Dividends tax: 15% nonresident tax
Stamp duty: 1.5%. Not applicable to stock market transactions.
Foreign ownership limits: None
Regulation on capital repatriation: Exchange controls—prior permission is needed from Central Bank.

Penalty on Currency Conversion: None
Number of listed companies: 6
Number of listed fixed instruments: 5
Number of stockbrokers: 2
Name and address of selected stockbrokers:

Swaziland Stockbrokers Ltd.
P.O. Box 2818
Mbabane, Swaziland
Tel: [268] 204-6163
Fax: [268] 204-4132

> African Alliance Ltd.
> P.O. Box 5727
> Mbabane, Swaziland
> Tel: [268] 404-8735
> Fax: [268] 404-8747

Tanzania

Name and address:	Dar-es-Salaam Stock Exchange
	P.O. Box 70081
	c/o Capital Markets & Security Authority
	Fourth Floor Twiga Building
	Samora Avenue
	Dar-es-Salaam, Tanzania
History:	The Dar-es-Salaam Stock Exchange was created in 1997. The development of this exchange is hampered by the enforced lack of participation by foreign investors and by a local investor community that lacks significant surplus funds and is not yet fully convinced of the value of investing in the stock market.
Market capitalization (6/30/99):	U.S. $187 million
Trading days:	Tuesday and Thursday
Trading hours:	10:00–11:00
Settlement:	Electronic trade date + 5
Currency:	Tanzanian shilling
Capital gains tax:	None
Dividends tax:	5%
Stamp duty:	None
Foreign ownership limits:	No foreign investors are allowed to trade on the exchange
Number of listed companies:	2
Number of listed fixed instruments:	None
Number of stockbrokers:	7

Names and addresses of selected stockbrokers:

> Fintrust Ltd.
> P.O. Box 6649
> 50 Mirambo Street
> Dar-es-Salaam, Tanzania
> Tel: (255) 51 117686
> Fax: (255) 51 116668

Orbit Securities Company Ltd.
Twiga House, 3rd Floor
Dar-es-Salaam, Tanzania
Tel: (255) 51 111785
Fax: (255) 51 113067

Stock Brokerage Agencies
P.O. Box 5237
Plot No. 9/2, Mandela Road
Dar-es-Salaam, Tanzania
Tel: [255] (5) 14-86-41
Fax: [255] (5) 14-36-08

Tanzania Securities Ltd.
P.O. Box 2130
NIC Life House, 5th Floor
Dar-es-Salaam, Tanzania
Tel: (255) 51 112807
Fax: (255) 51 112809

Vertex Financil Services Ltd.
P.O. Box 13412
CDTF-HQ Building
Ohio Street/Samora Ave.
Dar-es-Salaam, Tanzania
Tel: (255) 51 110392/116383
Fax: (255) 51 110387

Tunisia

Name and address:	Bourses des Valuers Mobilieres de Tunis (Tunis Stock Exchange) Centre Babel Block E Montplaisir 1002 Tunis, Tunisia Tel: [216] (1) 786-912/787-724 Fax: [216] (1) 789-189
History:	The Tunis Bourse was created in 1969, and both stocks and bonds trade on the exchange. Until 1996, the exchange maintained limits on the permissible share price movements. Share prices declined precipitously in the wake of the abolition of those limits, but shares on this exchange have retained their value in the United States.
Market capitalization (6/30/99):	U.S. $2.8 billion

Trading days:	Monday–Friday
Trading hours:	8:00–11:00
Settlement:	Trade date + 5
Currency:	Dinar
Capital gains tax:	None
Dividends tax:	None
Stamp duty:	None
Foreign ownership limits:	Foreigners may not participate directly on the exchange.
Regulation on capital repatriation:	None
Penalty on currency conversion:	None
Number of listed companies:	44
Number of listed fixed instruments:	70
Number of stockbrokers:	28

Names and addresses of selected stockbrokers:

Amen Invest
150 Avenue de la Liberté
1002 Tunis, Tunisia
Tel: [216] (1) 792-972/785-725
Fax: [216] (1) 786-663/786-663

Arab Financial Consultants
11 Rue Nouira
1000 Tunis, Tunisia
Tel: [216] (1) 334-994/334-224
Fax: [216] (1) 335-956

Best Invest
88, Av. Hedi Chaker
1002 Tunis, Tunisia
Tel: [216] (1) 845-766
Fax: [216] (1) 847-561

BNA Capitaux
Rue Kheireddine Pacha
1002 Tunis, Tunisia
Tel: [216] (1) 841-966
Fax: [216] (1) 348-763

Compagnie Financière Internationale de Bourse
51, Avenue Jugurtha
1002 Tunis, Tunisia
Tel: [216] (1) 840-253
Fax: [216] (1) 843-778

Compagnie Generale d'Investissement
25, Rue du Dr Calmette, Mutuelleville
1002 Tunis, Tunisia
Tel: [216] (1) 789-466
Fax: [216] (1) 789-990

Financement et Investissement
9 rue Med Ali Annabi
1002 Tunis, Tunisia
Tel: [216] (1) 841-034/841-253
Fax: [216] (1) 841-280

Le Capital
Angle 67, Avenue Mohamed V et 4 Rue du Niger
1002 Tunis, Tunisia
Tel: [216] (1) 800-144/802-223

Societe d'Intermediation et de Conseil Financier
Centre Commercial Galaxie 2000
Rue d'Irak, Bloc B, 4 etage
1002 Tunis, Tunisia
Tel: [216] (1) 800-985
Fax: [216] (1) 794-905

Societe Maxula Bourse
6 rue de Damas
1002 Tunis, Tunisia
Tel: [216] (1) 789-752
Fax: [216] (1) 787-288

Tunisie Valews
17 rue de Jerusalem
1002 Tunis, Tunisia
Tel: [216] (1) 792-794
Fax: [216] (1) 795-641

Uganda

Name and address:
Kampala Stock Exchange
The Uganda Securities Exchange
4 Nile Avenue
EADB Building
Kampala, Uganda
P.O. Box 23552
Kampala, Uganda
Tel: [256] (41) 342-818
Fax: [256] (41) 231-813

History:
The Kampala Stock Exchange was created in 1997 and is run under the jurisdiction of the Cap-

ital Markets Authority, which reports to the Central Bank of Uganda. The exchange's door opened to trading in January 1998. At the time, the exchange had just one instrument, a bond issued by the East African Development Bank.

Trading days:	Monday–Friday
Currency:	Ugandan shilling
Capital gains tax:	None
Dividends tax:	None
Number of listed companies:	None
Number of listed fixed instruments:	2
Number of stockbrokers:	11

Names and addresses of selected stockbrokers:

African Alliance CUJ Ltd.
Plot 34 Panworld Centre, Nkrumah Road
Kampala, Uganda
Tel: [256] (41) 231-092/250-378
Fax: [256] (41) 341-593

Baroda Capital Markets
Plot 18, Kampala Road
Kampala, Uganda
Tel: [256] (41) 233-680/233-683
Fax: [256] (41) 258-263

Equity Stockbrokers
c/o Orient Bank
Uganda House
Plot 10, Kampala Road
Kampala, Uganda
P.O. Box 3072
Kampala, Uganda

Trans Africa Finance and Securities
P.O. Box 22789
Udyan House, Jinja Road
Kampala, Uganda
Tel: [256] (41) 234-554/234-564
Fax: [256] (41) 234-575

Zambia

Name and address:

Lusaka Stock Exchange (LUSE)
First Floor, Lusaka Stock Exchange Building
2A Cairo Rd.
Lusaka, Zambia

P.O. Box 34523
Lusaka, Zambia
Tel: [260] (1) 228-391/228-537/228-594
Fax: [260] (1) 225-969
E-mail: luse@zamnet.zm

History:	The Lusaka Stock Exchange, one of the newest exchanges in Africa, was created in 1993 and opened in 1994. However, its first security, Chilanga Cement, was not listed until 1995. The number of securities traded on the exchange is expected to increase as up to 150 state enterprises will be privatized over the next few years. Additionally, a number of private companies are converting to public companies and issuing shares on the exchange.
Market capitalization (6/30/99):	U.S. $289 million
Trading days:	Monday–Friday
Trading hours:	10:00–12:00
Settlement:	Trade date + 3
Currency:	Zambian kwacha
Capital gains tax:	None.
Dividends tax:	15% withholding tax on dividends
Stamp duty:	None
Foreign ownership limits:	None
Regulation on capital repatriation:	None
Penalty on currency conversion:	None
Number of listed companies:	9
Number of listed fixed instruments:	2
Number of stockbrokers:	6

Names and addresses of selected stockbrokers:

Cavmont Securities Ltd.
P.O. Box 35476
Lusaka, Zambia
Tel: [260] (1) 227-763
Fax: [260] (1) 224-316
E-mail: cavmont@zamnet.zm

Finance Securities Ltd.
P.O. Box 37102
Third Floor, Chanik House
Lusaka, Zambia
Tel: [260] (1) 229-733/229-742
Fax: [260] (1) 227-544/224-450

Intermarket Securities Ltd.
P.O. Box 35832
Standard Chartered Bank Building, First Floor
Lusaka, Zambia
Tel: [260] (1) 227-227/231-334
Fax: [260] (1) 227-274
E-Mail: idhzam@zamnet.zm

Pangaea/EMI Securities Ltd.
P.O. Box 30163
First Floor Luse Building
Lusaka, Zambia
Tel: [260] (1) 238-709/710
Fax: [260] (1) 220-925
E-mail: ppzam@zamnet.zm

Zimbabwe

Name and address:	Zimbabwe Stock Exchange P.O. Box UA 234 Fifth Floor, South Hampton House Union Avenue Harare, Zimbabwe Tel: [263] (4) 736-861/796-225 Fax: [263] (4) 791-045
History:	The first Zimbabwe stock exchange was opened in 1896 to raise funds for gold mining. It closed after the end of the Boer War in 1902. Another exchange, the Umtali exchange, which also opened in 1896, remained active until 1924, when it closed after local mineral deposits dwindled. The next stock exchange opened in 1946 in Bulawayo. A second floor of that exchange opened in 1951 in Harare. Those two exchanges were consolidated in 1974 pursuant to a stock exchange act of 1974. The Zimbabwe government authorities permitted dual-listed companies (companies listed in Harare and a foreign stock exchange) in 1997, but investors were prohibited from transferring shares in those companies from Harare to foreign exchanges. Since June 1993, when the Zimbabwe Stock Exchange was opened to foreign investors, the stock exchange has been characterized by extreme volatility.
Market capitalization (6/30/99):	U.S. $1.5 billion

Trading days:	Monday–Friday
Trading hours:	9:00–10:00 A.M. & 11:45–1:00 P.M.
Settlement:	Trade date + 7
Currency:	Zimbabwean dollar
Capital gains tax:	10%
Dividends tax:	15% withheld at source
Stamp duty:	45c per Z$100.00
Foreign ownership limits:	No foreign investor may hold more than 10% of a listed security, and foreign investors, in the aggregate, may not own more than 40% of a listed security.
Regulation on capital repatriation:	None
Penalty on currency conversion:	None
Number of listed companies:	69
Number of unit trusts:	26
Number of listed fixed instruments:	6
Number of stockbrokers:	10

Names and addresses of selected stockbrokers:

Continental Securities Trading (Pvt) Ltd.
P.O. Box CY 255
Harare, Zimbabwe
Tel: [263] (4) 757-671/672
Fax: [263] (4) 757-679

Corporate Securities
P.O. Box 7245
Harare, Zimbabwe
Tel: [263] (4) 702-005/728-252/728-251/728-253
Fax: [263] (4) 702-006
E-mail: corpsec@harare.iafrica.com

Edwards & Company (Pvt) Ltd.
P.O. Box 524
Harare, Zimbabwe
Tel: [263] (4) 74 554
Fax: [263] (4) 60 502

Intermarket Stockbrokers (Pvt) Ltd.
P.O. Box 3290
Harare, Zimbabwe
Tel: [263] (4) 750-915/922
Fax: [263] (4) 759-369

Kingdom Stockbrokers (Pvt) Ltd.
P.O. Box 3205
Harare, Zimbabwe
Tel: [263] (4) 758-857/858/859
Fax: [263] (4) 758-228
E-mail: kingsec@harare.iafrica.com

Msasa Stockbrokers (Pvt) Ltd.
40 Union Avenue
Harare, Zimbabwe
Tel: [263] (4) 772-392/393/394/395
Fax: [263] (4) 749-690

Quincor James Capel
P.O. Box 1244
Harare, Zimbabwe
Tel: [263] (4) 794-452
Fax: [263] (4) 736-043

Remo Investment Brokers (Pvt) Ltd.
P.O. Box BE 271
Harare, Zimbabwe
Tel: [263] (4) 750-717/718
Fax: [263] (4) 759-804

Sagit Stockbrokers (Pvt) Ltd.
P.O. Box 21
Harare, Zimbabwe
Tel: [263] (4) 757-867/869/870/874
Fax: [263] (4) 750-564
E-mail: sagit@harare.iafrica.com

Appendix B

SELECTED AFRICA-FOCUSED PRIVATE EQUITY FUNDS

Africa Infrastructure Fund
Emerging Markets Partnership
2001 Pennsylvania Avenue, NW, Suite 1100
Washington, DC 20006
Tel: [1] (202) 331-9051
Fax: [1] (202) 331-8255

Africinvest
M. R. Beal et Compagnie Internationals, SA
B.P. 2969
Dakar, Senegal
Tel: [221] 214-474
Fax: [221] 214-897

Cauris Investment
West African Economic and Monetary Union
B.P. 1172
Lomé, Togo
Tel: [228] 21-42-44
Fax: [228] 21-72-69

Commonwealth Africa Investment Fund (COMAFIN)

CDC Capital Partners
One Bessborough Gardens
London SW1V 2 JQ, United Kingdom
Tel: [44] (171) 828-4488
Fax: [44] (171) 828-6505

Enterprise Fund—South Africa

Enterprise Capital Fund
P.O. Box 11177
55 Fax Street
Johannesburg 2001, South Africa
Tel: [27] (11) 498-2152
Fax: [27] (11) 498-2138

Ghana Enterprise Fund

Venture Fund Management Co., Ltd.
Fifth Floor Tower Block
Box 2617
SSNIT Pension House
Liberia Road
Accra, Ghana
Tel: [233] (21) 666-165
Fax: [233] (21) 664-055

Ghana Venture Capital Fund

Venture Fund Management Co., Ltd.
Fifth Floor Tower Block
Box 2617
SSNIT Pension House
Liberia Road
Accra, Ghana
Tel: [233] (21) 666-165
Fax: [233] (21) 664-055

Mauritius Venture Capital Fund

Mauritius Equity Investment Management Ltd.
Sixth Floor, Sir William Newton Street
Port Louis, Mauritius
Tel: [230] 211-4949
Fax: [230] 211-9393

Modern Africa Fund

Modern Africa Growth and Investment Company
1100 Connecticut Avenue, NW
Washington, DC 20036
Tel: [1] (202) 887-1772
Fax: [1] (202) 887-1788

and

30 Wellington Road, Parktown
PO Box 6872
Johannesburg 2000, South Africa
Tel: [27] (11) 488-2656
Fax: [27] (11) 488-1592

New Africa Infrastructure Fund

New Africa Advisers
103 W. Main Street
Durham, NC 27701
Tel: [1] (919) 688-8092
Fax: [1] (919) 688-9095

and

New Africa Advisors
P.O. Box 9431
1066 Building, 35 Pritchard Street
Johannesburg 2001, South Africa
Tel: [27] (11) 836-2027
Fax: [27] (11) 836-0029

New Africa Opportunity Fund

New Africa Advisers
103 W. Main Street
Durham, NC 27701
Tel: [1] (919) 688-8092
Fax: [1] (919) 688-9095

and

New Africa Advisors
P.O. Box 9431
1066 Building, 35 Pritchard Street
Johannesburg 2001, South Africa
Tel: [27] (11) 836-2027
Fax: [27] (11) 836-0029

South Africa Infrastructure Fund

Standard Corporate and Merchant Bank
First Floor, 78 Fox Street
Johannesburg 2001, South Africa
Tel: [27] (11) 636-0434
Fax: [27] (11) 636-1517

Southern Africa Enterprise Development Fund

P.O. Box 2241
Saxonwold 2132, South Africa
No. 32, Fricker Road, First Floor
Illovo 2196, South Africa
Tel: [27] (11) 283-1630/1/2/3/4
Fax: [27] (11) 442-9824

Tanzania Venture Capital Fund

Equity Investment Management, Ltd.
P.O. Box 2535
Plot 1404/ 45, Ghana Avenue
Dar-es-Salaam, Tanzania
Tel: [255] (51) 348-83*
Fax: [255] (51) 444-440

The Development Finance Company of Uganda

PO Box 2767
Plot 1, Lumumba Avenue
Rwenzori House, Second Floor
Kampala, Uganda
Tel: [256] (41) 256-125
Fax: [256] (41) 259-435

West Africa Growth Fund

Framlington Asset Management West Africa
Tour AMCI 12 etage gauche
01 B.P. 1273
Abidjan 01, Côte d'Ivoire
Tel: [225] (22) 32-16-64
Fax: [225] (22) 32-16-04

Appendix C

AFRICAN MUTUAL FUNDS

AFRICA

Africa Funds	Currency	Domicile	Manager	Address
Africa Emerging Markets	U.S. dollar		Emerging Mkts. Inv. Corp.	Arindam Bhattercharjee/ John Niepold 1001 Nineteenth Str., N 16th Floor Arlington, VA 22209–1722 U.S.A.
Global African Dvp (Glad Fund)	U.S. dollar	British Virgin Islands	Trigone	
Clavert New Africa/A CALVERT	U.S. dollar	United States	Calvert Asst. Mgt. Co.	The Calvert Group 4550 Montgomery Ave. Bethesda, MD 20904 U.S.A.
Simba Fund	U.S. dollar	Guernsey	Barings	
MS Africa Investment	U.S. dollar	United States	Morgan Stanley Asst. Mgt.	Michael Scwabe Morgan Stanley Asset Mgt. 1221 Avenue of the Americas, 22nd Floor New York, NY 10020–1001 U.S.A.
GT Africa A	U.S. dollar	Bermuda	LGT	
GT Africa A	U.S. dollar	Bermuda	LGT	

Merrill Middle East Afr/A	U.S. dollar	United States	Merrill Lynch Asset Mgt.	Grace Pineda Merrill Lynch 800 Scudders Mill Road Plainsboro, NJ 08536 U.S.A.
Merrill Middle East Afr/B	U.S. dollar	United States	Merrill Lynch Asset Mgt.	As above
Merrill Middle East Afr/C	U.S. dollar	United States	Merrill Lynch Asset Mgt.	As above
Merrill Middle East Afr/D	U.S. dollar	United States	Merrill Lynch Asset Mgt.	As above

EGYPT

Hermes Egypt Fund Limited	U.S. dollar	Bermuda	Hermes (Bermuda)	Hermes Fund Mngt. 58 Tahir St., Dokkki Giza, Egypt
Hermes Emerging Markets	U.S. dollar	Bermuda	Hermes (Bermuda)	As above
Egyptian American Bk. Mutual Fd.	Egyptian pound	Egypt	Egyptian Fd. Mgt. Grp.	Egyptian Fund Mngt. 3 Ahmad Nesin St. Giza Cairo, Egypt
Bank of Alexandria Fund One	Egyptian pound	Egypt	Egyptian Fd. Mgt. Grp.	As above

(continued)

AFRICAN MUTUAL FUNDS (Continued)

Africa Funds	Currency	Domicile	Manager	Address
Egyptian Gulf Bank Mutual Fund	Egyptian pound	Egypt	Hermes (Bermuda)	Hermes Fund Mngt. 58 Tahir St., Dokki Giza, Egypt
Cairo Bank Mutual Fund	Egyptian pound	Egypt	Hermes (Bermuda)	As above
American Express Mutual Fund	Egyptian pound	Egypt	Hermes (Bermuda)	As above
Delta Mutual Fund	Egyptian pound	Egypt	Hermes (Bermuda)	As above
Hermes Al Rajhi Egypt Mutual	U.S. dollar	Bermuda	Hermes (Bermuda)	As above
Egyptian Growth Inv. Co. Ltd.	U.S. dollar	Guernsey	Concord Misr Investm. Ltd.	Concord Int. Invsts. 18/F, Banque MISR Tower 135 Mohammed Farid Street Cairo 11511, Egypt
SAIB Growth Fund	Egyptian pound	Egypt	Prime Investments s.a.e.	Prime Investments 7 Midan Al Thawia Third Fl., Mohandisseen Cairo, Egypt
Egypt Investment Co.	U.S. dollar	Guernsey	Concord National (BVI) LTD	Concord Int. Invsts. 18/F, Banque MISR Tower 135 Mohammed Farid St., Cairo 11511, Egypt

KENYA

| Regent Undervalued Fund | | | | Regent Fund Management (U.K.) Limited Walter House 418–422 Strand London, England WC2R |

MAURITIUS

| Mauritius Ltd. | U.S. dollar | | Lloyds GSY | |

MOROCCO

| Maroc Privatisation | French franc | France | SMC | MAROC PRIVATISATION SBFI NATEXIS GESTION 21 Boulevard Haussmann Paris 75009, France |

NIGERIA

| Nigeria Emerging Market Fund | U.S. dollar | Cayman Islands | Intl. Asst. Transactions LP | |

(continued)

AFRICAN MUTUAL FUNDS *(Continued)*

SOUTH AFRICA

Africa Funds	Currency	Domicile	Manager	Address
The Cabot South African	U.S. dollar	British Virgin Islands	Cabot/Folkes	Albert Alletzhauser Portfolio Manager/Analyst Cabot Ltd. Representative Office Fifth Floor #88 Grayston Drive Sandton, 2146
Standard South Africa Hedge Ltd.	U.S. dollar	Jersey	Standard Bank	
SGF South Africa Mgd.	U.S. dollar	Cayman Islands	Syfrets Mgt.	
Genbel South Africa Ltd.	South African rand	South Africa	Genbel/Unisen	
SFM Lux	South African rand	Luxembourg	Standard Bank	
South Africa Omni	U.S. dollar	Bahamas	Magnum Fd. Mgt.	
New South Africa Fund	U.S. dollar	United States	Fleming	James Campbell Portfolio Manager Fleming Asset Mngt. 25 Cophall Ave., London, England EC2R 7DR–UK

Fund	Currency	Country	Manager	Contact
Old Mutual South Africa	U.K. sterling	England	Old Mutual	Peter Linley Portfolio Manager Old Mutual 80 Cheapside London, England EC2V 6AA–UK
Southern Africa Fund Inc.	U.S. dollar	United States	Alliance Capital Management	Greg Eckersly Portfolio Manager Alliance Capital P.O. Box 412434 Craighall 2024 Johannesburg, South Africa or Mark Breedon Portfolio Manager Alliance Capital One Mayfair Place Londong, England WIX 6JJ–U.K.
Credit Suisse South Africa	U.K. sterling	England	Credit Suisse	Isabel Knight Portfolio Manager Credit Suisse Beaufort House 15 St. Botolph Street London, England EC3A–77J–U.K.

(continued)

AFRICAN MUTUAL FUNDS (Continued)

Africa Funds	Currency	Domicile	Manager	Address
UBS Eqty. Inv. South Africa	U.S. dollar	Switzerland	UBS (Intrag)	Markus Bachman UBS Gessneralle 3 P.O. Box 8098 Zurich, Switzerland
S&P Southern Africa	U.K. sterling	England	Save & Prosper	
Five Arrows CFL S African Rd	South African rand	Guernsey	Rothschild-Five Arrows CFL	Ben Laidler Portfolio Manager Rothschild Five Arrows House St. Swithin's Lane London, England EC4N 8NR–U.K.
Five Arrows IRL S African Rd	South African rand	Guernsey	Rothschild-Five Arrows IRL	As above

Appendix D

AFRICA-FOCUSED BROKERS IN THE UNITED STATES

Arnhold and S. Bleichroeder, Inc.
1345 Avenue of the Americas, 44th Floor
New York, NY 10105-4300
Tel: [1] (212) 698-3000
Fax: [1] (212) 299-4490

Deutsche Morgan Grenfell
31 West 52nd Street
New York, NY 10019-6160
Tel: [1] (212) 469-6041
Fax: [1] (212) 469-5184

Fleming Martin, Inc.
320 Park Avenue
New York, NY 10022
Tel: [1] (212) 508-3800
Fax: [1] (212) 508-3834

HSBC Securities Inc.
140 Broadway
New York, NY 10005
Tel: [1] (212) 658-4000
Fax: [1] (212) 658-4365

Hudson Sloane & Co. L.L.C.

Three Park Avenue, 39th Floor
New York, NY 10017
Tel: [1] (212) 779-3088
Fax: [1] (212) 685-8872

ING Barings (U.S.) Securities, Inc.

667 Madison Avenue
New York, NY 10021
Tel: [1] (212) 409-1000
Fax: [1] (212) 409-1020

J.P. Morgan Securities

60 Wall Street
New York, NY 10260
Tel: [1] (212) 483-2323
Fax: [1] (212) 483-2323

Merrill Lynch

World Financial Center, North Tower
250 Vesey Street
New York, NY 10281
Tel: [1] (212) 449-1000
Fax: [1] (212) 449-8100

Standard New York Inc.

Citicorp Center
153 East 53rd Street
New York, NY 10022
Tel: [1] (212) 407-5136
Fax: [1] (212) 407-5029

Appendix E

INVESTMENT INFORMATION RESOURCES

International Finance Corporation (IFC)

2121 Pennsylvania Avenue, N.W.
Washington, DC 20433
Tel: [1] (202) 477-1234
Fax: [1] (202) 974-4384
Internet: www.ifc.org

Industry Contacts

General Inquiries: [1] (202) 473-9119
Agribusiness: [1] (202) 473-0558
Capital Markets Development: [1] (202) 473-8790
Chemicals, Petrochemicals & Fertilizer Department: [1] (202) 473-0573
Foreign Investment Advisory Service: [1] (202) 473-0411
Infrastructure Department: [1] (202) 473-0031
Oil, Gas and Mining: [1] (202) 473-0513
Technical and Environment Department: [1] (202) 773-0634

IFC Regional Contacts

ABIDJAN:
IFC regional Representative
West and Central Africa
B.P. 1850

Abidjan 01, Côte d'Ivoire
Tel: [225] (22) 44-32-44
Fax: [225] (22) 44-44-83

ACCRA:
IFC
Patrice Lumumba Road,
Roman Ridge
PMB CCC 21
Accra, Ghana
Tel: [233] (21) 776-245
Fax: [233] (21) 774-961

DOUALA:
IFC
Nigeria
Rus Flatters, B.P. 4616
Douala, Cameroon
Tel: [237] 42-80-33
Fax: [237] 42-80-14

HARARE
IFC Regional Representative, Southern Africa East
101 Union Avenue, Seventh Floor
Union Avenue, P.O. Box 2960
Harare, Zimbabwe
Tel: [263] (4) 79-48-60
Fax: [263] (4) 79-38-05

JOHANNESBURG
IFC Resident Representative, South Africa
Grosvenor Gate, First Floor
Hyde Park Lane, Hyde Park 2196
P.O. Box 41283, Craig Hall 2024
Johannesburg, South Africa
Tel: [27] (11) 325-0560
Fax: [27] (11) 325-0582

LAGOS:
IFC Resident Representative, Plot PC 10, Engineering Close
Off Idowu Taylor Street
Victoria Island, P.O. Box 127
Lagos, Nigeria
Tel: [234] (1) 61-20-81
Fax: [234] (1) 61-63-60

NAIROBI
IFC Regional Representative, Africa
Hill Park Building, Upper Hill
P.O. Box 30577
Nairobi, Kenya
Tel: [254] (2) 714-140
Fax: [254] (2) 720-604

African Enterprise Fund

Manager, West Africa Division, AEF
IFC
2121 Pennsylvania Avenue, N.W.
Washington, DC 20433
Tel: [1] (202) 458-5082
Fax: [1] (202) 676-9704

Manager, East and Southern Africa Division, AEF
IFC
2121 Pennsylvania Avenue, N.W.
Washington, DC 20433
Tel: [1] (202) 473-0535
Fax: [1] (202) 676-9707

Africa Project Development Facility (APDF)

World Bank-APDF
1818 H Street, NW, Room K 5203
Washington, DC 20433
Tel: [1] (202) 473-6673
Fax: [1] (202) 676-0387

Multilateral Investment Guarantee Agency (MIGA)

World Bank
1818 H Street, N.W.
Washington, DC 20433
Tel: [1] (202) 473-6168
Fax: [1] (202) 477-9886
Internet: www.miga.org

International Center for Settlement of Investment Disputes

World Bank
1818 H Street, N.W.
Washington, DC 20433
Tel: [1] (202) 458-1534
Fax: [1] (202) 522-2615

African Development Bank Group
U.S. Executive Director
African Development Bank Group
Avenue Joseph Anoma, 01 B.P. 1387
Abidjan 01, Côte d'Ivoire
Tel: [225] (22) 20-40-15
Fax: [225] (22) 33-14-34
Internet: www.afdb.org

U.S. Department of Commerce AfDB Liaison Office
U.S. Embassy, U.S. and Foreign Commercial Service
5 Rue Jesse Owens
01 B.P. 1712
Abidjan 01, Côte d'Ivoire
Tel: [225] (22) 21-46-16
Fax: [225] (22) 22-24-37

Director, Private Sector Department
African Development Bank Group
Avenue Joseph Anoma, 01 B.P. 1387
Abidjan 01, Côte d'Ivoire
Tel: [225] (22) 20-41-68
Fax: [225] (22) 20-49-64
Internet: www.afdb.org

Arab Bank for Economic Development in Africa
P.O. Box 2640
Sayed Abdul Rahman El Mahdi Avenue
Khartoum, Sudan
Tel: [249] (11) 7-3646/7-3498/7-3709
Fax: [249] (11) 7-0600

Economic Commission for Africa (ECA)
P.O. Box 3001-3005
Addis Ababa, Ethiopia
Tel: [251] (1) 51-7200
Fax: [251] (1) 51-4416

Islamic Development Bank Contact
P.O. Box 5925
Jeddah 21432, Saudi Arabia
Tel: [966] (2) 636-1400
Fax: [966] (2) 636-6871

United Nations Development Program (UNDP)

One United Nations Plaza
New York, NY 10017

United Nations Conference on Trade and Development (UNCTAD)

Palais des Nations
CH-1211
Geneva 10, Switzerland
Tel: [4] (22) 917-1234/907-1234
Fax: [4] (22) 907-0057

United Nations Industrial Development Organization (UNIDO)

Vienna International Center
P.O. Box 300
A-1 400
Vienna, Austria
Tel: [43] (1) 21-1310
Fax: [43] (1) 23-2156

Appendix F

AFRICAN INVESTMENT PROMOTION AGENCIES

Algeria

Agence de Promotion, de Soutien et de Suivi des Investissements (APSI)
Le Directeur du Guichet Unique
Boulevard du 11 Decembre 1960
El-Bair
Algiers 16030, Algeria
Tel: [213] (2) 92-51-27
Fax: [213] (2) 92-37-62
E-mail: apsi@hoggar.cerist.dz

Angola

Foreign Investment Cabinet (GIE)–Angola
Rua Cercoeira Lukoki 25
9 Andar
Luanda, Angola
Tel: [244] (2) 33-29-54
Fax: [244] (2) 39-33-81

Botswana

Botswana Department of Trade and Investment Promotion (TIPA)
Ministry of Commerce and Industry
Private Bag 00367
Gaborone, Botswana
Tel: [267] 35-1790
Fax: [267] 30-5375

Burundi

Ministry of Commerce, Industry & Tourism
Director, Private Sector
Development Project
B.P. 6138
Bujumbura, Burundi
Tel: [257] 21-34-47/48
Fax: [257] 21-34-46

Cameroon

Investment Policy Development Unit Director
Ministry of Industrial and Commercial Development
B.P. 15304
Douala, Cameroon
Tel: [237] 43-31-11
Fax: [237] 43-30-07

Cape Verde

Centro de Promção de Investimento e das Exportaçóes (PROMEX)
P.O. Box 89, Avenida Qua
Praia, Cape Verde
Tel: [238] 61-57-52
Fax: [238] 61-14-42

Côte d'Ivoire

Investment Promotion Center (CPI)
01 B.P. V152
Abidjan, Côte d'Ivoire
Tel: [225] (22) 21-40-70
Fax: [225] (22) 21-40-71

Egypt

General Authority for Investment (GAFI)
8 Adly Street
Cairo, Egypt
Tel: [20] (2) 390-0975
Fax: [20] (2) 390-7315
E-mail: oadel@gega.net

Eritrea

Investment Center of Eritrea in Asmara
P.O. Box 921
Asmara, Eritrea
Tel: [291] (1) 51-24-00
Fax: [291] (1) 51-43-96

Ethiopia

Ethiopian Investment Authority
Bole Road, P.O. Box 2313
Addis Ababa 2313, Ethiopia
Tel: [251] (1) 15-34-32
Fax: [251] (1) 51-43-96

Gabon

PROMOGABON
Ministry of Industry and Commerce
B.P. 3029
Libreville, Gabon
Tel: [241] 74-89-57/58
Fax: [241] 74-89-59
E-mail: promogabon@tiggabon

Gambia

National Investment Promotion Authority
Independence Drive
Banjul, Gambia
Tel: [220] 22-83-32
Fax: [220] 22-92-20

Ghana

Ghana Investment Promotion Centre
P.O. Box M193
Accra, Ghana
Tel: [233] (21) 664-276
Fax: [233] (21) 663-801
E-mail: kahwoi@ncs.com.gh

Guinea

National Center for Private Investment Promotion
P.O. Box 1518
Conakry, Guinea
Tel: (224) 42-23-71

Kenya

Investment Promotion Centre
National Bank Building
Harambee Avenue, 8th Floor
P.O. Box 55704
Nairobi, Kenya
Tel: [254] (2) 221-401/402
Fax: [254] (2) 336-663
E-mail: epzahq@africaonline.co.ke

Lesotho

Lesotho National Development Corporation
Private Bag A96
Maseru 100, Lesotho
Tel: [266] 31-20-12
Fax: [266] 31-00-38
E-mail: indc@pixie.co.za

Malawi

Malawi Investment Promotion Agency
Aquarius House
Private Bag 302
City Centre
Lilongwe, Malawi
Tel: [265] 78-08-00
Fax: [265] 78-17-81
E-mail: mipaII@malawi.net

Mali

Centre National de Promotion des Investissements
B.P. 1980
Boulevard Chelck Zayed
Laflabougou, Mali
Tel: [223] 22-22-79
Fax: [223] 22-80-85

Mauritius

Mauritius Export Development and Investment Authority (MEDIA)
P.O. Box 1184, Level 2 BAI Building
25 Pope Hennessy Street
Port Louis, Mauritius
Tel: [230] 208-5965
Fax: [230] 208-5965
E-mail: media@bow.itnet.mu

Morocco

Ministry of Finance and Investment
Office of Industrial Development
10 Rue Ghandi
B.P. 211
Rabat, Morocco
Tel: [212] (7) 70-84-60
Fax: [212] (7) 70-76-95

Mozambique

Investment Promotion Centre, Investment Facilitation Division
Rua da Imprensa 322 r/c
Maputo 4635, Mozambique
Tel: [258] (1) 42-25-25/30
Fax: [258] (1) 42-26-04
E-mail: nic@iwwn.com.na

Namibia

Namibia Investment Centre
Private Bag 13340
Windhoek, Namibia
Tel: [264] (61) 283-7315
Fax: [264] (61) 22-02-78/ 25-46-00

Nigeria

Nigerian Investment Promotion Commission
Plot 1181, Aguiyi Ironsi Street
Maitama District
P.M.B. 381
Garki-Abuja, Nigeria
Tel: [234] 9-413-4112
Fax: [234] 9-413-4112

Senegal

Guichet Unique Business
Ministere de l'Economie, des Finances et du Plan
Rue Rene Ndiaye
Dakar, Senegal
Tel: [221] 23-96-99
Fax: [221] 22-41-95

Seychelles

Seychelles International Authority
P.O. Box 991
Mathe, Seychelles
Tel: [248] 22-58-51
Fax: [248] 22-58-51
E-mail: siba@seychelles.net

Sierre Leone

Department of Trade, Industry and State Enterprises
Ministerial Building, George Street
Freetown, Sierre Leone

Tel: [232] (22) 22-65-22
Fax: [232] (22) 22-83-73

South Africa
Investment South Africa
P.O. Box 782084
Sandton 3146, South Africa
Tel: [27] (11) 884-2206
Fax: [27] (11) 313-3663
E-mail: brain@isa.org.za

Sudan
Public Investment Promotion Administration
P.O. Box 6286
Khartoum, Sudan
Tel: [249] (11) 77-01-56
Fax: [249] (11) 77-07-30

Tanzania
Tanzania Investment Centre
P.O. Box 938
Dar-es-Salaam, Tanzania
Tel: [255] (54) 372641/113365
Fax: [255] (54) 112761/113366

Togo
Centre Togolais de Promotion des Investissements
B.P. 3250
Lome, Togo
Tel: [228] 21-13-74
Fax: [228] 21-52-31

Tunisia
Foreign Investment Promotion Agency
63, Rue de Syrie
1002 Tunis Belvedere
Tunisia
Tel: [216] (1) 79-21-44
Fax: [216] (1) 78-29-71
E-mail: api@api.com.tn

Uganda

Uganda Investment Authority
P.O. Box 7418
Kampala, Uganda
Tel: [256] (41) 23-41-05/25-15-62
Fax: [256] (41) 24-29-03
E-mail: uia@starcom.co.ug

Zambia

Zambia Investment Centre
Director General
P.O. Box 34580
Lusaka 10101, Zambia
Tel: [260] (1) 25-52-41/3
Fax: [260] (1) 25-21-50
E-mail: bngandu@zamnet.zm

Zimbabwe

Zimbabwe Investment Centre
109 Rotten Row
P.O. Box 5950
Harare, Zimbabwe
Tel: [263] (4) 759-9114
Fax: [263] (4) 759-917
E-mail: zic@harare.iafrica.com

Appendix G

AFRICAN PRIVATIZATION AGENCIES

Angola

GARE
Rua Serqueira Lukoki No. 25—Ninth Floor
Luanda, Angola
Tel: [244] (2) 39-04-96/39-34-35
Fax: [244] (2) 39-29-87

Benin

Ministry of Finance
Technical Secretariat
B.P. No. 8140
Cotonou, Benin
Tel: [229] 31-36-78
Fax: [229] 31-23-15

Burkina Faso

Privatization Commission
01 B.P. 6451
Ouagadougou 01, Burkina Faso
Tel: [226] 31-26-30
Fax: [226] 30-42-81

Cameroon

Secretaire du Comite Privatization Link
SNI Building, Ninth Floor,
P.O. Box 1452
Yaounde, Cameroon
Tel: [237] 23-97-50
Fax: [237] 23-51-08

Cape Verde

Privatization and Regulatory Capacity Building Project
P.O. Box 323
Praia, Cape Verde
Tel: [238] 61-47-48/61-23-19/61-70-81
Fax: [238] 61-23-34

Chad

Commission Desengagement de l'Etat
Government of Chad
N'Djamena, Chad
Tel: [235] 52-33-78
Fax: [235] 52-33-78

Congo

Comite de Privatisation
Immeuble de l'A.R.C., 7e étage
B.P. 1176
Brazzaville, Congo
Tel: [242] 83-28-64
Fax: [242] 83-33-26

Côte d'Ivoire

Cellule de Privatisation
Rue de Lindenie Villa 36
Abidjan, Côte d'Ivoire
Tel: [225] (22) 22-22-24/22-22-31
Fax: [225] (22) 22-22-35

Djibouti

USREP, Ministry of Finance
Djibouti, Djibouti
Tel: [253] 35-70-25
Fax: [253] 35-65-01

Ethiopia

Ethiopian Privatization Agency
P.O. Box 11835
Private 10134
Addis Ababa, Ethiopia
Tel: [251] (1) 15-03-70
Fax: [251] (1) 51-39-55

Gabon

Cellule de la Privatisation
B.P. 178
Libreville, Gabon
Tel: [241] 76-39-03
Fax: [241] 72-65-96

Ghana

Divestiture Implementation Committee
F. 35/5 Ring Road East
North Labone, P.O. Box C 102
Cantonments
Accra, Ghana
Tel: [233] (21) 77-20-49/77-31-19
Fax: [233] (21) 77-31-26

Guinea

Ministry of Planning and Finance
Avenue de la République, Face à l'Hôpital Ignace DEEN
B.P. 2066
Conakry, Guinea
Tel: [244] (41) 3597

Kenya

Executive Secretariat and Technical Unit
Investment Secretary/Coordinator
Department of Government Investments
Seventh Floor, Anniversary Towers
University Way
P.O. Box 34542
Nairobi, Kenya
Tel: [254] (2) 22-21-27/57/68
Fax: [254] (2) 21-69-45

Lesotho

Privatization Unit
Maseru, Lesotho
Tel: [266] 31-79-02
Fax: [266] 31-75-51

Madagascar

Commission Technique a la Privatisation
Secretaire Technique
1er étage Immeuble Fiaro,
Ampefiloho
B.P. 8400
Antananarivo, Madagascar
Tel: [261] (2) 226-6667
Fax: [261] (2) 226-6669

Malawi

Privatisation Commission
CDL House
Independence Drive
P.O. Box 937
Blantyre, Malawi
Tel: [265] 62-36-55
Fax: [265] 62-12-48

Mali

CERDES
B.P. 160
Avenue Moussa Traore
Quartier du Fleuve
Bamako, Mali
Tel: [223] 22-81-83
Fax: [223] 22-81-83

Mauritania

Cellule de Rehabilitation du Secteur (UTRE), Parapublic
Director
Nouakchott, Mauritania
Tel: [222] 25-20-43
Fax: [222] 25-0706

Mozambique
Enterprise Reform Unit
Ministry of Planning and Finance
Rua da Imprensa, No. 256, Predia
22 Andares - 7 Andar, 708/710
CP No. 4350
Maputo, Mozambique
Tel: [258] (1) 42-65-15/6
Fax: [258] (1) 42-15-41

Niger
Direction des Entreprises, Publiques Portefeuille de B.P. 389
Niamey, Niger
Tel: [227] 73-43-36

Senegal
Cellule de Gestion de l'Etat
B.P. 4017
Dakar, Senegal
Tel: [221] 823-3428
Fax: [221] 822-5631

Sierra Leone
Public Enterprise Reform and Divestiture Commission
P.O. Box 1025
11, Rowdown Street
Freetown, Sierra Leone
Fax: [232] 222-29/ 22667

Swaziland
Public Enterprise Unit
Head
Mbabane, Swaziland
Fax: [268] 42141

Tanzania
Parastatal Sector Reform Commission
Second Floor, Sukari House
Sokoine Drive/Ohio Street
P.O. Box 9252
Dar-es-Salaam, Tanzania
Tel: [255] (5) 13-42-96, 11-54-82, 11-62-68
Fax: [255] (5) 13-30-46/39-481

Togo

Commission de Privatisation
B.P. 2748
Lome, Togo
Fax: [228] 21-43-05

Uganda

Public Enterprise Reform and Divestiture Commission
IPS Building, Sixth Floor
Plot 14, Parliament Avenue
Box 10944
Kampala, Uganda
Tel: [256] (41) 25-01-08
Fax: [256] (41) 25-99-97

Zambia

Zambia Privatization Agency
Nassar Road, Box 30819
Lusaka, Zambia
Tel: [260] (1) 22-11-92
Fax: [260] (1) 22-52-70

Zimbabwe

National Economic Planning Commission
Government of Zimbabwe
Harare, Zimbabwe
Fax: [263] (4) 79-59-87

Selected Bilateral Information Sources

Overseas Private Investment Corporation (OPIC)
1100 New York Avenue, N.W.
Washington, D.C. 20527
Information Hotline: 1-800-424-OPIC
OPIC FactsLine (fax-on-demand service): [1] (202) 336-8700
Internet: www.opic.gov

U.S. Trade and Development Agency
1621 North Kent Street, Suite 300
Arlington, VA 22209-2131
Tel: [1] (703) 875-4357
Fax: [1] (703) 875-4009
E-mail: info@tda.gov
Internet: www.tda.gov

Appendix H

AFRICA INVESTMENT REFERENCE SOURCES

Books

AFRICAN STOCK EXCHANGES HANDBOOK

- provides an overview of Africa's capital markets complete with contact information for selected brokerage firms.

- Publisher: Focus News Services
  34 Clarges Street
  London W W1Y 7PL
  Tel: [44] (171) 355-1300
  Fax: [44] (171) 495-1332
  E-mail: africafocus@africafocus.demon.co.uk

- U.S. Contact Information
  Tel: [1] (202) 638-7030
  Fax: [1] (202) 638-6784

EMERGING STOCK MARKETS FACTBOOK

- IFC compendium which provides an overview and comparison of the World's stock exchanges, including those in Africa

- Publisher: International Finance Corporation
  c/o The World Bank Info Shop
  1818 H Street, N.W.
  Washington, DC 20006

Tel: [1] (202) 458-5454
Fax: [1] (202) 522-1500
Website: www.worldbank.org (select publications)

Magazines

BUSINESS IN AFRICA

- Monthly magazine that provides up-to-date articles and analysis on business activity in Africa, with special emphasis on Southern Africa

- Publisher: Goldcity Ventures Limited
  P.O. Box 1357
  Rivonia 2128
  South Africa
  Tel: [27] (11) 807-0948
  Fax: [27] (11) 807-0919
  Internet: www.businessinafrica.com

AFRICAN BUSINESS

- Monthly magazine focused on business in Africa
- Publisher: IC Publications
  P.O. Box 261
  Carlton House, 69 Great Queen Street
  London WC2B 5BN, United Kingdom
  Tel: [44] (171) 404-4333
  Fax: [44] (171) 404-5336

AFRICAN REVIEW OF BUSINESS AND TECHNOLOGY

- Monthly magazine focused on industry in Africa
- Publisher: ARBT
  Alain Charles House
  27 Wolfred Street
  London SW1E 6PR, United Kingdom
  Tel: [44] (171) 834-7676
  Fax: [44] (171) 973-0076

AFRICAN COMMUNICATIONS

- Monthly magazine focused on telecommunications, communications, and telephony in Africa

- Publisher: AFCOM International, Inc.
  10560 Main Street, Suite 510
  Fairfax, VA 22030
  Tel: [1] (703) 691-3570
  Fax: [1] (703) 691-3572

Newsletters

EMERGING MARKETS AFRICA

- Fortnightly report on African capital markets

- Publisher: Emerging Markets Business Intelligence
  Glebe House, 12 Glebe Road
  London N8 7DB, United Kingdom
  Tel: [44] (181) 372-8932
  Fax: [44] (181) 374-1153
  E-mail: 100766,2735@compuserve.com

AFRICA FINANCING REVIEW

- Provides insight, analysis, and "unbiased opinion" on issues related to finance in Africa, particularly Africa's capital markets

- Publisher: African Financing Review
  31 Dunstan Road
  London NW11 8AG, United Kingdom
  Tel: [44] (181) 731-8392
  Fax: [44] (181) 731-8221

LOCATE AFRICA

- Newsletter of the African Investment Promotion Agency Network

- Publisher: AFRIPANET Foundation
  With support from the World Bank's MIGA
  c/o Investment Center
  Ministry of Trade and Industry
  Windhoek, Namibia
  Tel: [264] (61) 229-933
  Fax: [264] (61) 220-278

DEVELOPMENT BUSINESS

- Fortnightly guide to consulting, contracting, and supply opportunities around the world; is an important guide to publicly funded projects in Africa

- Publisher: United Nations
P.O. Box 5850
Grand Central Station
New York, New York 10163-5850
Tel: [1] (212) 963-1516
Fax: [1] (212) 963-1381
E-mail: dbusiness@un.org

ADB BULLETIN

- Bimonthly publication of the African Development Bank, intended to inform stakeholders, the public, and officials of partner institutions and staff, of development goals, strategies, and achievements of the ADB and its constituencies.

- Publisher: Communications Unit
African Development Bank
01 B.P. 1387
Abidjan 01, Côte d'Ivoire
Tel: [225] (22) 20-41-18
Fax: [225] (22) 20-40-06
Internet: www.afdb.org

AFRICA CONFIDENTIAL

- Fortnightly newsletter about economic, commercial, and political events in Africa

- Publisher: Miramoor Publications Ltd.
73 Farrington Road
London EC1M 3JB, United Kingdom
Tel: [44] (171) 831-3511
Fax: [44] (171) 831-6778

HART'S AFRICA OIL AND GAS

- Fortnightly news and analysis from the growing African energy market

- Publisher: Hart Europe
  Rosemount House
  Rosemount Avenue
  West Byfleet
  Surrey KT14 6NP, United Kingdom
  Tel: [44] (193) 234-4424
  Fax: [44] (193) 235-5927
  E-mail: mdixon@harteurope.co.uk

SOUTHERN AFRICA REPORT

- A bimonthly assessment for decision makers

- Publisher: Southern Africa Report Association
  P.O. Box 261579
  Excom 2023
  Johannesburg, South Africa
  Tel: [27] (11) 646-8790
  Fax: [27] (11) 646-2596
  E-mail: LESDV@aol.com
  Website: www.sanalysis.com

SOUTHERN AFRICAN INVESTOR

- Monthly investor periodical which discusses recent and projected investment projects in the Southern Africa region

- Publisher: Investor Responsibility Research Center (IRRC)
  1350 Connecticut Avenue, NW
  Washington, DC 20036
  Tel: [1] (202) 833-0700
  Fax: [1] (202) 833-3555
  Website: www.irrc.org

SOUTHERN AFRICAN ANALYSIS & ADVICE

- A bimonthly assessment for decision makers

- Publisher: Dr. Les de Villiers
  with Professional Management Review (PMR - Johannesburg)
  194 Putnam Road
  P.O. Box 1587
  New Canaan, CT 06840
  Tel: [1] (203) 966-9645

Fax: [1] (203) 966-6018
E-mail: LESDV@aol.com
Website: www.sanalysis.com

THE NETWORKER

- Monthly newsletter of the West African Enterprise Network

- Publisher: WAEN
SSNIT Tower Block, 5th Floor
Private Mail Bag,
Ministries Post Office
Accra, Ghana
Tel: [233] (21) 78-01-86/23-40-07
Fax: [333] (21) 23-40-07/66-91-00
E-mail: ababio@africaonline.com.gh

The Internet (Additional Web Sites)

- www.sourceafrica.com   African information research resource

- www.woyaa.com   Africa information search engine

- www.africasia.com   Online site of IC Publications, publishers of *African Business, New African,* and *The Middle East*

- www.usafrica.org   Online site of Africa Growth and Opportunity Act Coalition

- www.galaxy.einet.net   Country-by-country business information

- www.privatization.net   Online site of newsletter *Privatization News*

- www.africapolicy.org   Online site of the Africa Policy Information Center, providing Africa policy-related information from 1978 to the present

- www.ita.doc.gov   Online annual Country Commercial Guides prepared by the U.S. Department of Commerce

Business Associations

Corporate Council on Africa
1660 L Street, NW, Suite 301
Washington, DC 20036
Tel: [1] (202) 835-1115
Fax: [1] (202) 835-1117

African Business Roundtable
86, Grayston Drive, Sandown 2196
P.O. Box 652257, Benmore 2010
Johannesburg, South Africa
Tel: [27] (11) 884-0436
Fax: [27] (11) 884-0133

Committee of French Investors in Africa (CIAN)
190 Boulevard Haussmann
75008 Paris, France
Tel: [33] (14) 562-5576
Fax: [33] (14) 256-7933

The Business Council Europe-Africa-Mediterranean
c/o B.A.B.A (United Kingdom)
45 Great Peter Street
London SW1P 3LT, United Kingdom
Tel: [44] (171) 222-1077
Fax: [44] (171) 222-1079

West African Enterprise Network
SSNIT Tower Block, Fifth Floor
Private Mail Bag, Ministries Post Office
Accra, Ghana
Tel: [233] (21) 666-165/ 780-521
Fax: [233] (21) 780-521/ 669-100

East African Enterprise Network
c/o National Coordinator
Uganda Enterprise Network
Kampala, Uganda
Tel: [256] (41) 250-907
Fax: [256] (41) 343-682

Southern African Enterprise Network
c/o Managing Director
Corpus Globe Advocate
The Globe Building
Longolongo Road
Lusaka, Zambia
Tel: [260] (1) 235 480
Fax: [260] (1) 238 657

Index